Rome Fell Today

*This book is affectionately dedicated
to our good friend, Tom Allen*

ROME
FELL TODAY

*Robert H. Adleman
and
Colonel George Walton*

LESLIE FREWIN : LONDON

Grateful acknowledgement is made for permission to reprint the following copyrighted material:

Selections from *I Was There* by Admiral William D Leahy. © 1950 by William D Leahy. © 1950 by The Curtis Publishing Company. Published by McGraw Hill Company. Reprinted by permission of Brandt & Brandt.

Selections from *Command Missions* by Lucian King Truscott. © 1954 Lucian King Truscott. Published by E P Dutton and Company. Reprinted by permission of Curtis Brown Ltd.

Selections from *But For the Grace of God* by Rt Rev Msgr J Patrick Carroll-Abbing. © 1965 by Boys' Town of Italy, Inc, and used by permission of the publisher, Delacorte Press.

Selections from *The Goebbels Diaries* by Lois P Lochner. © 1948 by the Fireside Press Inc. And from *Triumph in the West* by Arthur Bryant. © 1959 by Arthur Bryant. Both reprinted by permission of Doubleday and Company, Inc.

Selections from *Not So Wild a Dream* by Eric Sevareid. © 1946 by Eric Sevareid. Reprinted by permission of Alfred A Knopf Inc.

Selections from *Anzio—Epic of Bravery* by Fred Sheehan. © 1964 by the University of Oklahoma Press. Reprinted by permission of the University of Oklahoma Press.

© 1968 and 1969 by Robert H Adleman
and Colonel George Walton

First published in Great Britain 1969 by
Leslie Frewin Publishers Limited,
One, New Quebec Street, London W1

Reprinted lithographically by
Taylor Garnett Evans, Watford
and bound by William Brendon,
of Tiptree, Essex

09 098350 5

Contents

Preface   IX

Foreword   3

I   May 30 - 1, 1944   9

II   December 1941 - July 1943   31

III   July 10 - August 17, 1943   69

IV   September 1943   89

V   October 1 - December 20, 1943   107

VI   December 25, 1943 - January 25, 1944   139

VII   February - May 1944   169

VIII May 1944   199

IX   May 28 - June 3, 1944   223

X   June 5 and Beyond   261

      Acknowledgements   285

      Chapter Notes   289

      Bibliography   313

      Index   323

The correspondent hunched over his typewriter. For six months he'd been sweating out the dirty war in Italy and now that the biggest prize had fallen, his lead sentence just wouldn't come. He wanted to say something about the glory of Rome, the grandeur of it so long sullied by Mussolini and Hitler, and as of this day it was free. The Americans had just taken the first of the Axis-dominated capitals. It meant something that made the words he knew seem scanty. After a while, he shrugged and began tapping out: 'Rome fell today. ...'

Rome Fell Today

A FOREWORD

SINCE World War II there has been a growing tendency to consider the battle fought in Italy as an almost bottomless pit which sucked in much of the strength and guts of the Allied effort. The ranking American officer in that campaign, General Mark W. Clark, has had the stereotype of the hungrily ambitious military man fastened to him so securely that he was denied the office of Chief of Staff — a post which seemed inevitably his before the public (and many of his troops and associates) began blaming him for Italian mountains and the bloody Rapido River.

But the focus shifts for all of us. The campaign that achieved its dramatic climax with the fall of Rome takes on additional dimensions as each year passes. Some of the events and decisions that seemed so unfortunate in 1943 and 1944 we now understand as not only logical under the prevailing circumstances but historically inevitable.

The Italian campaign was operated by neither angels nor devils, but by competent men doing what they considered their best under terribly difficult circumstances. The decisions were planned and executed by lonely generals because everything in the world's news conspired to isolate them. The issues and accomplishments elsewhere were often clear-cut and dramatic. In Italy, everything bogged down in the mud. It was the ideal place for a commanding officer to acquire an inferiority complex. Mark Clark and the British general, Sir Harold Alexander, were not only under pressure to win, they were also never allowed to forget that other theater commanders were hungry for their men and materiel. Douglas MacArthur, for example, rarely missed the opportunity to point out to visiting correspondents the stupidity of denying him the tools that were being frittered away in Italy.[1]

The libraries and archives contain innumerable descriptions

of the battles in which these assets were used. Therefore, at this late date, we will serve no purpose by once again going up on one Italian hill and down another with a rifle company, recrossing a river with a division, or repeating the boat-by-boat description of an invasion by a corps. Battles will be described in the following pages in only enough detail to supply dimension to the men who fought them. This is not meant to indicate that these battles were unimportant, because any place where many men fight and die is a major place. But the primary effort in these pages will be to discover *why* and not *how* this polyglot force came to be knocking on the gates of Rome.

The Fifth Army, led by General Clark, had the distinction of being the most truly international force ever gathered under an American banner. Foreign elements often constituted half its strength and the exotic combination of British, French, Italian, Brazilian and other national units presented command problems that were both unique and difficult.

No other Allied army spent as much time in continuous action against the enemy as the Fifth.[2] It went ashore at Salerno in September 1943 to become the first American lance into Germany's "Fortress Europe." For almost two years thereafter it fought in Italy under conditions so cruel that more than one correspondent began his story with the shocked description of men living like animals in the field.

Fifth Army activities must constitute the thread of continuity in any account of the capture of Rome so it follows that one of our chief concerns will be General Mark Clark, who became a storm center almost as soon as he stepped ashore at Salerno. There will be other leading roles, because the Italian campaign was rich in sources of charismatic excitement such as Clark's courtly and enigmatic English superior officer, General Alexander. Pope Pius XII became a controversial figure even before the war ended. Criticisms of his official conduct finally flared into the open with the staging of the play *The Deputy* and the publication of the serious charges listed in Saul Friedländer's book *Pius XII and the*

Third Reich. And, certainly, no all-star cast is complete which does not include "Smiling Albert" Kesselring, the German general who never stopped protesting his love for things Italian while dictating the type of campaign which raked such bloody furrows through the country.

As a private individual, General Clark is so personally charming that it is almost impossible not to reject the verdict of one former staff officer who said that "he was a goddamned study in arrogance!" Take an example. During the research phases of this book, we brought up in a conversation with him the consistently repeated charge that he was so publicity-conscious that pictures of him always had to be taken from his left side. This is a seemingly trivial point, but it is amazing how many times in the course of our interviews and research this foible was used as a launching point for an attack on the man.

In answer, he smiled in an almost boyish way. "Oh," he said, "I guess that's right. But what the hell, most people think they look better one way or another in a picture."

You get the feeling of uncompromising honesty. You also get the feeling, when talking to Clark, of an almost complete military instrument. He rarely reads a book, watches sports and westerns on television to the exclusion of anything else, and apparently has never lost loyalty to any person or institution after he once concluded that such loyalty was merited.

In a search for authenticity, we have tracked down and read almost every scrap of information appearing in the thousands of reference books, published biographies, memoirs, and critiques which deal with the period. We have studied at the national archives in Alexandria, Virginia, and other primary sources for research in military history. Hundreds of interviews with almost every major surviving character have been conducted by us, and those meetings supplied the accuracy for the conversations that have been reconstructed. As a result, the reader can safely assume that every unannotated conversation or remark quoted in this book was furnished us by either a participant in or a witness to the event under discussion.

However, in spite of these pains, it is necessary to point out that an honest history, like an honest newspaper report, is a difficult product to produce. You must arrive at an average or, if you like, a "consensus" which reconciles many frames of references before a story or a report can be considered authoritative.

Historians, biographers, and memoir-writers must be evaluated in light of their own prejudices, and sometimes it becomes unpleasantly obvious that these writings are little more than special-purpose pleadings. Sometimes they are downright dishonest.

As for personal recollections, after twenty years they often acquire a gloss which suppresses ugliness, dwells on glory and is adulterated with folklore. A Texan named Lee F. Allison, in answer to the questionnaire which went to a cross-section of Fifth Army survivors, wrote quite honestly, ". . . war must be, in some ways, like childbirth — all the bad, horrible, and uncomfortable things fade in your memory and just the funny and better things remain."

Even impressions recorded during the actual time of battle are not always trustworthy. A battle is not one linear event existing in a vacuum. It is a mosaic made up of apparently unrelated major and minor experiences, and it is a rare commanding officer who is sure of even the important details of an operation. Only the passage of time brings order and clarity to the battlefield.

This also holds true for the journalists on the scene. Their impressions are filtered through censorship, emotional involvement with the units to which they are attached, and a sizable number of other factors which include personal prejudice. A glance through the accounts published in major magazines and newspapers during this period proves that many men can see one event in many ways. As Will Lang, now the chief of *Life*'s regional news bureaus and then a correspondent who slogged almost every inch of the way alongside Fifth Army troops, said during a discussion of the merits of certain generals, "After all, there are no perfect correspondents either!" Which, of course, is another way of saying that the complete picture cannot be found in any one source, and, further, the truth has an uneasy way of shifting its address from generation to generation.

Much of the material in the following pages reflects the generous willingness of certain historians, military men, diplomats, and journalists to share their expertise. In some instances, our conclusions may differ from theirs, but we would have had difficulty in arriving at *any* judgments if they had not devoted some part of their busy days to helping us understand that part of the larger picture with which they were concerned.

Among those we would especially like to thank are General of the Armies Dwight D. Eisenhower, General Mark W. Clark, General Robert W. Porter, Jr., Lieutenant General Geoffrey Keyes (who died shortly after this manuscript was completed in 1967), Major General Fred L. Walker, Major General George E. Lynch, Major General John E. Sloan, and Major General Robert T. Frederick.

Ambassador Robert Murphy's discussion of the political and military considerations was of immeasurable help to us in understanding the background of the Italian campaign.

And we are deeply grateful for the critiques of Eric Sevareid, Bill Mauldin, Will Lang, Harry Sions, Peter Tompkins, and Dr. Robert W. van de Velde. We are particularly indebted for his cooperation to Dr. Ernest F. Fisher, Jr., Office of the Chief of Military History, Department of the Army, Washington, D.C.

CHAPTER I

MAY 30–31, 1944

Rome must now fall. Generals Alexander and Clark would soon receive the key to the city, but surely it was General Walker who turned the key. From him they were really receiving it.[1]

— ERIC SEVAREID

THE word had spread among the headquarters personnel of the 36th Division that the Brass from above, the VI Corps commander, Major General Lucian K. Truscott, Jr., and the big boss of the Fifth Army himself, Lieutenant General Mark W. Clark, were meeting with the Old Man in the unit's makeshift war room.

To those in the know, there could be only one purpose for the meeting; to discuss the Old Man's plan to break the stalemate that was keeping the Allied armies from pouring through the passages to Rome.

Everyone realized that the Old Man, Major General Fred L. Walker, had been chafing under the knowledge that his 36th was regarded by many of the higher brass as a hard-luck outfit worth only a place in the reserve of other divisions in the final march on the big prize of the Italian campaign. Now, Walker had an idea how the 36th might be able to turn the key in the door to Rome.

For the past few days he had been puzzling and mulling over his plan and he finally had it down pat. He knew how to slice through that tight ring which the retreating Germans had drawn around the city. Truscott and Clark would have to listen to him.

Max E. Shaffer of Fort Worth, the division photographer, was called to the war room where the generals were meeting. He describes the scene:

"As I recall, it was on May 30, 1944, in the early afternoon, and I had just finished processing some negatives when General Walker's orderly came to my section and said I was wanted in headquarters. This didn't seem too unusual to me at the time, and as always I grabbed my camera, stuffed some film packs in my pockets, and took off with the orderly. When we got to the tent where the division chief of staff had his office, the Chief of Staff told me General Walker was in what amounted to a war room with some other generals and that I was to just slip in, stand around and not attract any attention. Above all I wasn't to say a damn thing unless asked, and to keep my ears open. The Colonel said I had a job to do but I wouldn't get the details until this meeting was over.

"When I went in the war tent I saw General Walker, and he was then talking to General Truscott. General Walker looked at me and nodded, and continued his conversation. As I recall, General Clark was also there.

"I did my best to blend in with the tent walls and not do anything that would make any one in the tent notice me. The generals were poring over a map and General Walker seemed to be doing most of the talking. Walker was explaining a plan or a maneuver to Truscott and I believe it was Clark who commented to Walker, 'Fred, it won't work, you will get a hell of a lot of men killed for nothing.'

"Walker replied, 'I know it will work, and in fact I am so sure it will that I will stake my reputation on it.' General Walker then continued to say that one of his regiments had found this opening and had been watching it for some time, and they were all sure that it was unguarded and open.

"This type of discussion continued for what seemed to me about a half of an hour. General Walker never gave an inch, and continued to insist that his plan was sound and workable. I got the impression that Walker was asking permission to try some sort of maneuver on our front, but was being denied permission by Corps and Army to commit his forces in the manner he wanted to. I was aware by the tone of the general conversation that the talks were coming to an end and that General Walker had not received permission to carry out his plan.

"At about this point I believe it was General Truscott that started to leave and then turned to General Walker and said, 'Fred, I won't give you permission to do this; if you do it on your own and you fail, the axe will fall,' or something like that. I believe that General Clark then said, 'Fred, I can't OK this. If you do it and succeed, we are on our way to Rome; but if you fail, you will have to bear the brunt of what comes with the failure, and your action will be without my approval or the approval of Truscott.'

"They all shook hands and left the tent, leaving General Walker and the Chief of Staff and myself. General Walker then turned to me and said, 'Shaffer, come here.' I walked over to the map and General Walker said to the Chief of Staff, 'Explain this to the Sergeant and tell him what we want him to do.'

"The Chief of Staff then told me of the General's plan to infiltrate some troops, he didn't say how many, through a gap that had been found in the German lines. These troops were to get on some high ground behind Velletri and cut the German supply lines into the town. My part in this was explained by General Walker coming back and saying he wanted me to photograph every damn thing in this maneuver that I thought would help to tell the story of what was happening, from start to finish.

"General Walker said to me, 'Sergeant, I suppose you heard the conversation regarding what we are going to do,' and I told him that I did. General Walker then said, 'Well, if we make this breakthrough we will have opened the door to Rome, but if we don't, you know what can happen to me as a result of trying this without the approval of Corps and Army. So what I want you to do is be able to furnish as much photographic coverage as possible regarding all aspects of this, in order that we can at least show how we tried and maybe place us in a better position if we fail.'

"I still had not learned what unit or units were involved or how many troops were involved. General Walker asked me if I understood what I was to do and I said that I did. General Walker said he wanted me as far forward as I could get with the troops that were infiltrating but not to stay too near the command element.

"I left the General and his chief of staff and went back to the PIO and gathered up as much film as I could carry. Before I left, General Walker had told me that this entire maneuver was being carried out in secret and that I was not to discuss it with anyone. I informed the PIO officer that I was going to make a trip to the line and get some photos and he didn't question me or press me for any details. I left the division area with just the clothes I had on, plus a field jacket, the pockets stuffed with film. I didn't have a weapon, in fact very seldom had one, a fact which caused a number of field grade officers on the line to have fourteen kinds of fits. I joined a rifle company that was on foot leaving their regimental area. At the time I wasn't even sure which regiment I was with. I joined them at an assembly area and I assumed that my presence was expected. I later learned that I was with one of the units of the 142nd."[2]

For the sake of those who are unfamiliar with the composition of United States Army units, it should be explained that an army is composed of two or more corps. A corps is composed of two or more divisions and a division has three regiments. Special purpose units can be added at any level, but if these segments are kept in mind, the disposition of troops should not be hard to follow.[3]

The campaign in Italy so far had consisted of a series of fights to oust the Germans from positions in the high ground. But each time the mission had been accomplished, the Germans had withdrawn masterfully to a prepared position in another mountain range behind them. Now it seemed that the same agonizing situation was again coming into focus. The forces of Generalfeldmarschall Albert Kesselring had established their positions in the last range of hills before Rome.[4] The 36th Division was confronted by a particularly massive block in that chain, the redoubtable Mount Artemesio.

General Walker's plan in effect suggested that during the night, elements of the 36th Division could infiltrate through the gap that he had discovered, climb the mountain from the rear, and, by commanding these heights, destroy the German garrison in the town of Velletri which was nestled at its base.

This was not the first time that the tiny village of Velletri represented the key to a campaign. Almost exactly two hundred years before, an Austrian offensive against the combined Spanish and Neapolitan army in Italy was trying to break through it on its march downward to Naples. Here, too, a surprise night infiltration around the flanks of the Alban Hills was the tactic chosen. The attack stopped short of success when it bogged down into bitter hand-to-hand fighting in the narrow streets.

Major General Fred L. Walker, a career soldier in command of the 36th, which was a Texas National Guard Division, had been a former instructor of General Clark's at the Army War College and was now his subordinate. Walker felt that he had professional reasons for worrying whether the proposed infiltration would come off.[5] Under his command, the division had been badly bloodied almost nine months before, when the Fifth Army came ashore at the tip of the Italian peninsula at Salerno and, in succeeding battles, had never earned the respect of the other outfits

dmit that their short- lifficulty of the jobs e that his career could ed action. This is what e will fall."

ker recalls, "we were actions for the reason ve to and through any roops.

nt a number of times, el Reese, who was the some of the troops in st in front of Velletri, and in that particular d visibility was very t. He wandered off in tes he came back and I le said, 'Well, I'm just German patrol in this cane and when we saw each other, they ran and I ran. So I'm just lucky to be here.'

"I mention this merely to show how close the lines were at that time and how the patrols encountered each other in that thick cane and brush.

"On one occasion, I visited the first battalion of the 141st, which was up over on the right flank of the regiment and the executive officer and I made an exploration of the front. I discovered that there were practically no actions on this front and was told that his patrols had been up front quite a little distance but that they had encountered no resistance although they did occasionally hear German firearms.

"This gave me the idea that perhaps the front was not held strongly by the Germans. I returned to the Division Headquarters, thinking all the time that I ought to investigate the situation. So I took a look over the front in a plane, one of the little artillery reconnaissance planes, and I could see no evidence of any troop encampments or field works or activity; and then the idea began to grow. I thought, 'Well, I am going to look into this further.' So I went back to division headquarters and I asked the map section to study the air photographs and see if they could find any evidence of any enemy activities in that area. They did so and reported to me that they could find nothing of any consequence. So then I lay awake most of the night trying to figure out with myself as to what I should do about this. So the next morning, as I remember, I called Colonel Stovall, who was the division engineer, and asked him to make a reconnaissance of that area and let me know whether or not it would be possible for me to support an advance over that area with tanks and artillery — whether there were any roads or not that would permit that.

"He made a reconnaissance in a plane and came back and reported to me that it *would* be possible for him and his engineer battalion to make an improvised roadway if the infantry should be ordered through that area, so that the artillery and tanks could cross.

"With this information, I felt that I had an idea that was practical. The idea came to me that now you've got a proposition, you've explored it, you know what it's like, and it's worthwhile presenting it to your superiors. But before I did, I talked to my staff and told them that I was contemplating this movement and asked each one of them what they thought of it.

"As a result of my conversations with them, I was reinforced in my own idea. In the meantime, I had received orders to move the division to the left in rear of the 45th and the 34th divisions with the objective of relieving one of those divisions that had been fighting for some time and needed to be relieved because they were not making any headway. This order I received from General Truscott at a conference at his headquarters along about ten or eleven o'clock at night.

"When I received that order, I began to think, 'Well now let's see, this looks like something I don't want to do. I have taken a beating at the Rapido River and I don't want to take another beating.' But anyway next morning I issued the orders for the movement of the division to the left behind the 45th and 34th divisions and directed that the movement begin at one o'clock. Troops were packing up, getting ready to move. The headquarters troop was the first to move and they had already taken position on the road but had not yet gone, when General Truscott came by to see how we were getting along with our movement to the left.

"When he came along, I said to him, 'I have been investigating the front in front of 36th and I have come to the conclusion that we can go through there a lot faster than we can go through the front where you have ordered us behind the 45th and the 34th. It looks like we can get through with much greater speed and really break the lines.'

"He asked me a few questions and I answered them and he concluded by saying that 'I think you have something there. I'll let you know.' So I sent word to the reconnaissance troops not to move but to wait until I gave them further orders.

"This, as I remember, was about eleven o'clock. About an hour or so later he called me on the telephone and said, 'I've talked to General Clark and General Clark has OK'd your proposal, and you are authorized to cancel the order to move to your left and to go ahead on *your* plan. *But you had better get through.*' That was the end of our conversation.

"With that I hurriedly issued orders to the various units and assembled the commanders. They assembled at my headquarters at about four o'clock and I issued new orders for the movement through our front."[6]

At the time when General Walker made his move the overall campaign had reached an embarrassing stalemate. Although the Allied attack boiling out of the Anzio beachhead had just linked with the Fifth and Eighth armies thrusting up the peninsula, the German lines defending Rome refused to give. A costly headlong battering through the enemy lines seemed the only answer.

For four fruitless days Truscott's VI Corps punched and pawed along the southern slopes of the Alban Hills in a vain attempt to secure the high ground overlooking the Eternal City. The most newsworthy prize in the Italian campaign was Rome and Clark wanted the American Fifth Army to get the sole credit for its capture.[7] But the British Eighth Army was rapidly reaching a position where to shut the door on their help would have made him the subject of serious criticism. Beside himself with impatience, he began to shift his units in an effort to find the combination that would open the German defense.[8]

Behind their lines the Nazi soldiers crouched in readiness. One of their captured combat reports noted:

. . . many ravines and natural caves offered protection for the local reserves against even the heaviest artillery fire as well as against bombings from the air and made it possible not only to keep those reserves available close by for employment in automatic counterthrusts, but also to move them about easily and in all directions.

Systematic observation by all services made it possible to concentrate and direct the fire of the artillery and of our heavy weapons in such a way as to effectively counteract the enemy's approach and his movement into position.

On 29 and 30 May [the Allied attacks] broke up into individual thrusts, frequently made without any coordination in time and place. During the attack for the C-position near Velletri, altogether thirty-eight attacks and thrusts worth mentioning were reported; all of them were either repelled, or wherever penetrations had occurred, these were immediately wiped out by counterthrusts.[9]

The German commander, General Heidrich, of the 1st Parachute Division, issued a communiqué to his soldiers which read in part:

With overwhelming superiority in men and materiel, the enemy is attempting to cut off considerable parts of the German forces and so bring a victory within his grasp. *He will not succeed* . . . he will not be able to force the decision which, with heavy losses, he has been seeking. The war will not be decided by territorial gains in Italy.[10]

But, in spite of General Heidrich's heartening words, there is evidence that the Germans were not unaware of their last-ditch position. An Irish priest whom the civilians behind the lines found to be a source of steady strength, the Rt. Rev. Msgr. J. Patrick Carroll-Abbing, wrote in his diary that "something was definitely in the air. There was a perceptible note of discouragement among the Germans, a sense of expectancy, a new tension during the Allied bombardments. I found myself moving from one part of the front to the other, trying to contact the isolated groups of civilians before the situation changed."[11]

On the Allied front, General Walker was being told to take his Texans over into the reserve position mentioned above. It was considered that the 36th, being relatively rested, could be then used to exploit a possible breakthrough.

This was a "safe" move for Walker and it should have been attractive to him. The fifty-seven-year-old officer was aware of the general opinion voiced later by Colonel Robert Porter, the deputy chief of staff of II Corps in Italy: "My feeling was that this outfit had never really found themselves. Certainly everybody over there had tough jobs. They never had the breaks — the breaks always went against them, and I know that our staff was almost superstitious about this. They felt that anything ever given to the 36th was going to go wrong. I know, particularly, that our operations and intelligence people thought this way and breathed a sigh of relief whenever the 36th would go back into a rest area because they felt that then things would begin to sort themselves out."[12]

The reputation of the 36th[13] was not improved by an incident which occurred earlier that week. During the night, one of the division's highest-ranking officers awoke to go to the latrine. His closest friend, sleeping next to him, heard the stir and, believing that it was caused by German infiltrators, clawed for his gun and shot his friend in the chest. The story spread rapidly through the Fifth Army, few soldiers ignoring the opportunity to add ribald comments about the "trigger-happy 36th."

There were very few in Italy who regarded the 36th Division with respect. After their performance at the Salerno landing, General Clark ordered Walker to replace many of his original National Guard staff officers.[14] The implication that they were incompetent was unmistakable. Walker regarded this as a reflection on himself, and his feelings toward his former student turned into bitterness. When the replacements arrived, there was talk that he spent considerable time trying to ascertain which, if any of them, were plants sent by General Clark to spy on him.

The replacements didn't quiet the division's reputation for dissension or nepotism. One of Walker's sons was the division G–3, a sensitive post which is primarily concerned with operations and planning. Clark made another visit to Walker's headquarters in an effort to change the assignment, saying, "Fred, gosh, I just don't think it's right,"[15] but unwilling to further antagonize the man who had been his mentor, he didn't forbid it by direct order. Walker's son later became embroiled in an argument with the division's intelligence chief and thereafter the two key section heads spoke only through intermediaries to each other.

Another of Walker's sons became his father's aide, and a staff officer recalls: "I was assigned to the 36th at the time and one day while the pressure was off, a group of us decided to take a bath in the creek. Among them was Walker's son. We were all knee-deep in the water when suddenly a headquarters officer came down carrying a gas mask. Ignoring the rest of us, he addressed himself to young Walker. 'Your father wants you to put this on,' he told him."[16]

According to recollections by various other headquarters officers, Walker's feelings toward Clark were further discolored by-the belief of the older man that Clark had reneged on a promise to give him the first available corps command, a position which could have meant a promotion to the rank of lieutenant general.

Robert van de Velde, then a II Corps intelligence officer and now a faculty member of the Woodrow Wilson School at Princeton, offers this analysis of the 36th as it stood before Velletri:

"The 36th was never given a chance to recover from its initial sad experience at Salerno. An outfit that takes a beating in its first or early days of combat never seems to recover until it has a success. The 36th just never had the success necessary to bring it back together and restore its confidence in itself. It could have been a great division. What the hell, all of them started out pretty much the same, and very often it just depends on which division is where at any given moment. Some of them become great and some don't.

"I don't think that there is a tremendous amount of difference in the ability of officers. There are, obviously, personality and capability differences, but no general (and people usually talk about units in the names of their commanders) stands alone. These chaps have to depend not only on their immediate staff, but their subordinate commanders and so on down the line. So, when you talk about Clark or Walker, you are really talking about, in each case, a group of men. If you take that group and match it against a similar group somewhere else, the chances are that the average ability will not be too different. But there is, of course, in history that precise moment when a commander's ability — some special gift or art or skill that he has developed or was born with — shows up."[17]

Velletri was Walker's moment in history. Reluctant to stick his professional neck out any further, aware that the echelons above him planned to relegate his division to a safe secondary role, Walker nevertheless found that that intangible "special gift or art or skill" would not let him rest.

General Walker's and Sergeant Shaffer's recollections vary somewhat, but the fact remains that permission for the infiltration was reluctantly but finally given. Clark and Truscott were hungry to eliminate the last roadblock on the road to Rome. If Walker could take Velletri, the ring around the city could be snapped at minimum cost.

The 141st, 142nd, and 143rd infantry regiments made up the 36th Division. Walker's battle plan sent the 142nd, under the command of Colonel George E. Lynch, through the two-mile-wide gap he had discovered between the left flank of the German 1st Parachute Division and the right flank of the 76th Panzer Corps, and to then turn north and west. The 143rd would follow, fanning out to the southwest, while the 141st was to approach Velletri from the west. In effect, the 36th was about to encircle the last enemy garrison before Rome.

At noon on May 30, Colonel Lynch was still unaware that Walker's new plan had been substituted for his previously received orders. While he was issuing final instructions to his subordinate commanders to implement the old plan, his briefing was interrupted by a messenger from Walker. "The General wants to see you right away," he was told. Lynch recalls: "The division attack plan was simple and direct. Given orally, it was a short, mission-type order, uncluttered with the detail that goes into a written directive, simply a 'where-to-go' order without any 'how-to-do-it.' "[18]

Private First Class Richard J. Kennedy, now a master sergeant in the Air Force, was there when Lynch returned with his news. "He told the officers and men alike," says Kennedy, "that we must go behind the city of Velletri . . . make a fifteen-mile hike through the Alban Hills, and infiltrate enemy lines without firing a shot. This was hard to take, but Colonel Lynch said, 'If anyone wants out, get out now. This is your last chance.' We all got our packs and equipment and started walking."[19]

Now committed, Walker was impatient that the maneuver should begin with the least delay. He went to Lynch's headquarters in order to push the troops forward as fast as possible. He recalls that: "I told the battalion commander, 'Now is the time for you to get going. Get going rapidly, because we don't want to waste any time.' Well, they didn't move as fast as I felt that they should have, so I said to one of the lieutenants, 'Lieutenant, get your troops up, get them on their feet, and get them going.' And he went about his business and nothing happened. After a few minutes, he came back near me again and I said, 'Lieutenant, get your troops up and get them going,' and he answered without the slightest hesitation, 'General, I'm going, but I'm *not* going until I get ready.' And I realized that when he made that statement, he was telling me, 'General, mind your own business.' So I withdrew and let him handle the job."[20]

The regiment, in column form, began to glide out in the weak moonlight. Leading elements crossed the highway shortly after midnight, the men spaced as far apart as visibility allowed. The regimental headquarters report for that day departed from its usually stiff military phrases in order to describe the trek:

The route followed was off the trail through parallel rows of grape vineyards which afforded good cover. Out to the left toward Velletri there was a steady exchange of machine-gun fire where we knew the 141st Infantry Regiment was engaged. Occasionally a shot spoke loudly at or near the column and there was a moment of breathless anticipation as to what might follow. Passing by some of the houses en route dogs howled and even a jackass brayed. But the time of greatest tension happened around 0300 when mass enemy air action

hovered overhead. During the night there had been single planes
obviously on reconnaissance but at this time the enemy was over in
great numbers. Antiaircraft shot up its sparkling display of defensive
fires. The planes hovered threateningly near. Then the inevitable
flares were dropped to light up the area as broad daylight. They were
not too far off. Or so it seemed. Of course everyone in our foot
column hugged the ground and waited. Bombs were bursting and the
chatter of strafing action grew louder. But it was soon apparent that
we were not the enemy's target that time. In fact, it was very
favorable to us as it focused attention away from our sector to over in
front of Velletri where it was taking place. The flares lasted about a
half-hour after which we moved on again while the drone of the
planes gradually faded out.

The next concern was the fact that daylight would soon be upon
us. The bulk of the mountains were still before us. At 0415 the first
gray light of day began to dim out the stars. The head of the column
was just starting up the slopes. A broad open field had to be crossed
before climbing the hills. But in the early morning haze it would have
been difficult to distinguish the moving column. Our pace hurried.
There was no one to oppose us. The infantrymen clambered up the
slopes.[21]

As part of the security measures for the mission, Colonel Lynch
issued a directive strange to infantrymen: "I told them that in
order to minimize the chance of new men disclosing our show by
firing at noises in the dark, all troops were to move with loaded
magazines but no ammunition in the rifle or pistol chambers until
the break of dawn. Any killing was to be done by bayonet, knife
or other quiet means. Traveling between the two leading battalions
all night, I did not hear a single shot until after dawn."

Lynch recalled another, and lighter, moment occurring during
the nocturnal march: "We heard some rustling in the bushes to the
right of us, and then someone out there called, 'Who's that?' One
of my group answered that we were regimental headquarters.
There was silence for a moment and then we heard the voice in the
bushes say, 'Come on boys, we're *way* behind.' "[22]

Eric Sevareid and *Life* photographer Carl Mydans accompanied the march. Sevareid remembers seeing General Walker just before it began: "The advance Command Post of the division now consisted of several bearded officers squatting under a railroad trestle studying a map. General Walker gave me a curt nod and continued pacing back and forth under the trestle. He was a solemn, self-contained man and this was the first time I had ever observed him in a state of perturbation."[23]

A 143rd Regiment platoon sergeant named Hubert A. Simons also saw Walker that night. "The main thing I remember is that I wanted a smoke bad, so I got down on the ground and took my raincoat and covered up and lit a cigarette. Someone came along and kicked me, so I jumped up real quick and there stood General Walker. He said, 'Sergeant, don't you know better than to smoke tonight? We are trying to get around behind the Germans and they might see you and give away what we are trying to do.' I felt real bad."[24]

Correspondent Kenneth Dixon adds a macabre footnote to the men's interpretation of the order to keep silent. "Pfc. Dick Kennedy, a nineteen-year-old 'Texan' from Chicago, tapped me on the shoulder as he crawled past me up the line and pointed over to the right.

" 'That guy must know you, reporter. He's smiling.'

"There had been no outcry ahead, but a German soldier was propped up against a tree, wearing two grins in the moonlight — a white one where his teeth were bared and a dark red one three inches below. I kept crawling."[25]

When asked about the incident, Kennedy recalled: "Yes, there were several sentries eliminated without any noise, using wire and knives. Sentries were crawled upon and jumped from the rear. The thumb and the index finger holding the German's nose and the other three fingers of the left hand placed over the mouth, jerking the head full back exposing the jugular. Holding the knife in the right hand, the blade was swiftly inserted between the vein and the neck bone. As it was pushed through the skin and behind the jugular and air pipes, the knife then came out under the chin.

The guard bled to death without a sound except bubbles of blood."[26]

The division photographer, Max Shaffer, picks up the narrative: "We marched all night. It seemed to me that almost all of this march was through one large draw. We had all been cautioned to maintain absolute silence, and when the troops learned what we were doing, this became the quietest bunch of guys I have ever seen. All night long I never heard so much as a small clink from a piece of equipment. We started the long climb later on in the night and just before dawn broke I realized we had reached our objective, the hills behind Velletri. Mount Artemisio.

"This march gave me a very odd feeling, because a large body of men [had] marched all night through German lines and not one shot had been fired at us.

"When we reached the top of the hills behind Velletri, some of the troops were sent down toward the town to some high ground closer to town while a platoon was sent down to some overhanging ground on the highway. This roadblock was later reinforced before noon of that day.

"We still had not fired a shot at dawn, nor had a shot been fired at us. We could look down on the town and had a very good view of the highway approaches to the town from the German side. This was the Rome highway, Highway 7.

"I got the impression from the troops that I was with that they were rather enjoying this operation. For some of these soldiers, it was the first time that they felt they had the Germans in the palms of their hands and they planned to make the most of it."[27]

The few hours following daybreak are best described by the men who were there. Sergeant Latham Jones, a member of a tank destroyer battalion, said, "Next morning we were in a clearing a hundred yards from the road when a German command car stopped at the road junction. The officer got out smartly, pulled the road map out of his case and looked at it for a few minutes. Then he slowly raised his head and stared at us for about a half a minute, then studied the map for fifteen seconds, then zoomed back out in the direction of Rome. We were laughing so hard we couldn't fire on him."[28]

James L. Minor, a lieutenant colonel commanding the 1st Battalion of the 142nd Infantry, vividly reconstructs this scene: "Before daylight we were dug in and ready for anything. Our plans were made and we had our weapons so situated that in case we caught a convoy coming out of or going into Velletri, our bazookas and heavy MG's would knock out the lead and last vehicle and then we would mow the other vehicles in between all to pieces. We did not have to wait long. Just after daylight, a German ration and ammunition convoy came into the trap from the direction of Marino and headed for Velletri. We worked our strategy as planned and it turned out perfectly. We knocked out the first and last vehicle and then shot up all the others. There was utter confusion among the Germans and we killed a bunch of them and captured the remainder. We and the other 'Dogfaces' immediately cleared the highway of all the vehicles and debris and were ready for the next convoy or vehicles of any sort. Needless to say, we all ate real good for the next several days as the German ration trucks were loaded with all kinds of goodies and foods such as strawberries, peaches, cherries, etc. This was repeated often throughout most of the morning and we shot up an untold amount of German vehicles of every sort, killed a number of Germans and captured a bunch more.

"Up until just before noon, there had not been one single vehicle come out of Velletri. They were all going into Velletri. I guess the Germans in Velletri finally awakened to the fact that something was wrong because just before noon a convoy of about eighteen German tanks appeared around the turn in the road coming out of Velletri with a German officer standing in the first tank, arms folded 'Hitler type.' The men were in position and they were to fire on my orders; bazookas first at the first and last tank and then everything we had was to cut loose. After the last tank had come around the turn from Velletri, I gave the orders to the bazooka men to fire. Their hits were perfect, knocking out the lead and last tank, and then we cut down on the tank convoy with everything. The Germans were completely confused — they began jumping out of the tanks and running and we mowed 'em down. We captured all of the German tanks along with some Germans. The thing I will always remember about this incident was the German officer in the lead tank — when the bazooka round hit he squirted out of the turret like a cork out of a champagne bottle."[29]

It was a field day for the artillery observers who had accompanied the infantry to the peaks. Given an unobstructed view of the German positions, they spent the day directing Allied fire into the city and the crowded network of roads behind the enemy lines. W. A. Garrard described the havoc caused by the shelling: "About eight that morning, it was still quiet and it looked as if every German in Velletri was coming out of the buildings to assemble into regimental formations. They began loading their equipment into trucks as if they were going to march out in parade formation. It was obvious that they did not know that we were waiting for them in the mountains above. Our observers brought down the divisional and corps artillery on the Krauts. The barrage must have lasted about fifteen minutes. After it was lifted and the smoke cleared, the streets of Velletri were littered with dead Krauts and wrecked equipment."[30]

When the 141st Infantry made its attack on the town that afternoon, hundreds of prisoners were routed out of the extensive fortifications, tunnels and reinforced gun positions — unmistakable evidence that the Germans had assigned Velletri major importance in their defense line.

Captain Jack L. Scott, of Oklahoma City, remembers, "When I arrived in Velletri, a fire fight was going on. Standing in the center of the square, directing things, was General Walker. He had beat us into the city."[31]

By nightfall, all of the objectives had been gained and three thousand men were firmly entrenched south of what had been the Germans' last defense line before Rome. The losses to Walker's forces had been amazingly light, and now, after many months of agonizing inching forward, the way to Rome was clear. By taking Velletri in this fashion, Walker had saved the Allies the fearful costs of continued frontal assaults. General Truscott later noted that "this was the turning point."[32]

There were others who found pleasure in the feat over and above its considerable military worth. Lieutenant General Geoffrey Keyes, the commanding general of II Corps, was especially proud because, as Colonel Porter explained, "General Keyes always had a warm spot in his heart for the 36th. When they took Velletri, all of us felt proud, because it was as if we had an erring son who had suddenly found himself."[33]

His Texans had always been unshakably loyal to General Walker. Not one of them showed any inclination to dilute his triumph. The brilliant engineer who had cut through the road that had supplied the fighting elements, Colonel Oran C. Stovall, spoke for most when he observed: "Generally the army commander is credited with winning the battle, but in many cases, if the truth were known, the troops played a far greater part than the commander. But the battle of Velletri was all Walker's; it was his plan, he directed it and he led it. He put his head in the noose for instant hanging if it failed to work. For my part, I was only the pick-and-shovel boy trying to do what the boss wanted done."[34]

These sentiments were not confined to the officers. Almost every questionnaire answered by the enlisted men of the 36th contained high praise for Fred Walker. For example, the photographer, Shaffer, said: "In looking back on Velletri, now I realize that at no time did I ever doubt that what we were trying in going through the German lines could be done. In all the action around Velletri I never heard a man express doubt regarding the maneuver. I never heard a man grumble about any part of it, and almost every man I talked to was sure of what they were doing and many of them were aware that General Walker was behind this operation all the way."[35]

This was Fred Walker's "brilliant moment," and it has dwarfed every other triumph or setback in his career. It is given to very few men to achieve more than one masterpiece in a lifetime.

Rome fell within the next week. It was a prize that many men and many units had raced to achieve. A paragraph written by John P. Delaney contains an eagle's-eye view of the closing phase of the competition:

In its final stages, the drive for Rome developed into pretty much of a rat race. The II Corps — including the 88th, 85th, and 3rd Divisions, and the 1st Special Service Force as its major components — was moving up in the Highway 6 area. To the west, the IV Corps cleaned up what was left of the opposition and drove on Rome from that direction. In back of the line troops, jammed bumper to bumper, came all the rear echelon units from as far back as Naples. Rome was the ripest plum in Italy in the way of civilization and fancy billets and no one wanted to be left out. For months before the May jumpoff headquarters and rear outfits had pored over street and building maps picking the choice spots in the city for new quarters. Some far-sighted brass even had selected apartment sites and villas as their main objectives in their own personal drives. Now that the city was almost in our hands, every vehicle that could roll was loaded with office supplies and equipment and headed up Highway 6."[36]

But what set them racing to Rome? And what reason was there for the Allies to be fighting the bloody Italian campaign in the first place?

CHAPTER II

DECEMBER 1941–JULY 1943

Our men, General Marshall, Admiral King, Secretary Stimson and, certainly, General Ike were all cross-Channel from the very beginning. Anything else was unwelcome diversionary tactics. So, when Mr. Roosevelt took the position to go for the North African thing, he did it with a very reluctant staff.

But I think it proved to be the only thing we could have done under the circumstances, because Dieppe demonstrated that we were in no position to make a Channel crossing. Our losses would have been horrendous. So, with Mr. Roosevelt fearful that Stalin was going to quit on several occasions, plus Stalin's insistence that we have a second front, the only thing we were physically able to do at that time was the North African enterprise.

But I felt you had an honest difference of opinion.

— AMBASSADOR ROBERT MURPHY[1]

THE "race" mentioned by John Delaney is more than a bit of imagery. In 1944, to any observer lucky enough to have a vantage point in Italy in which he didn't have to endure the choking dust in summer or inch through mud that was really freezing slime in winter, the drive on Rome did indeed have the aspects of a race: a horse race.

The competitors were the divisions of England, New Zealand, France, Poland, Brazil, and a host of other wildly disparate nationalities. The Americans had two formidable units in the VI Corps and II Corps, each spurred by a hard-driving professional.

From their positions of overall command, Clark and Alexander should not have appeared as participants in the race. But the histories and memoirs of the period unmistakably indicate their emotional involvement. Clark wanted the honor of the first entry into Rome reserved for members of the Fifth Army, and there is abundant evidence that Alexander would not have been displeased if the British Eighth shared the first day of capture.[2]

And always hovering not too far from the arena during this stage of the campaign were the "Big Three" — Franklin D. Roosevelt, Winston Churchill, and Josef Stalin. Obviously, their daily interest was diluted by important happenings in other parts of the globe, but the conclusions they reached at Quebec, Teheran, London, Washington, and other places established the ground rules for the Italian campaign. The major political decision of World War II was that it would be fought by a close alliance of America, Great Britain, and Russia.[3] Such a concept made it inevitable that the war in Europe would receive priority over the Pacific fight.

History tells us that the alliance worked much better than might have been expected. English and American leaders engaged in a running dispute over priorities of targets, but the arguments never strayed far from the level of a family scrap.[4] Relationships with Russia were a different matter. In the early days of the entente, there was always a considerable fear that Russia would cave in, give up the fight because of the frightful punishment she was taking, and be forced to sign a separate peace.[5]

This fear caused President Roosevelt and, occasionally, Winston Churchill to concede so many points to Stalin that, to this day, their activities during the period are regarded, in some quarters, as suspiciously soft-headed.[6]

The fact remains that Russia fought the good fight. She signed no separate peace even though the Nazi hordes tore at her vitals through most of the first half of World War II. And, after the Germans lost impetus, she mounted the counterattack which rolled westward like a tidal wave. In the absence of this quite amazing display of fortitude, England might very well have gone under, leaving America standing alone to fight both European and Asian wars.

« 2 »

The Fifth Army's road to Rome properly begins with Mark Clark losing his pants in North Africa. Landed on a lonely beach by submarine during the German domination of that continent, he was there because Roosevelt and Churchill, meeting in Washington with their staffs shortly after the Pearl Harbor attack and again six months later, had agreed to shelve an immediate cross-Channel invasion in favor of regaining control of the Mediterranean through the occupation of French North Africa.

This was not an easy decision to reach. The Americans wanted to invade Europe immediately. The British were unwilling to antagonize a potent ally, but were fearful of the dangers of mounting such an attack before it had been assured of success. A recent raid on Dieppe had persuaded them that such an undertaking would be suicidal at this stage of the game, and the penalty for losing, they felt, would be an immediate invasion of their homeland.[7] This conflict of views resulted in a long and bitter controversy. Spurred on by Stalin's insistent demand for a pressure-relieving second front, it eventually resulted in the Italian campaign. And, like many compromises, it ended by pleasing no one.

Winston Churchill arrived in Washington in June 1942 to meet with President Roosevelt and the American generals, and, hopefully, to scuttle BOLERO, the American proposal for an immediate buildup of United States forces in the United Kingdom in preparation for the early invasion of Nazi-dominated Europe. Churchill was against this plan. He passionately believed that it was premature and that if the project went wrong in France or Belgium, the results could be so disastrous that the war might be lost.[8]

In an effort to convert the Americans to this viewpoint, he called upon every bit of eloquence he could muster. And Churchill, at his best, was an almost irresistible force. Harry Hopkins, the executive assistant to the President, was later to say, "We have come to avoid controversy with Winston; we find he is too much for us."[9]

The trip was successful. To the considerable disappointment of General George C. Marshall, the quiet administrative genius who built the American World War II armies into the largest war machine the world had ever known, President Roosevelt agreed to postpone the invasion until 1943 and, instead, initiate the planning and execution of an assault, code-named TORCH, on North Africa.

Roosevelt's agreement was not entirely due to his conviction that it represented the proper military strategy. Continually pushed by Stalin to provide an immediate second front and never quite forgetting that he needed tangible evidence of military accomplishment to help him win a favorable balance in the coming Congressional elections, he saw that a successful major American military effort would result in needed political capital.

General Marshall later recalled, "When I went in to see Roosevelt and told him about [planning for] TORCH, he held up his hands in an attitude of prayer and said, 'Please make it before Election Day.' However, when I found we had to have more time and it came afterward, he never said a word. He was very courageous."[10]

General Marshall was unhappy with the concept of TORCH. But even as he continued to offer reasons for an early invasion of France, the Chief of Staff remained busy with the creation of the giant that became the American army. Although Marshall has had severe critics, it has never been disputed that the subsequent success of our field forces was due primarily to his enormous ability to visualize all of the ramifications involved in attaining a goal and then, almost unerringly, select the proper men to plan and execute it.

One of the young officers who earned Marshall's attention was Dwight D. Eisenhower. Colonel Eisenhower, as Chief of Staff of the Third Army, had distinguished himself during the summer maneuvers of 1941. Marshall had been told that the young man "possessed broad vision, progressive ideas, . . . and lots of initiative and resourcefulness."[11] Ike lived up to his advance billing and, at the conclusion of the exercises in September, was promoted from colonel to brigadier general.

Other men who were to play important parts on the march on Rome came to the Chief of Staff's attention during this period. The ability that Major General George S. Patton displayed during the Louisiana maneuvers to mount and execute slashing armored attacks outweighed the distaste Marshall felt for the man's flamboyance, profanity, and what he later described as "an irrational obsession with war."[12] Patton was marked for high command.

Self-effacing Omar Bradley, who was to lead II Corps in Sicily; Courtney Hodges; Terry Allen; "Beetle" Smith — these were the names of other men who Marshall knew would grow into the leadership that victory required. Marshall had never forgotten the smugness with which green American troops landing in France during the First World War had proclaimed, "Lafayette, we are here," and then persisted in a string of blunders which lasted until they had gained enough experience to handle themselves in combat in a workmanlike manner. If he had to accept it, he was determined to wring out of the North African adventure the training he felt his men would need when later on they set out across the English Channel.[13] And, when General Marshall thought of training, he thought of Ike's close friend Mark Clark.

« 3 »

Because so many of Clark's later activities in Italy were molded by his experiences during this period, it is pertinent now to isolate and identify them.

One of his great sources of pride is the fact that there have been three generations of Clarks graduated from West Point: his father, Colonel Charles G. Clark, in 1890; he himself in 1917; and his son, William, in 1945. Actors point up their heritage by claiming, "I was born backstage in a trunk." Clark was born in 1896 at Madison Barracks, New York, where his father was then stationed.

He never questioned that he would follow his father's career. His entry into West Point provoked no spasms of doubt or soul-searching. He was where he wanted to be and he thoroughly enjoyed all four years of it. Six feet, two inches tall, so thin that he had to choose baseball rather than football as his major sport, the possessor of a craggy face led by a nose of noble proportions, he was the embodiment of the Western American folk-hero. Later in North Africa, one impressed Frenchman described him as "an absolute Gary Cooper." His appearance may provide a key to some of the reactions to him. During some particularly violent negotiations with the French commanders in North Africa, an OSS operative on the scene put down in his diary, ". . . at this bit of defiance, Clark put on his grim movie actor's face."[14]

To this day Mark Clark's love for sports and his appreciation of the American West partially indicate that he is not one given to intellectual pursuits. It is doubtful, in the words of one of his friends, "that Wayne reads more than two books a year." Clark's closest friends have always referred to him by his middle name, "Wayne," which seems to be a softer and, perhaps, more affectionate gesture than one of those determinedly colorful nicknames affected by so many military professionals.

He is a considerate man. Throughout the almost forty years of his marriage to Maurine Clark (she died in 1966), they spent few days together in which he did not pick a bunch of flowers to present to his beloved "Reeny."[15] Many journalists found him self-seeking, haughty, and at times a stuffed shirt, but the response from every enlisted man who ever had close contact with him is one of respect and affection for his thoughtfulness.

He is not a wit, but he is a man of constant good humor. He feels no compunction about telling a self-deflating story if it is funny enough. He once recalled that after having retired as commanding general in Korea, he was walking down a New York street, when he became aware that a woman was following him. "Finally," he says, "she caught up with me and reached for my hand. She said, 'I've always admired you. I've always followed your career.' I blushed modestly and mumbled something and then she added, 'God bless you always, Senator Kefauver.' "

Wounded in World War I, in which he served as a battalion commander, Clark followed the usual post-to-post trek of the professional between wars. He was marked by his superiors during this period as capable of key responsibilities, and was picked for attendance at the Command and General Staff School and the Army War College. Just prior to the outbreak of World War II, he again came to the attention of his superiors when, as a major in charge of the plans and operations section of the 3rd Division, his training of the unit resulted in a very successful simulated amphibious assault landing on the beaches of Monterey, California.

This performance yielded one of the mystical "lucky breaks" which studded Clark's meteoric career. Brigadier General Leslie McNair, soon to be placed in command of the Army Ground

Forces, was intensely interested in amphibious warfare. Hearing about the 3rd Division's activities at Monterey, he wrote to the young officer who had played such an important part in them. A continuing correspondence followed. When McNair received his new assignment, he requested that Clark head his plans and operations section.

Then another factor intersected: McNair was quite deaf. Because Clark couples ability with great personal charm, he was asked to represent his chief in a series of important conferences, many of them taking place in General Marshall's office. Thus, Clark came to the attention of almost everyone who counted those days in Washington. By 1940, Clark was a brigadier general, having been jumped to that rank from lieutenant colonel.[16]

This rapid rise was almost unquestionably due to solid performance. General Marshall recalled after the war ended: "General Clark played a very determining part [in developing the army's training programs]. As a matter of fact, the method of raising these divisions, building them up, was largely worked out by General Clark. He would sit across the desk from me up in the Chief of Staff's office and we would work out the details."[17]

Naturally, sudden prominence like this carried with it the unavoidable ill will and jealousy of certain seniors. General Marshall's biographer, Forrest C. Pogue, noted: "To members of the Personnel and Plans divisions of the War Department, already upset because their functions were being shifted to GHQ, the Chief of Staff's tendency to listen to this newcomer was especially frustrating. They, as well as many generals in the field, . . . growled as Clark rose rapidly toward the top in the Washington hierarchy. Like many men near the source of power, Clark grew both in self-confidence and in capacity to exasperate his contemporaries and former superiors, gaining many powerful enemies."[18]

Clark, describing his reactions in a later conversation, observed, "A young fellow with a war on is just praying for a chance to get into combat and do things. I wasn't about to say 'No, I won't accept' to anything. But I was overwhelmed. I began to realize it when they were assigning these senior people to me all the time. Colonels — my seniors all the way back to West Point — would be in the field and I'd go out [to see them] as a brigadier general. Now I've thought about this, the way I was catapulted, I just made a hell of a lot of people mad."[19]

There was one friend, not yet powerful but destined to play a major role in Mark Clark's life, who didn't growl at the lanky man's success. Dwight D. Eisenhower, who had been at West Point with Clark and was now an obscure lieutenant colonel in the field, wrote to Clark at the War Department in 1940:

It is perfectly okay with me if the personnel section . . . is aware of the fact that I have an ambition to command one of the next armored regiments to be formed. They will probably think me a conceited individual, but I see no objection to setting your sights high . . . I do hope to avoid Staff and to stay on troop duty for some time to come. And since I notice that in the original assignments they gave one of the armored regiments to a lieutenant colonel, I will hope that they might think that much of me also."[20]

The closeness of Clark and Ike has been an enduring relationship. General Eisenhower summarized it once by saying that he and Wayne had always been close friends, that although he was a couple of classes ahead of Clark at West Point, he later became friendly with Clark's mother, who asked him to keep an eye on her boy. And, as a matter of fact, the friends always looked out for each other. When Clark was made a brigadier general, he immediately began plumping for Ike to get his star. When Ike went to Europe to survey the military situation, naturally he asked his friend to go along with him. After graduation, the two men and their wives kept in touch throughout the peacetime years. When Marshall, in anticipation of the oncoming war, began to search for fresh new talent to replace the older men who had been holding the fort at the War Department for the past two decades, one of his first choices was Eisenhower. Ike had come to his attention at an earlier time, but Clark's jogging of his elbow on Ike's behalf during the buildup certainly helped along the process of natural selection.

Clark recalls Ike's entry into the ranks of the generals: "I was conducting the critique of the big Louisiana maneuver where they had Lear and Krueger's army pitted against each other. There were two thousand officers in the audience, and while I was talking, someone handed me a telegram dealing with promotions. I looked at the list for brigadiers and there were about twenty names on it. Ike, who was chief of staff to General Lear during this maneuver, was third on it. And so I read the list, purposely skipping Ike's name. I got through the list and said, 'That's it, gentlemen.' I could see Ike sitting down in front of me. He had been expecting to be on the list. Then I said, 'Oh, I'm sorry. I omitted one name. Dwight D. Eisenhower,' and I saw his lips say silently, 'You son-of-a-bitch!' "[21]

Ike's subsequent career resembled the upward path of a sky-rocket. Possessing unusual talents as a planner, an administrator, and a diplomat, he was promoted into prominence over the heads of hundreds of senior officers. As a matter of fact, his promotion to major general preceded Clark's.

"I was McNair's chief of staff by then," says Clark, "and we were going ahead doing our job by building the divisions. Ike and I collaborated all the time . . . at his house or my house. He was doing planning and I was training. Then one day Marshall sent for us to go to Europe and make some recommendations for command of the troops we had building up there."

The trip was a productive one. On the basis of their findings, Eisenhower was selected as the commanding officer of the American Forces in Europe. To head the ground forces then grouped under the banner of II Corps, his immediate selection was Mark Clark.

Maurine Clark described the departure of her husband and his friend on this new path:

"On a rainy morning, dark and gray, Bill [their son] and I

went with Wayne to the airport from which he was to leave for that strange, menacing war whose course and ending and tragedy none could foresee. There he joined Ike for the flight to England. It was like a dream, frightening and unreal, to think that in a moment or two Wayne, whom I could see and hear and feel; Wayne, who was standing there with his arm around me; Wayne, who was grinning and trying to give me a final word of cheer, would step into that airplane and be lost to me, gone from my sight and touch for nobody knew how long.

"Ike said good-by and left Wayne, Bill, and me standing alone in the rain, trying so desperately to think of something meaningful to say, something that could be treasured as a parting memory. Nothing came and finally Wayne kissed me and was gone. Bill and I turned to walk toward the automobile. But a figure came hurtling through the rain, out of the mist. It was Ike, trying to do just a little more to help me keep my chin up, kissing me once again and saying, 'Don't worry about Wayne, I'll take good care of him.' And then they were gone."[22]

The British, spurred perhaps by the desire to make psychological capital out of the potential strength of their American ally, lionized Eisenhower. But Clark was so little noticed that William Dickinson, now managing editor of the Philadelphia *Bulletin* and then a United Press correspondent in London, said, "Clark was a complete unknown. After an impressive reception at the Guildhall, everyone had heard of Eisenhower, but no one ever heard of Clark in those days."[23]

Clark's duties in England included the indoctrination of the officers coming over in almost daily boatloads to form cadres for the various headquarters of the growing command. One reserve officer was repelled by some of the attitudes: "I'll never forget," he says, "Clark's getting up in front of his staff officers in the beginning days in England and saying, 'Boys, just relax, there's going to be plenty of jobs for everybody.' This was a group of 305 officers who had no assignment but headquarters . . . and every single one of them was so rank-conscious, it was just awful.

They'd been waiting all these years for a war to start so they could get a promotion. It was so obvious it was just terrible. Some of them, though, turned out fairly good."[24]

Winston Churchill lost no time in cultivating the two young American generals. He noted in his diary:

When on August 24 I returned from Cairo to London, much remained to be decided about the final shaping of our plans and on the following day Generals Eisenhower and Clark came to dine with me to discuss the state of the operation.

I was at this time in very close and agreeable contact with these American officers. From the moment they arrived in June I had arranged a weekly luncheon at Number 10 on Tuesdays. These meetings seemed to be a success. I was nearly always alone with them, and we talked all our affairs over, back and forth, as if we were all of one country. I set great value on these personal contacts. Irish stew turned out to be very popular with my American guests, and especially with General Eisenhower. My wife was nearly always able to get this. I soon began to call him "Ike." For Mark Clark and Bedell Smith, the latter of whom arrived early in September as Chief of Staff to Eisenhower, I coined the titles "the American Eagle" and "the American Bulldog." We also had a number of informal conferences in our downstairs dining-room, beginning at about ten o'clock at night and sometimes running late.[25]

Churchill's peccadillos fascinated them. Clark told Ike's aide, Harry Butcher, in a mixture of awe and amusement how the Prime Minister guzzled his soup with speed and loud noises at meals, knocked over a highball glass at the dinner table with his elbow and completely ignored it, and then, later in the evening, told a servant to bring him a fresh pair of socks and exchanged them for the ones he was wearing without ever missing a conversational stroke. One of these evenings had a peculiar highlight when the Prime Minister walked to an open door, rubbed his back vigorously against it and cheerfully remarked, "Guess I picked 'em up in Egypt."[26]

Churchill used these meetings as an opportunity to continue the vigorous prosecution of his views that a North African expedition would be preferable, as a next step, to an invasion across the Channel. Rightly assuming that the two men were a direct conduit to Marshall and Roosevelt, he brought out every argument to keep the Americans firm in their resolve to go through with the project.[27] Will Lang, then a correspondent in the European Theater and now chief of the *Life* regional news bureaus, offers this explanation of Churchill's attitude: "I feel fairly sure that Churchill was just aghast at the possibility of casualties on the order of [those] which the British suffered in World War I. It took them generations to get over it — if you consider that they ever got over it at all."[28]

Clark, who is about as pragmatic as a man can get, was entertained but not swayed by Churchill's eloquent pyrotechnics. Even though he agreed with the Prime Minister's position, it was his own decision. Describing it, he said, "We were right in the middle of this battle between Churchill and the Americans. When General Marshall or Admiral King or Harry Hopkins came or sent messages about this cross-Channel thing, I answered, 'We're as anxious to get into battle as you are.' But, having just come from America, I knew everything we had, being responsible for the training. So I kept sending messages back to them listing what I needed for this thing, knowing full well that there wasn't any capacity for them to deliver it.

"In my opinion, it [the invasion of France] would have been catastrophic at this time. We had no means whatsoever to cross the Channel. None whatsoever.

"You see, here was this overwhelming desire that American troops get into the war. Stalin was putting the heat on all the time — 'When are you going to fight?' and 'When are the Americans going to get their feet wet?' So, they finally decided in Washington that we had to get into battle. Preferably before Election Day.

"Anyway, we got to work on the planning for North Africa. Ike and I had an apartment together — two bedrooms and a living room in which Ike and I would walk up and down talking and planning half the night. I'd say, 'We haven't got enough air support for this Oran thing' or 'We haven't got this or that,' and he'd make a note of it and say, 'Well, we'll take those up with the Prime Minister tonight.'

"When we'd get to Churchill, we always got a decision. Brother, did that bird make decisions! I can tell you that as we got closer to D-Day, he'd be back and forth with the President on the wire almost constantly. He'd send for me. He'd be in his office walking up and down and he'd say, 'I'm about to dictate a message to your President. I want you to listen to it and tell me if you think I've expressed myself clearly and if you think he will understand it.' And I'd do the best I could.

"One night at 10 Downing Street he asked me if we were going to meet the appointed D-Day date for North Africa. I told him I doubted it, that I had been talking with General Eisenhower and it didn't look like we could meet the date for the landing because of the delay in loading our ships in Scotland. He said, 'Why is there this delay?' I answered, 'Because your people have been making us load at night without any lights whatsoever in order to avoid bombing.' This was about one in the morning, but without any hesitation he got the head of their naval operations on the phone and said, 'How soon can you get over here?' And he'd drag him over. He kept dragging his department heads out all night. After they hashed it back and forth, and he had satisfied himself, he issued an order to leave the lights on, effective the following night.

"I feel that one of the greatest privileges of my life was the fact that I was able to know Churchill. He was a great man. A great man."[29]

Field Marshal Sir Alan Brooke, chief of the Imperial General Staff (a position comparable to that of General Marshall), also admired the Prime Minister, but like so many of the other members of Churchill's staff, found that dealing with him could be a difficult proposition. Brooke noted in his diary:

Winston's lack of "width" and "depth" in the examination of problems was a factor I never got over. He would select individual pieces of the vast jigsaw puzzle which we had in frcnt of us and concentrate on it at the expense of all others. When I used to say, "But can't you see that if we concentrate on B, plans A and C will be affected?" he would reply, "I do not want to see A and C. Can't you see that B is the vital point?" I used to reply that B was certainly important at the time, but reminded him that last week A had been of major importance and that probably next week C would require most attention. These arguments were useless, and he would continue examining B as if A and C did not exist.[30]

Another view was supplied by Field Marshal J. C. Smuts, the South African leader whom Churchill respected more than almost any other living man. Someone once asked General Smuts what technique he thought would be most helpful in dealing with the Prime Minister. Smuts answered, "Well, I think he would have to have a command of rhetoric. But even then he would always be talked down."[31]

However, the Prime Minister's personal physician, Lord Moran, supplies the view that may come closest to defining the man's greatness:

What his critics are apt to forget is that you cannot measure inspiration. That is why it is not easy to bring home to the military hierarchy the list of assets which easily tilt the balance in his favour: the strength of will that has bent all manner of men to his purpose; the extraordinary tenacity — the Americans call it obstinacy — with which he clings for months, and if need be for years, to his own plans; the terrific force of personality that can brush aside all doubts and hesitations, and sweep away inertia, refusing to listen when weaker men begin to whine about difficulties; above all else, the superb confidence he exuded in 1940. When the Prime Minister set out to inspire the country with his will to win he made up his mind that it must begin in his own bedroom. I have been with him there at all hours, I have seen him take a lot of punishment, and not once did he look like a loser. Not once did he give me the feeling that he was in any way worried or anxious as to the outcome of the fight. Gradually I have come to think of him as invincible.[32]

« 4 »

In July 1942, when the American chiefs reluctantly but finally withdrew their objections to the North African invasion, General Marshall named General Eisenhower to command the project and set about to provide him with the best subordinate commanders he could find. Patton, of course, was a must. Although he regarded the man's needless profanity, obscenity, and gaudy showmanship as serious defects in a commander, "the Chief of Staff saw behind the officer's adolescent caperings the skill of a professional, who added to years of training a natural talent for fighting and the ability to make men go beyond what they believed themselves capable of doing in battle."[33] Terry Allen, Walter Bedell Smith, and Lloyd R. Fredenall were other additions to a staff which Mark Clark headed as second-in-command. Omar Bradley joined it about six weeks later.

The next few months were devoted to hectic activity. Once it had been agreed to go ahead with the North African adventure, the list of moves and decisions needed for its successful implementation seemed endless.

General Eisenhower's naval aide, Captain Harry Butcher, noted in his diary at one point that "a million details are needed to arrange an expedition like TORCH. How Clark keeps his good humor, I don't know." Butcher also mentioned that one of the highlights of a birthday party held for Beetle Smith was Clark's initiation of a crap game with a pair of dice he had brought back with him after a recent flying visit to America, but Clark "was unable to make them perform as advertised."[34]

On October 17, a telegram was received by Clark and Eisenhower in their London headquarters which was destined to alter dramatically the conduct of the coming operation and to turn Mark Clark from a little-known second-in-command into a highly identifiable public personality. The telegram was from Robert Murphy, the diplomat who had represented American interests in France after its capture by the Germans and who was now in Algiers after having been secretly detailed by Franklin Roosevelt to assess the possibilities of bringing French North Africa into the war against the Nazis. It said, in effect, that if an American delegation were to land in North Africa prior to the massed assault by American troops, a deal might be worked out under which the French would offer only token resistance and then come into the war on our side. This show of resistance would be necessary since (Murphy indicated) the French generals were sure that their homeland would be immediately penalized by an even stiffer occupation if the Germans became persuaded that there had been a sellout.

Murphy stipulated that the delegation should be headed by a high-ranking officer thoroughly familiar with the TORCH operation. The trip would be made by submarine to a cove near Algiers, and the guides detailed to beacon them to the shore by lantern light would then conduct them to a secluded beach house where Murphy and the French representatives waited.

Clark volunteered for the difficult and dangerous assignment. It was a job that had to be done and he was uniquely the man to do it. But, years later, his wife revealed that the event represented a major emotional experience for him. "He is not given to over-dramatizing himself or his experiences," she wrote, "but this one really got him. He showed it in a letter given to his aide to be delivered to me only in the event that Wayne did not return from the submarine trip. It was later Wayne sent it on to me. It was perhaps the most sentimental letter he ever wrote me."

The letter read:

DARLING SWEETHEART —

I am leaving in twenty minutes on a mission which I volunteered to do when it was suggested that a general officer do it.

If I succeed and return I will have done a fine deed for my country and the Allied cause. Of course you know my life is dedicated to military service and now that my opportunity has come for that service I go forward proud of the opportunity which has been given me.

If I do not return know that I loved you and our Bill and Ann. Only one request I make. You have been an angel on earth to me — continue being that and do everything you possibly can for our Allied cause. Only in so doing will you find solace, and only by all so doing, will Victory be won.

God bless and keep you.

WAYNE[35]

A handful of Englishmen were detailed from Lord Mount-batten's Combined Operations Command to man the submarine. They were not told what the mission would be or the names of the men they were to transport. One of the Englishmen, Captain Godfrey B. Courtney, relates: "We were sitting around speculating about our mission when we heard a noise forward. My eyes popped when I saw a U.S. Army officer with the two stars of a major general on his shoulders. There were four other Americans, and after they had passed by our bunks Livingston nudged me and whispered, 'This is going to be the craziest thing yet.' I had been expecting almost anything, but nothing like this, and I was inclined to agree with him. The tall chap with the general's insignia was not built for a submarine. He kept bumping his head against the knobs and the bulkheads."[36]

While headquarters on both sides of the Atlantic waited for reports of the mission's progress, Harry Butcher noted in his diary: "There was a mess-up in the time for Clark's rendezvous. Colonel McGowan [Robert Murphy's code name] and the party had been at the secret meeting place a night too soon and they are supposed to meet tonight or tomorrow night. This means Clark has to lie around in a sub. I know he has his dice, for they are his good-luck pieces. He probably will have the crew's money."[37]

Later, when the party had gone ashore and were in the meeting with the Frenchmen, the group had been alarmed by a policeman's knock on the door. Everyone scuttled for the dusty cellar where they waited, guns in hand, for the policeman to conclude his inspection. At one point Captain Courtney began to strangle with the need to suppress a cough. Clark, who had been nervously chomping on a wad of chewing gum, took it from his mouth and stuffed it in the Englishman's. It kept their presence a secret.[38]

The trip was a success. The meeting opened the door to French cooperation once the combined American and British assault forces came ashore in North Africa. There was even a dash of humor to broaden the dramatic mission. Clark, not wishing to be encumbered, had taken off his pants (which contained several hundred dollars in gold) and had placed them in the bottom of the small boat in which they were paddling back to the submarine. A heavy wave capsized the small craft, and Clark's pants, to the glee of the crew and of the public who read about it later, were lost. No spectacle, it seems, is more irresistible than a man of high rank shivering in his underwear. Only General Marshall was not amused. Although pleased by Clark's accomplishment, he frowned at the light note which accompanied it. "It's not the kind of publicity a general should get," he said.

Back in England, Clark reported on his success to a delighted Churchill. Later, when he was presented to King George, the first royal question concerned those lost pants. As a practical matter, most quarters seemed pleased that a note of humor had been injected into an essentially grim project which many American planners estimated had no more than an even chance for success. Everyone was aware that if the first major combined effort should fail, the balance of the war could be severely affected.

To complicate the situation, there still remained the thorny political situation in North Africa. Much historical attention has been devoted to the "Darlan deal" and to the conflicting positions of de Gaulle and Giraud.[39] But it is worth distilling the various imponderables into the one basic question which still plagued the Allies even though Mark Clark's mission was judged a success: Would the French guns be aimed toward the invading American

Army? Clark's mission appeared to have paved the way, but at the time Eisenhower and his planners were forced to concede that the chances of armed resistance versus token opposition ran fifty-fifty.

« 5 »

In the early hours of November 8, three amphibious forces totaling approximately one hundred thousand men, sailing through submarine-infested waters from England and America, began their attacks on a front which included Casablanca, Oran, and Algiers as primary targets.

General Marshall credited the intense attention paid to Anglo-American collaboration for much of the landing's success. Several days later, in a speech delivered to the American Academy of Political Sciences, he declared:

In the past two days, we have had a most impressive example of the practicable application of unity of command, an American Expeditionary Force . . . supported by the British fleet, by British fliers, and by a British Army, all controlled by an American commander-in-chief, General Eisenhower, with a deputy commander also an American officer, General Clark. . . . The instructions of the British Cabinet to guide their Army commander serving under General Eisenhower furnish a model of readiness of a great nation to cooperate in every practicable manner. I go into detail because this should not be a secret. It will be a most depressing news to our enemies. It is the declaration of their doom.[40]

Clark learned a great deal from this operation. Later, in Italy, he attempted to establish the same operating circumstances for his Fifth Army, but by this time the war had gone on too long and grown too difficult to permit selfless cooperation between allies. The North African adventure was to be Clark's last exposure to an atmosphere free from various national self-interests.

Because political considerations intensified at the same pace as the military ones, President Roosevelt appointed Robert Murphy as his personal representative at Eisenhower's headquarters.

While he appreciated the military virtues of his field commanders, Roosevelt was aware that, politically, they were babes in the woods.

Murphy, in responding to the suggestion that the British, during that period, tended to categorize the American leaders as amateurs, once admitted: "Yes, that was their attitude. And, in some respects, there was some justification for it — especially in the field of intelligence. There's no doubt about it, we were amateurs. I still remember, for example, an American captain with an intelligence unit, very soon after we got to Algiers, walking into one of the big banks and demanding certain information. Before they even had a chance to answer, he pounded his .45 revolver on the counter while shouting, 'I'm going to shoot all of you if you don't answer my question right away!' This is amateur, really amateur. That's what they had in mind."[41] Clark's aide, Lieutenant Jack Beardwood, noted in his diary that, on one occasion, while Clark was talking to General Giraud, he told his interpreter to say, "Old gentleman, I hope you know that from now on your ass is out in the snow."[42]

In describing Mark Clark, Murphy added: "Sometimes Wayne rubbed people the wrong way. He can be a very tense and explosive person and sometimes tends to say the first thing that comes into his mind. In his relations with people like General Alexander, this frequently became a problem. Sometimes he felt that the British were hanging back — unwilling to take chances — and he'd express his feelings about it in no uncertain terms. But I don't believe that this detracted from his very sound thinking and approaches. The decisions he made were almost always the right ones. He's an ardent man, and when he believes in a thing wholeheartedly, he commits himself completely to it. If the other fellow doesn't match his commitment, he's apt to be abrasively critical.

"Like many of the other officers in our headquarters, he didn't have much of a background for a highly sophisticated political situation. We'd never had an Anglo-American headquarters before in our entire military history, and nothing in the experience or education of our officers had prepared them for it.

"Sometimes this inexperience became a terribly awkward thing. For example, on the second day of the North African operation, we had this conference with Admiral Darlan and the other French leaders. All of them understood English. I was acting as Clark's adviser, and at one point of the proceedings he became exasperated and began pounding the table and shouting, 'I'm going to send all of you sons-of-bitches to jail if you don't start agreeing!' It was one of the worst possible things to do under those circumstances. Another time, Darlan once said privately to me, 'Will you do me a favor? Tell General Clark I am a five-star admiral and not a second lieutenant.' "[43]

Clark, when asked to comment on this report, answered, "It's certainly true. But you must remember that I went in as a youngster, having been promoted quickly into command. None of us had much experience in this type of thing — we had been picked almost completely on our past records, and we just didn't have the background for all this pulling and hauling in different directions. For example, we were backing General Giraud and he was balking because he wanted the title of overall commander. I told Ike to give him my job, because I wanted to go back to my corps, anyway. But then finally he acquiesced and then we found that we had the wrong guy for the job of knitting the French together. Anybody would kill him on sight and I had to hide him out for a month.

"And then we started getting criticism from back home because we made a deal with Admiral Darlan. The President was upset and Churchill was upset [because Darlan had been prominently identified as a Vichyite and thus was suspected of being sympathetic to the German masters of France], but finally I said, 'The hell with it, I'm going to do this exactly the way I see it!'

"Darlan was an opportunist. I don't think you could trust him in the early days. He was waiting to see which way to jump — how many guns we had, how many tanks, what we were going to do, etcetera. His pussyfooting got so bad there that I finally exploded and said, 'We're not going to tolerate this any longer!' And, boy, it brought him around!

"You see, this was a matter of Americans being killed. The Germans were pouring into Tunisia and the French were operating the trains and I was getting obstacles every way I turned. It was a question of getting the troops to meet that threat up there and I didn't know anything about this kid-glove stuff, so I have no doubt that I did and said many things that were undiplomatic. But after it was all over, I got the impression in talks with Mr. Churchill and the President that they felt you had no alternative, really, to doing business with that fellow.

"You see, I may not have known anything about diplomacy, but I knew we were getting a runaround. I knew that Giraud was the wrong man and that General Juin wasn't big enough and that Darlan was the boy calling the signals. Ike and I worked out a code which I used to report to him during these conferences. I remember how we worked it out. We were sitting on our bunks one day before I went in and we had a couple of scotches and Ike said that we ought to have a code name for Churchill and all the other leading figures. We figured out forty or fifty names and when we came to these guys I had to deal with, we put down YBSOB, which meant 'yellow-bellied sons-of-bitches.'

"Well, the messages kept going back and forth between us after that and, of course, a copy of all of them went to Mr. Churchill and the White House.

"Finally, the President sent a message to Ike which said, 'I'm reading Clark's dispatches with interest, and I sympathize with his pressures, but there is a word that appears in all these dispatches which occurs so often that I'm led to believe that it's not a typographical error. Please explain.'

"Now, Ike could have explained, you know, but he thought it was funny to buck it over to me with a note that here was a message from the White House and would I please answer it direct. I was so exhausted that I thought, 'Well, here goes, I'll shoot the works,' and I sent back an answer to the President which said, 'General Eisenhower has asked me to reply direct to your message on so-and-so. You are correct. The word YBSOB is not a typographical error. Translated literally, it means 'yellow-bellied sons-of-bitches.' Respectfully, Mark W. Clark.'

"I waited for the axe to fall after that and within forty-eight hours I got an answer back from the President. It said, 'I read your letter and thoroughly understand it. I wish that I had had a similar word when I first came to Washington.' "[44]

The North African campaign had begun on November 8, 1942. Eisenhower's fears were unrealized, and after French support had been secured, an Allied column headed for Tunisia. But the Germans, mounting a huge counteroffensive on February 14, 1943, forced the American troops back through the Kasserine Pass and, within a week, had advanced almost a hundred miles before being brought to a halt.

By the middle of March, the Allies had regained the offensive. In southern Tunisia, the United States II Corps, commanded by Lieutenant General George S. Patton, Jr., turned the flank and the rear of the German lines while General Sir Bernard Montgomery sent elements of the British Eighth Army through the desert to outflank the Axis position and to break into the eastern coastal region of central Tunisia.

The campaign, which some military historians consider the turning point in the war in Europe, was won by May 10, 1943. The victory opened the Mediterranean Sea to the Allies' shipping and provided them with positions from which to mount future attacks on occupied Europe.[45]

« 6 »

There were other consequences of this successful operation. It provided a first-rate training opportunity for the troops and commanders who would later inch so painfully up the Italian peninsula, and it marked the time when the divergent aims and motivations of the British, French, Russian, and American leaders first came into focus.

The differences flared into the open at Casablanca. A meeting was opened on January 14, 1943, on African soil, at which Roosevelt and Churchill and their staffs were to decide on the next target in the struggle to defeat the Germans.[46]

At the conference, the Americans, perhaps reflecting a national impatience, were eager to mount a cross-Channel thrust into France and, by using a battering ram at Germany's doors, bring the war to a quick finish.[47] As a matter of fact, Marshall and his staff were beginning to regard the obvious reluctance of the British to accept the merits of this plan as evidence of some dark holdover from an Imperial past.[48]

The anxiety of the American leaders was heightened by the suspicion that Franklin Roosevelt was peculiarly susceptible to British blandishments. General Joseph Stilwell, speaking from another theater of war, bluntly noted: "Besides being a rank amateur in all military matters, F.D.R. is apt to act on sudden impulses . . . We'll do this, we'll do that, we'll do the other. Blow hot, blow cold. And the Limeys have his ear while we have the hind tit."[49]

An even more conservative view, although phrased more delicately, is found in the memoirs of General Albert C. Wedemeyer: "We had gone to Casablanca without an agreed or clearly defined position among the American Army and Navy representatives. Nor did President Roosevelt bring mature leadership to our Joint Chiefs of Staff. While permitting them freedom to state their personal views, he seldom gave them any specific knowledge of his own plans and policies. So once again we had no assurance that the President would support our choice of concentration, and, on the military level, we were without agreement among ourselves as to how to convince the British of the danger of frittering away our combined resources on indecisive, limited operations."[50]

And a final observation from the vantage point of elapsed time is rendered by Professor Thomas A. Bailey in his acclaimed critique *Presidential Greatness:* "Franklin Roosevelt, fairly oozing infectious confidence, was a geyser of warmth, buoyancy, cheerfulness, friendliness, and captivating personal magnetism. He would first-name important men at their first meeting. Observers said, with pardonable exaggeration, that with his dazzling smile he could charm the birds out of the trees. Fully aware of this marvelous talent, he delighted in turning it on and off, much as one would manipulate a perfume flagon. He enjoyed sending people away so spellbound that they forgot the complaint they had brought. He was eager to meet Joseph Stalin, the hardened old conspirator of the Kremlin, and charm him out of his nasty Communist ways. 'I can handle that old buzzard,' he is said to have remarked privately. He finally managed to meet the Russian premier at Teheran and then at Yalta, but the record does not reveal that he succeeded in melting his steely adversary."[51]

This American resistance both infuriated and frustrated the British. The usually suave Sir Harold Alexander called General Eisenhower "a Goddamned dumbbell"[52] and the Chief of the Imperial General Staff, Sir Alan Brooke, who had never considered Marshall as being especially intelligent (although he admired him as a man), patiently repeated over and over again his conviction that the Allies were pitifully unprepared for this venture, since they lacked combat-ready divisions, landing craft, and sufficient air support. Alan Brooke was certain that if the Americans were to have their way, a Channel crossing at this time would prejudice, perhaps fatally, the entire conduct of the war.[53]

As usual, the truth seems to have lurked somewhere between the extremes. Knowing what we now know about German capabilities, the human costs of such an invasion, even if successful, would have dwarfed the actual number of casualties reported in the June 6, 1944, landings. One British leader said to General Marshall during this period, "It's no use — you are arguing against the Somme," referring to England's loss of the pick of her young men in World War I.[54] The English insisted that they could not again suffer such a bleeding. There was never any doubt in the minds of Churchill and his staff that the English people would not, and in fact could not, stand it.[55] To emphasize the point, the Prime Minister repeated on several occasions within the hearing of Ambassador Robert Murphy, "What the hell are you going to do with your victory if you're going to lose all your manpower?"[56]

There were other pressures. Charles de Gaulle felt that the English reluctance to accept American views was inspired by the desire to deny France a place of European eminence once the Germans had been defeated.[57] Russia harbored an attitude which Marshal Stalin reduced to writing in a letter of February 16, noting that since the suspensions of operations in Tunisia, twenty-seven German divisions had been diverted to the Russian front. He added, with heavy sarcasm, "In other words, instead of the Soviet Union being aided by diverting German forces from the Soviet-German front, what we get is relief for Hitler!"[58]

Another consideration was pointed out by General Marshall in a 1957 letter to the American historian Professor Samuel Eliot Morison, stating that the great lesson he learned in 1942 was that in wartime, the politicians have to do *something* important every year.[59]

The final item in contention was the suspicion that Great Britain wanted to make sure of the mastery of the Mediterranean for her own commercial purposes. When General Clark was once asked his opinion of whether or not this played any part in Churchill's thinking, he answered, "If it didn't, I'd have been very much surprised."[60]

To rebut this accusation of self-interest, quite a few historians, most of them English, have declared that Churchill's preoccupation with a Mediterranean-based thrust up through the Balkans was evidence of his farsightedness — that in reality it was a desire to bar the postwar spread of Communism to Western Europe. This is simply not true. The fear at this time was not that Russia would expand, but that she would collapse. It was not until 1944 that

British policy can be described as deliberately aimed at frustrating Communist ends.

Great Britain has for centuries been a sea-oriented power. Certainly, Churchill was convinced that control of the Mediterranean meant control of the Western world, but the most logical summary of the governing factors belongs to General Eisenhower, who, despite Alexander's impatient outburst, is essentially the reasonable man willing to consider all aspects before making up his mind. During a discussion of British attitudes, he said that later he had come to agree that Churchill had something on his side when he wanted to go into the Mediterranean. For a hundred years, up till World War I, Britain had kept the peace throughout the world with a relatively small army and a large fleet of ships. The only place he could recall offhand where they got into a major land engagement was at Khartoum, and there they were beaten badly. In World War I, they had no opportunity to use this fleet in a major fashion. As a result, an entire generation was decimated, and they were reluctant to endure any more hard fighting on land. That was why, he felt, that they fought so hard against OVERLORD (the cross-Channel invasion of France).

After the British had spent two years standing and fighting alone, the Americans had come in as big boys with all the armaments and everything else. They didn't like being relegated to second place at all.

But most important, the general felt, was this distaste for a large-scale land war. Churchill was always pessimistic about OVERLORD, although at one time or another during the campaign, he did say, "I am hardening toward this enterprise."

The full reporting of these attitudes is necessary here because, directly and unmistakably, they later affected the conduct of the Italian campaign.

The English eventually won their point. On January 23, Eisenhower, who had been appointed to command the enterprise, received this directive:

The Combined Chiefs of Staff have resolved that an attack against Sicily will be launched in 1943, with the target date as the period of the favorable July moon.

« 7 »

In preparation for the oncoming campaign, the Fifth Army, which had been activated a few weeks before, on January 5, was given to Mark Clark to command. Clark had his third star pinned on him in North Africa by his good friend Ike, who had flown over from Gibraltar especially for the occasion. At forty-six, Mark Clark was the youngest lieutenant general in the history of the United States Army. His jurisdiction extended over 225,000 square miles of parched African earth and a force of men drawn from every branch of the military establishment, a force that had neither enough training nor experience for what would lie ahead.

How did Clark react? Despite critics who maintain that arrogance is the anchor point of his personality, his first thoughts were of the bitter gall that was probably being swallowed by his former senior, George Patton.

"I knew Georgie from way back," recalls Clark. "He had come from West Point to Fort Sheridan, where my father was a battalion commander. I was around fourteen years old and I certainly admired him. Georgie had married a lot of money and he had polo ponies and all the other things that a young lieutenant just didn't have. I always felt that way about him. Then when they made me commander of the Fifth, and Georgie's corps was assigned to it, the first thing I did, I got right in my plane and flew to Casablanca to see him. I told him, 'Georgie, it's the gosh-darndest thing. I feel you should have had it. I just feel terrible and I want you to know that it's probably as tough on me as it is on you.' He said, 'Wayne, I don't know anybody I'd rather fight alongside of than you. You're going to need some headquarters officers, and if you want any of mine or anything else, I'll help you.'

"Then later," Clark continued, "after Ike had decided to create a Seventh Army for the invasion of Sicily and had put Patton in command, I offered Georgie the training centers I had brought into existence for my Fifth. I trained Patton's men because I had the centers. We spent all our time together, overseeing the amphibious training and I said many a time, 'Georgie, anything you see that you think we can do better, don't hesitate to tell me or tell my people.' So Georgie and I never had any differences whatsoever."[61]

<< 8 >>

There is one more friendship that played a part in the history of the Fifth Army. How decisive it was is a matter that is still being questioned, since one of the men was and remains a shadowy figure. Certainly, this relationship took place on a level far below that of Churchill and Roosevelt, or Eisenhower and Clark, or Clark and Patton, but it is no less germane, since it stands as an example of how incidents and men of negligible headline value can influence such gigantic events as the capture of Rome.

Few senior officers in the Italian campaign were as wholeheartedly admired as Robert William Porter, Jr. One measure of his ability is that although he was only a colonel when the war ended, he is today a four-star general with command responsibilities for a large part of the Western Hemisphere. A man mentioned frequently with respect and affection, General Porter is a slender, bespectacled, soft-spoken individual who would appear to be infinitely more at home in a high-school principal's office. Today Porter seems light-years away from the World War II soldier who became the boon companion of the cruel ex–Foreign Legion captain Nicholas Vladimir Malitch — a White Russian whom many Americans came to suspect as being a double or even a triple agent.

Perhaps the best description of Porter was offered by Robert van de Velde, then a II Corps staff officer: "I think he was the best-liked, the most human of the senior officers. In many ways, he's a strange sort of a man. His enunciation was a bit overcareful, he was meticulously correct in his own dress, but anything that might be considered 'sissy' about him was quickly dispelled in anyone who knew him. He was one of the most gutsy guys I've ever known.

"One of the things that stand out in my recollection [of the war] was Porter taking a bath every morning. Even though it was wintertime in the mountains, he'd stand stark naked outside his little half-ton trailer scrubbing himself clean with snow.

"Without question, Porter was one of the greatest influences on the younger officers. He taught them more about the process of military planning and strategy and the necessity for intelligence and the careful coordination of staff functions, than they could have gotten anywhere else. He was a hard taskmaster. Sometimes he seemed to be involved in 'make-work,' but it was all instructive, and I particularly remember the young G–2 and G–3 officers sitting around him on logs or rocks, taking almost daily lessons in what was going on and why new plans might be needed — what the alternatives were and why one choice was better than another.

"He's the personal hero of the war to many others besides myself. In all my years of military service I've never met a man more dedicated to the finest type of military professionalism. He is a man of high intelligence, not possessing the 'military mind,' but a man who thought militarily. He was a fine tactician and, given the opportunity, a strategist almost without peer. Even in the heat of a campaign, he was sensitive to the people who were below and around him. In a sense, his junior officers were his acolytes. They never went out blind: they knew why he wanted information from another commander, where it fitted into the bigger picture, and why it was necessary. He was also a first-class human being. I've never heard him speak ill of another man."[62]

The story of his meeting with the Russian Malitch is told by Porter: "Our activities in Algeria were such that we needed someone to work with the French police and military forces to help control the movements of Arabs in the pay of the Germans in and around our camp. As G–2 [head of intelligence] of the 1st Division, I finally decided that the thing to do was to obtain a liaison officer from the Supreme French Headquarters in North Africa. The opportunity came sooner than I expected. My chief, General Allen, and I attended a dinner party during an inspection trip where I sat next to [Hooker A.] Doolittle, the American consul, during dinner. He told me of his adventures in getting out of Tunis ahead of the Germans and that one of the men who had been quite useful to him was a French Foreign Legion officer who was Russian by birth and had been demilitarized by the Germans after the fall of France.

"This man had been left without any means of livelihood, after having been ordered to remain in Tunisia. He had gone into the pay of the U.S. government, where the information he had supplied had been most useful. However, the Consul General said that the man was an inveterate gambler and if we should employ him, to be careful never to lend him any money.

"Because of this last statement, I decided that he would not be too useful. But General Allen, who had heard the story from across the table, leaned over and said, 'Bob, I would like you to pursue the lead on this Captain Malitch.' Doolittle heard the statement and said, 'Well, Malitch will be in the hotel tonight. I can get him if you want to take a look at him.' General Allen said that he did.

"Malitch arrived later — a typical French Foreign Legion officer. This was in the middle of winter and he had on a leather jerkin which came halfway down between his knees and his hips, the big Legion cap, and heavy crepe-soled shoes. You could see he was suffering from some form of arthritis, but he had a most intelligent face and a twinkle in his eye. General Allen was immediately attracted to him.

"Malitch wore his hair in a pompadour. He had large brown eyes, sharp features, and a leathery skin. The most striking thing about Malitch at first appearance was his hands — he had exceed-

ingly long fingers and he had a way of using his hands which gave
a great deal of meaning to his conversation. He didn't have all of
his teeth; some were missing from prominent places. When he was
younger, he had probably been very handsome. Now he had the
appearance of being somewhat second-handed.

"General Allen looked him over and said, 'I'm looking for a
French liaison officer who is intelligent, knows the country, speaks
some Arabic, is a keen observer of things military, and has the
judgment and wisdom to be seen and not heard unless he's called
on for a recommendation. Do you think that you can fill this
bill?'

"Nic answered, 'Yes, sir.' The General then asked him what
languages he spoke and he said, 'Well, I speak Russian, which is
my native tongue. I speak French, German, Italian, Arabic, Spanish, and a leetle English.'

"After the interview was over, a French liaison officer who was
with us began to chuckle. He told General Allen that there were
times when Nic was a 'bit erratic.'

"On the way to Algiers next day, we were going through the
mountains. The driver had tired, so I took the wheel. General
Allen was stretched out on the back seat taking a nap when he
suddenly sat up and said, 'Bob, go to General Mast and get
Malitch to be our liaison officer.' I said, 'I'm not certain we want
him.' He answered, 'Well, that's an order. Get Malitch.' 'Yes sir.'

"Well, we finally got Malitch. He showed up a few weeks later,
wearing light clothes that were completely unfit for the climate
and carrying an empty suitcase.

"We were leaving in three hours on a reconnaissance of southern Tunisia. General Allen and I wanted Malitch to go along
because of his ability to speak French, and we were going to go in
the French-controlled area. We had to open up the QM company
trucks to get long-handled underwear and various American
equipment that would keep him warm in an open jeep with the
windshield down. This put Malitch in American uniform as a
matter of emergency, and at the end of the war Malitch was still

wearing an American uniform. To show that he did have military status, we also pinned an American captain's bars on him and he wore these, too, till the end of the war.

"In this first expedition with the command group of the 1st Division, Malitch proved himself. He was very useful — he knew the country, could make the French telephone system in the back country of Tunisia and Algeria work, and he spoke Arabic and had a pretty basic knowledge of German. His English, though, left much to be desired. In the years that we were associated together, his English never really improved much.

"Malitch joined our headquarters in early January 1943. The Chief of Staff promptly assigned him to the G–2 section, since it seemed to be my responsibility to look after him. He had a great nose for news, was very friendly, and was well liked by all because he never seemed to be too tired to go on another errand. He had a way of evaluating events which was useful from the intelligence point of view, and he went out of his way to make himself useful around the headquarters. He did bear out Mr. Doolittle's profile of him, however. As soon as a pack of cards was taken out in a tent, whether it was the middle of the day or the middle of the night, Malitch was always available to play bridge, poker, or any game — particularly if there was an opportunity to do a little gambling while the play was in progress.

"Soon after he joined, we moved our headquarters into Tunisia and joined the French 19th Corps. We left Captain Malitch, initially, at French headquarters to be our liaison officer. However, we got very little information from him because the French were reluctant to tell him a great deal. At the same time, his serial number indicated that he was in the pay of the French intelligence services.

"In the operations in southern Tunisia, Malitch was a powerhouse of strength. He quickly developed a close friendship with Bill Darby of the Rangers. One time Darby had captured a prisoner, an Arab who was spying on his camp. He was hidden in an OP about a hundred yards from this camp. He brought the man to our headquarters. Malitch agreed to interrogate him. I was busy, so Darby went in to watch the interrogation. Apparently the man did not respond well. Malitch argued and talked and raved with no results. Suddenly, he spoke to a guard that was with him. The guard held the man and Malitch nipped him on the lobe of his ear and the man started to talk promptly and spilled quite a story as to the location of the Germans all through the area. This information was used within an hour after Malitch got it out of this Arab and was the basis of Darby's successful attack on a German outpost, which actually permitted us to get forward and capture the town of El Guetter and put us in position to withstand the attack of the German 10th Panzer Division three days later in the El Guetter area.

"During the same period, Nic came rushing into the command post one day and said, 'Vat you thing — I got the most amusing sight for you out at the Staff Dismount.' I asked him what it was and he said, 'Vell, I cannot describe it and it won't last long so you'd better hurry.' He took off to the Staff Dismount, I following at a trot. We got there to find among the Italian prisoners that had been captured that morning a lieutenant colonel, complete with the bedbug-infested mattress which he had been using in a jeep with two of his soldiers. He was the soul of propriety and dignity. I went up and introduced myself to this officer and asked him if he was being properly taken care of. He said that yes, he was, courtesy of Captain Maleesh of the American Army.

"Realizing that these men might be valuable, Malitch had picked the men off the road and got the colonel and his two orderlies into the jeep and the colonel had been installed in a French colonel's house with his two orderlies and then Malitch went to work to find out what he could about the situations of the Italians in Tunisia. He worked about an hour until I discovered it and ordered the colonel turned over to our regular interrogator. But, within that hour, Nic had gotten a great deal of valuable information for us dealing with the overall situation in Tunisia.

Three days later, from the Corps interrogators, I obtained the same information.

"I never got the full story of his life from Nic, but I understand he was born on a big farm near the Crimea. His father was a wealthy man — had big landholdings and also oil interests. As a young boy, Nic went to school in Moscow and Petrograd. He graduated from the Russian Military Academy and was about seventeen when World War I came along. He was a young officer in the Guards First Cavalry Division, commanded by a brother of the Czar. He was wounded in several actions and actually was recovering from wounds in Paris at the time of the Revolution and never had been able to get back.

"Malitch was a great provider. He could always find the finest foods in the village, the best cooks. And during active operations, if a cow got in a minefield, Nic had a way of being there to see that a quarter of beef got to the General's or Staff Mess.

"During the fighting against the 10th Panzer Division, I had sent him as a liaison officer with the French cavalry regiment which had agreed to protect the south flank of the 1st Division in a valley about twenty miles south of our location. This valley was a long narrow affair in the desert and would have been a good access road into Gafsa and could have cut our line of communications if we had not had someone in the valley watching that flank. I kept Malitch well informed on the situation in front of us and he did the same with me. Some of his messages were really amusing. During the actual attack of the 10th Panzer Division and our counterattack, I sent Malitch a message telling him that there would be a counterattack coming in upon us and we would go and attack ourselves. He sent me quite an estimate of the situation which ended up something like this: 'This is a very fine outfit, where men are fit and ready to go. I cannot say as much for the Colonel. He is fit, but mostly for alcohol.'

"When we left Tunisia and moved back to Oran to prepare for operations into Sicily, Malitch left Tunisia with us and came back to the Oran area, and then subsequently moved up to Algiers with us and went into Sicily. He'd become a very important element in the G–2 section by that time."[63]

Thus: Porter and Malitch. And Clark, Eisenhower, Patton, Alexander, Montgomery, and thousands of others . . . all on the road to Rome, pausing only briefly at that poverty-stricken way-stop which is Sicily.

CHAPTER III

JULY 10–AUGUST 17, 1943

---

*After all, the world is wide, and intelligent thought
will readily supply an unlimited number of well-
sounding names which do not suggest the character
of the operation or disparage it in any way and do
not enable some widow or mother to say that her son
was killed in an operation called "Bunnyhug" or
"Ballyhoo."*

— WINSTON CHURCHILL[1]

THE assault on Sicily was code-named Operation HUSKY. In spite of the Prime Minister's caution against too-descriptive code names, the attacking Allies found it necessary to employ a ground force which reached 467,000 at its huskiest peak against a defending German army that never totaled at any one time more than 60,000 men.

It was not a campaign calculated to bring military credit either to Montgomery, who commanded the British Eighth Army, or to Patton, at the head of the American Seventh.[2] Unimaginative and overcautious, the operation took thirty-eight days, and, at that, well over two-thirds of the defenders, carrying the bulk of their materiel, were able to escape to the Italian mainland to fight another day.

During this campaign, Sir Bernard Montgomery laid the foundation for the solid dislike of him which characterizes almost every American general who had contact with him during World War II. Even after the passage of two decades, one of the highest ranking officers snorted, "Monty was and is a stupid man!"[3] He was considered vain, egotistical, difficult, a show-off, and not really worth the credit accorded him by the British press. The Americans believed that Montgomery rarely moved or fought until the odds were strongly in his favor.[4]

As late as 1966, the Royal Air Force Marshal in World War II, Lord Tedder, declared that the North African battle of El Alamein, in which Montgomery's army decisively defeated General Erwin Rommel's forces, "should have started four days earlier."[5]

In Sicily, Patton too dissipated some of the public esteem he had earned by his imagination and daring in Africa. A man of unquestioned personal bravery, he nevertheless remained aboard ship for two days while his men swarmed onto the beaches in the beginning of the campaign.[6] The generally held opinion was that while Patton was great in mounting and winning sweeping attacks, he just didn't have the zest for the close infighting dictated by small arenas.

During the campaign, Drew Pearson leaked the news to a startled American public that Patton, in a fit of hysterical anger, had slapped a soldier hospitalized for combat fatigue. Concerned for his career, Patton turned to General Alexander but was told, "George, this is a family affair — I can't give you any advice. You must ask General Eisenhower."[7] Eisenhower refused to bow to the considerable cry for recall, and kept him in command. Ike felt that Patton was a needed combat leader and shielded him on several other occasions where Patton's uncontrollable temper led him into the same kind of trouble.[8]

Not until late in the war did Ike finally lose patience with Patton. After the mercurial cavalryman had made some unfortunate remarks which seemed to link the Nazis with the American Democratic party, Ike finally shipped him out, saying that Patton had better get the hell over to the Historical Section, or somewhere where no one could hear him talk.

When Patton moved up to the command of the Seventh Army, his place at the head of II Corps was taken by Major General Omar N. Bradley, who had neither the relish nor the desire for Patton's flamboyance. A sincere and quiet man, he made his mark through solid ability. Because his tenure in II Corps brought him into the Mediterranean theater, this illuminating comment by the journalist Will Lang becomes pertinent.

Discussing the role of public relations in a general's career, Lang said, "Well, Eisenhower has an exceptional personality, and it helped him get elected President of the United States. Omar Bradley had much the same thing. In a sense it was a quality of humility. I mean, Omar, for example, dressed by preference like a GI, but he was not unaware of the effect. He wore a dirty field jacket, one of those knitted wool caps underneath his helmet, and, except for his aide, might have passed as an elderly rifleman. This impressed the GI's because it wasn't phony. They saw that he tried to live as they did, and he did so over a long period of time. But he was also aware, let's not forget that."[9]

For the first time, Eisenhower also came in for criticism. He had been thrust into the role of super-hero by a public hungry for such an image, but now the British, led by Sir Alan Brooke,[10] began to hint politely that Ike had certain deficiencies as a strategist and tactician. This undercurrent was later given substantial American impetus by some of the men close to General MacArthur, a man who apparently never forgave his former subordinate for attracting the lion's share of the public's affection.

But only a first-rate soldier-statesman could have held together the sprawling complex of United States and British forces. There was no necessity for Ike to be a strategist. He already had too many of these on his combined staff. He showed consistent sensitivity to the possible pitfalls of a combined operation. Once he called an American general on the carpet after hearing about a dispute in which the man had been engaged. "I don't care if you call him a Limey," he said, "and I don't care if you call him a son-of-a-bitch, if that's what he is. But I damn well am not going to have you or anyone else putting the two together. You called him a 'Limey son-of-a-bitch' and that's why I'm firing you!"[11] The general was sent back to America the following day.

Eisenhower's diplomacy and Bradley's humility would become problems for Mark Clark in the coming Italian campaign. His noticeable lack of either of these virtues acted as a magnet for the criticisms of those who were frustrated by the Allies' agonizingly slow progress up the peninsula.

« 2 »

In a Washington conference which began May 12, 1943, Roosevelt and Churchill had already agreed to fashion future operations in a form which would knock Italy out of the war and after much travail, finally reached a firm decision to invade France in approximately twelve months. While the battle in Sicily was being won, the national leaders met again to decide succeeding steps. Coming together on August 14, 1943, at Quebec,[12] the President, the Prime Minister, and their chief advisers set the date for OVERLORD for May 1, 1944. And, because Mussolini, after having been recently deposed, had fled to the north of Italy under the protection of Adolf Hitler, the question of a large-scale campaign in Italy finally had to be faced and answered.[13]

One of the great sources of uneasiness for the other conferees was the insistence of Roosevelt and Churchill that their phrase "unconditional surrender" be strictly construed by diplomats and military men on both sides of the battle. The use of this term and the attitude that it implied have been severely criticized. The point is made in almost every memoir written by the men who participated in these events that in the face of this uncompromising position the Axis had no choice but to fight to the very end. Italy, they say, would have found it much easier to cross over to our side but for the opportunity the phrase gave the Germans to illustrate how difficult the path would be. The assertion is sometimes made that Germany would have capitulated much earlier had it not been for the apprehension engendered by this term.[14]

But what is seldom mentioned in these arguments is that Roosevelt and Churchill were united in sincerely detesting that aspect of the German personality which had caused it to precipitate two worldwide holocausts within two generations. The term "unconditional surrender" may have been a tactical mistake, but it represented an honest statement of feeling by two eminent men.

Franklin D. Roosevelt may have been the diplomatic dabbler he has been painted in so many of the recitals of his era, but it is hard to believe that there was anything superficial in his desire to restore and keep peace in the world. State Department documents, classified top secret until the end of 1966, show him to be an implacable foe of the Nazi ideology. In one note to Cordell Hull, dated April 1944, he said: "Germany understands only one kind of language."

Most of Roosevelt's associates, even the Russians, begged him to moderate his stand. The Soviet foreign minister, Vyacheslav Molotov, wrote that the term "affords enemy propaganda [the opportunity] to play on the natural fear of the unknown." The Russian appeal had no effect on Roosevelt, and there was no question that he was also expressing the exact sentiments of Winston Churchill when he wrote during this period to the War Department: "It is of the utmost importance that every person in Germany should realize that this time Germany is a defeated nation. I do not want to starve them to death but, as an example, if they need food to keep body and soul together, they should be fed three times a day with soup from Army kitchens. That will keep them perfectly healthy and they will remember that experience all their lives."

At another time, he sent a memorandum to the Joint Chiefs of Staff in which he said, "Please note that I am not willing at this time to say that we don't intend to destroy the German nation."[15]

Apart from the agreement of Churchill and Roosevelt to require an unconditional surrender, the old arguments continued between their two countries. The British wanted to stay in the Mediterranean and perhaps, Churchill suggested, make a further attack on the "soft underbelly" of Europe by thrusting into the Balkans, where Greece, Turkey, Yugoslavia, and other nations could all unite in a rush through Germany's back door.

The Americans considered this to be an almost dishonorable position — a breach of previously agreed-upon concepts. They refused to entertain any thought of a further campaign which did not put primary stress on a cross-Channel attack, and here they knew they would be seconded by the Russians, who did not consider that the second front they wanted so desperately could consist of anything less.[16]

Eisenhower had reconciled the two views in his own mind by agreeing to a limited Italian sortie involving the capture of the port of Naples and the airfields around the city of Foggia in the southern Italian boot.[17] Such a move offered strategic help to

OVERLORD, since the bases could be used for air strikes over occupied Europe and would insure the free passage of Allied shipping through the Mediterranean.

All sides saw varying degrees of value in a simultaneous attack into southern France which would draw German strength away from the Normandy beaches while the primary attack was in progress.[18]

There was only one area of general agreement. Everyone considered that a landing at the foot of Italy, with the further intent to occupy and capture the whole country, would be so stupid, wasteful, and unproductive a venture that it was not worth serious consideration. But this is what they did.

It happened because men simply do not control their own destinies. Some apparently unrelated occurrence can occasionally precipitate a chain of events which will gut and destroy the most carefully considered plans of the most eminent men.

It occurred that summer of 1943. The lifelines of two absent men bisected the planning sessions of the Allied leaders and, as a result, hundreds of thousands of soldiers of all nationalities went to Italy to fight a major campaign with few equals for misery, discomfort, and frustration.

The factors were these. On July 25, 1943, King Victor Emmanuel fired Mussolini, and, at almost the same moment in history, Albert Kesselring convinced Adolf Hitler that the territory south of Rome could and should be defended against the expected Allied invasion.

Mussolini's removal took the initiative away from the Allied conferees. Confronted with the undoubted political capital to be gained from an Italian surrender, they began to improvise a plan which would contemplate Italy as a comrade-in-arms rather than an enemy.

Marshal Pietro Badoglio, who had taken Mussolini's place, initiated a series of secret meetings with General Eisenhower and his staff. In effect, Badoglio told the American and English generals, if you will make a show of strength in Italy — if you will invade us — we can announce a plausible surrender and the Germans will not punish our country too severely, because we will obviously have had no control over events.[19] And so the Allies were once again facing the same arrangement which they had made with the French forces in Africa. It had worked then, and they were hopeful that it could work a second time.

Simultaneously, Hitler, after reaching the conclusion that Kesselring had been duped into believing that the Italians would help him fight for Italy, decided to pull back. He saw no reason to divert to the south of Italy any of the divisions needed so desperately on the Russian front.

But Kesselring was able to change his master's mind. He convinced Hitler that Italy presented a logical arena in which to begin the reversal of the Allied string of victories. He all but promised Hitler that the war could be settled on favorable terms if a German victory were won in Italy. And, after grumbling that "that fellow Kesselring is too honest for those born traitors [the Italian politicians] down there,"[20] Hitler gave in to the field marshal. Unquestionably the Fuehrer was also swayed by two prospects which any abandonment of Italy south of Rome would create: he would be forced to write off large numbers of German troops sure to be quickly captured in retreat, and he would be faced for the first time with giving away territory without a fight. Both prospects were abhorrent to him.

So the Italian campaign assumed its final proportions. The Germans found it desirable to repel an Allied invasion which was being mounted for private considerations; the British, loathing the Italians for their part in nearly severing the Empire's lifeline, accepted the campaign because the occupation of Italy enhanced the possibility of a thrust through the Balkans; and the Americans, aware that a substantial Italian electorate at home would enthusiastically welcome the emergence of Italy as an ally rather than an enemy, agreed that a show of strength on the mainland was desirable.

It may have been unintentional, but the actions of King Victor
Emmanuel and Marshal Badoglio amounted to a remarkably
adroit harnessing of these motivations. Expert observers like Peter
Tompkins labeled the King and his new prime minister as a pair
of monstrous double-crossers who had gone along with Mussolini
just so long as it was profitable and who then sought to cross sides
without getting in the way of a single bullet.[21] There is no question that the two were remarkably successful in gulling Kesselring
into believing that it was their firm intention to fight side by side
with him to repel the anticipated invasion of the peninsula. Up
until the radio flashed the news that Italy had surrendered, Kesselring was basing his defense plans, in part, on the employment
of the Italian army.[22]

Robert Murphy, one of the men negotiating with the Italian
surrender party, became aware at an early stage that the primary
concern of the King's representatives was not the terms of surrender, but the measure of damage the Germans might do to their
country after the crossover became known. They kept asking,
"Are you strong enough to protect us?" It was obvious to Murphy
that the surrender party assumed that the Allies intended to
commit all their available strength to the Italian mainland and
that they would occupy Rome within a very short time.[23]

Here, too, the King used the very best tactics available to him to
accomplish his primary purpose: to stay on the throne as long as
possible. Whenever Murphy, acting under instructions from
Roosevelt, pressed him to announce his abdication, the King
would invariably answer that the decision could be announced
more impressively from Rome. Once, when pressed so vigorously
by Murphy for an immediate statement that he finally became
aware that Roosevelt and Churchill did indeed mean to terminate
the thousand-year-old occupancy of the throne by the House of
Savoy, he answered, with tears in his eyes, "A republican form of
government is not suited to the Italian people. They are not
prepared for it either temperamentally or historically. In a repub-

lic, every Italian would insist upon being president, and the result would be chaos. The people who would profit would be the Communists."[24]

It was not until October 12, 1943, that the Italian government officially declared war on Germany, but by that time the pattern had been molded. Italy, a historic battlefield, was now destined for its most convulsive experience. By this time, the stakes were too high for either side to back out of the arena. Perhaps if England and America had been acting in perfect concert, they might have been able to employ the fall of Mussolini as the means of quickly and painlessly separating Italy from the war. Also, perhaps, the allegiance of the sixty-one divisions who constituted the Italian army could have been secured by the Allies. As it was, a lack of leadership left the soldiers and their officers in a state of uninformed panic.[25] After a few days of indecision, only seven demoralized Italian divisions were left to the Allies.

Teutonic competency did not permit Hitler and his generals to allow this period of Allied uncertainty to affect what they conceived to be their national destiny. While Kesselring continued to insist that the Italians would remain his brothers-in-arms, the German General Staff put FALL ACHSE (i.e., "Axis Project") into effect[26] — a plan which had been developed and continuously modified in anticipation of exactly the events now occurring. The decision to leave southern and central Italy undefended was reversed and, as a result, the pathway was opened to the bloody battlefields of Cassino, Anzio, and the Rapido River.

Within a month, the German concept of opposing Allied landings just long enough to disengage their divisions stationed in the Boot would be altered and hardened into a pattern of bitter resistance to every forward Allied step. By mid-October, the Germans would have nineteen divisions in Italy, eight more than the Allies, and Dr. Joseph Goebbels noted in his diary: "The Fuehrer is firmly determined to wipe the slate clean in Italy . . . The only thing certain in this war is that Italy will lose it."[27]

« 3 »

An artilleryman who learned to fly at forty-nine, Field Marshal Albert Kesselring became the chief of the Luftwaffe General Staff and earned Hitler's respect and friendship for the leadership he displayed in the campaigns in Poland and the Netherlands and Belgium.

He was a devout Roman Catholic. He made frequent public protestations of his affection for things Italian and his relationships with Pius XII were considered uniformly correct by both the German and Italian leadership. Early in the campaign, American journalists, who so often attempt to reduce complex personalities to simple denominators, fastened on him the nickname "Smiling Albert," because he was reputed to grin easily and often.[28]

For psychological reasons, Allied leadership denigrated his abilities whenever possible.[29] An American VI Corps intelligence report found in the national archives considered him "incapable of leading infantry units . . . is only in command of SÜDFRONT [the southern front] for prestige. He is a personal friend of Hitler."[30]

The stocky and balding Kesselring had detractors within his own ranks. General Frido von Senger und Etterlin, who commanded the resourceful defense of Monte Cassino, felt that his superior was "invariably too optimistic and that, as a result, it was difficult to have an objective discussion with him on any given situation."[31]

It is true that Kesselring was overly confident on occasion.[32] He had misread both the Allied strength and intentions in the Sicily landings, and when the British and Americans finally came ashore on the mainland at Calabria and Salerno, his estimates of the strengths needed to repel them were clearly set at minimums. However, there is good evidence to support the belief that this might have represented an intelligence failure rather than a tactical blunder. He was never aware, for example, that there was a

substantial network of espionage agents in Italy reporting directly
to Himmler and Hitler, completely bypassing his own headquarters.[33] And, too, suspicion exists that the estimates being fed
him by Admiral Canaris, head of German military intelligence,
were incorrect in certain important particulars. This may be explained by the belief of some writers that Canaris was either
sympathetic to the Allied cause or even perhaps a double agent on
the Allied payroll.[34]

But whatever the sources of criticism against Kesselring, they
did not include the men fighting him in the field, who found him to
be a master of defensive tactics and whose strategic use of the
terrain approached genius. Mark Clark considered him one of the
ablest officers in the German army and was admittedly happy
when Kesselring was later transferred to command the Western
Front in Germany.[35] General Porter, in discussing the battles for
Cassino, said, "Fighting against all the airpower we could muster
and our maximum effort on the ground, the moves he made show
that he had a genius for logistics and maneuver. Allied propaganda [at the time] did everything possible to tear Kesselring
down — make him look like a Boy Scout — but the people in our
headquarters held him in respect. He bloodied our noses every
once in a while."[36]

Relations between Kesselring and the Vatican remained undisturbed throughout this period, with the sole exception that after
an Allied bombing raid on Rome on Monday, July 19, 1944, the
Curia made every effort to have the Field Marshal's and other
command posts evacuated from the city.

This bombing was considered strategically necessary by both
the British and American air staffs.[37] There were two major
marshaling yards in Rome being used by German forces as freight
loading centers for ammunition and troops destined for present
and potential fighting fronts. In planning the raid, scrupulous care
was taken to confine it to military objectives. As a final precaution
against a possible popular outcry, the bombing crews and the
reporters accompanying them attended religious services con-

ducted by chaplains who had been encouraged to stress the need for the operation. One Catholic padre, in what may have been an excess of zeal, shouted, "Give them hell over there!" to a departing bomber crew.[38]

The American magazine *Newsweek* in reporting the event stated: "For three years the Allies had forborne. In those three years Mussolini had clamored for and received the privilege of bombing London. Axis planes had not forborne, because of religious and esthetic sensibilities, assaults on Rotterdam and Cairo. In those three years, the Fascists had made Rome one of the greatest of Italy's military centers. Now they could no longer hide their capital behind the skirts of the Papacy or civilization's reverence for the grandeur of Rome."[39]

An international reaction appeared after the attack but, to the relief of the Combined Chiefs, it was not nearly as severe as had been feared. One respected Catholic-oriented magazine of comment, *Commonweal*, declared that there is no philosophy which makes it look "as if Catholics thought there must be one justice for Rome and another justice for all other cities in the world. [The Catholic] will make no distinction between the bombing of Rome and that of the most miserable Calabrian village."[40]

Pope Pius XII showed little inclination to treat the operation as a *cause célèbre*. He contented himself with rebuking both sides for failing to make Rome an open city, but by doing so he precipitated an international discussion of the city's status.

To understand the position of the Pope, it is necessary to describe the Lateran Treaty which the Italian government had concluded with the Holy See on February 11, 1929. By the terms of the document, the part of Rome which comprised the Vatican and St. Peter's, known as Vatican City, became regarded as an independent sovereign state. As a result, throughout the war, diplomatic representatives of both belligerent parties resided within its walls without interference. The treaty also extended to the rest of the properties owned by the Church in other parts of

Rome, and the Pope showed no disposition at any time to abdicate his authority over these extraterritorial pieces of ground.[41]

For the record, it must be stated that the Germans observed this reservation of sovereignty with scrupulous care. Hitler might rage, as he did on July 26 after hearing about Mussolini's dismissal: "I'm going into the Vatican right now. Do you think the Vatican bothers me? We'll grab it at once. First of all, the whole diplomatic corps is in there. I couldn't care less. That bunch is in there, we'll drag them out, the whole swinish pack of them . . . What of it? . . . We can apologize afterwards, that's nothing to worry about. . . ."[42] But cooler heads prevailed and no act took place which could give the Vatican reason to denounce the German hierarchy. Goebbels and Ribbentrop, especially sensitive to world opinion, were the chief calming agents. Goebbels noted in his diary: "I would regard such a measure as exceptionally unfortunate because of the effect our measures would have on the whole of world opinion."[43]

Marshal Badoglio, evidently finding his courage in the Vatican's continued control of its territorial prerogatives, declared on August 14 that Rome was an "open city." This had the effect of persuading the Romans that their city would remain inviolate, and they went on about the business of living as if Badoglio's declaration had not been strictly unilateral. An Italian resistance leader, who seized on the news of surrender as his cue to rouse his fellow Romans into a popular insurrection against the Germans, found only a handful of volunteers willing to support him.[44]

Kesselring read this air of quiescence as a signal that there was no need to fear trouble at his back while he devoted himself to the job of securing southern Italy from the Allies. He gave orders to continue the respectful treatment of the Vatican area and made the Vatican territory off-limits to all German military personnel.[45] It was not until the Allied landing in Anzio in January 1944 that he recommended the demolition of all the bridges across the Tiber, the destruction of all electrical power installations and the razing of all industrial installations within the city. But even then he insisted that none of these objectives should be accomplished in a manner that might affect the facilities required by Vatican City.[46] Why did the Vatican receive this preferred treatment? Was it only public-relations pressures that caused the Germans to refrain from the ruthless conduct which had characterized their domination of all of the other territories they had occupied?

There are some writers and historians who believe that it was due to something more than a sensitivity to world opinion. In recent years, the play *The Deputy* has created storms in America and Europe because in it the playwright, Rolf Hochhuth, painted Pope Pius XII as an irresolute egotist who didn't care nearly as much for the victims of Nazism as he did for his own public image and the security of the papal throne.

In his blunt indictment *Pius XII and the Third Reich: A Documentation,* Saul Friedländer makes the point at great length that Pope Pius XII, who had spent many years in Germany as papal nuncio, had a strong affinity for that country which was not diminished by the advent of the Nazi regime and that, further, the Pope was so convinced that Stalin and the Communists represented a greater threat to Catholicism than world domination by Hitler and the Germans that he was willing to go to any lengths to set the two sides in conflict.[47] Friedländer produced a whole series of documents purporting to prove that the appeasement policies of the Catholic Church were no less craven than the policies followed by the English government under Chamberlain, and under the most charitable of constructions, all that might be said for Pius XII was that he was a skillful politician.

There were other sources which echoed Friedländer's conviction that from the moment Eugenio Pacelli became Pius XII in 1939, "he did all that could be done to promote the rapprochement between the Vatican and the Third Reich which he had wanted when he was only Secretary of State."[48] One American magazine, the *Christian Century,* stated: "That Vatican diplomacy will work against the evolution of democracy through the peace as it has in the events leading to the war is evident from the reported nature of

Lt-General Mark Clark (above), Commanding General of the Allied 5th Army, and Lt Francis Buckley are cheered by 5th Army troops when they meet in the Pontine Marshes area, reuniting the main army with the beachhead forces. (Keystone)

(Below) General Eisenhower (in jeep) receives a warm welcome from British troops during a visit to the front. (Keystone)

(Above) *Members of the German garrison who attempted the defence of Anzio lie dead in the streets as 5th Army troops move in, March 1944.* (Below) *German soldiers, hands raised in surrender, run towards the Allied line as the town of Cisterna is captured in October 1944.* (Keystone)

the feelers its emissaries have recently been putting out in Washington and London. It appears also from the indirect plea of the Pope for a soft peace for Germany contrasted with his silence when the democracies stood in the perilous position where Hitler now stands."[49]

When the Pope appealed, in a September 6 broadcast, for a negotiated peace, the same hostile observers immediately accused him of really attempting to win for Germany a settlement something short of a genuine defeat. In effect, they said, "the Pope has now decided that the Allies will win and, therefore, he is attempt-.ing to render the last bit of aid to Germany in his power . . . that is, acting as a peacemaker in her behalf."[50]

Many voices have been raised to dispute these accusations. A majority of the rebuttals, of course, are Catholic in origin. For example, Admiral Franco Maugeri, of the Italian navy, in his book *From the Ashes of Disgrace*, provides a definitive sampling of this position when he pays "tribute and homage to the service rendered the cause of freedom and democracy by the Vatican and its Head throughout the grim years of war. Pius XII, by word and by deed, constantly championed and protected the enemies of the barbarian tyranny. Members of my own family found refuge in one of the Catholic colleges in the heart of Rome. Nor was this aid limited to those of the Catholic faith. Countless numbers of Italian Jews and non-Italian Protestants were given refuge within the walls of Vatican City itself, and the Church contributed millions upon millions of lire to ransom Jews caught in the bloody talons of the German beast."[51]

But another source is so obviously free from a pro-papal bias that it would be submitted by almost any lawyer as a blanket answer to the indictment. This is the private diary of Dr. Joseph Goebbels, in which, at various times during this era, he made these notations:

I have received confidential information to the effect that the Pope has appealed to the Spanish bishops under all circumstances to see to it that Spain stays out of the war. He supports his argument with humanitarian phrases. In reality he thereby gives expression to his enmity for the Axis. It is clear nonsense for a spiritual and ecclesiastical power to meddle so much in political and military questions. After the war we shall have to see to it that as far as our country is concerned at least, such attempts at interference are rendered impossible.[52]

I proposed to the Fuehrer that he forbid visits of German soldiers to the Pope. This series of visits has really become a public danger. The Pope, of course, embraces every opportunity to receive German soldiers in order to impress them with the whole pomp of the Vatican's ceremony. Besides, the present Pope is clever enough to use these things for obvious propaganda. He speaks German fluently and his outer bearing naturally creates the desired impression with naïve soldiers, and especially officers. That's why this evil must be stopped.[53]

Through an undercover informant I learn that the Pope intends to enter upon negotiations with us. He would like to get into contact with us and would even be willing to send incognito to Germany one of the cardinals with whom he is intimate. Apparently he believes we are momentarily so badly off that we would be willing to make him essential concessions. There can, of course, be no thought of it.[54]

Dr. Goebbels is not the only source which indicates that the Pope was not pro-German. A cloak-and-dagger story appearing in the New York *Times* detailed how the Pope, in 1939, agreed to act as an intermediary between the government of Great Britain and a group of conspirators plotting to overthrow the German dictator. This action, in a report delivered to the American Historical Society, was described as "one of the most astounding events in the modern annals of the papacy."[55] And there were other testimonials. Hundreds of Allied soldiers and airmen downed behind German lines found sanctuary in the Vatican. The Hon. Harold Tittman, who was chargé d'affaires of the American mission to the Vatican during the German occupation of Rome and who spent the entire period as the only American diplomatic representative in Vatican City, recalls giving a Christmas party in 1942 for the twenty American escapees who were then taking refuge in the Vatican: "Once the escapees had reached the haven of Vatican City, they were allowed to stay and were housed in the barracks of the Swiss Guards."[56]

« 4 »

On September 3, the British, under Montgomery, came ashore at Calabria. The Americans, under Mark Clark, followed six days later at Salerno.

CHAPTER IV

SEPTEMBER 1943

The Italian campaign was hastily improvised. Following the capture of Sicily there was no sure way of knowing how the Germans would react, and I think it was generally hoped that they would just crawl back and all of Italy would fall right into our laps.

Well, this was specious reasoning. The same type of thinking had been followed and proven wrong in the invasion of North Africa when it was not expected that the Germans would come in to help the French. They did and we had a hell of a campaign on our hands as the Germans improvised, and improvised very well.

Then at Sicily it was expected that the Germans would pull out and we would then just be dealing with what was left of the Italian army. Well, they didn't, and it was an expensive, if short, campaign.

Then once again we followed the same reasoning. When we landed on the Italian beaches, we had assurances from Badoglio that his battalions would fold. They did, but the Germans had anticipated that, and they moved in again very fast. So we found ourselves with a very long and very difficult campaign. I can't imagine any high command undertaking a campaign like this if they knew, which they did not, that the Germans would put up a stiff resistance.

— WILL LANG[1]

MARK CLARK remembers the first day of the first assault by the Allies on the Europe that was held by the forces of Adolf Hitler:

"I got aboard Vice Admiral Henry Hewitt's flagship, the *Ancon,* and sailed out of North Africa. I remember at dusk looking out over the sea and seeing a hundred silhouetted ships carrying my men and my thought was: 'Thank God I'm not in command yet — it's up to this admiral to put us ashore.'

"You see, in the military schools, they always worry about this question of who's in command at what time during an amphibious operation, but we didn't have a bit of that at Salerno. Hewitt was in command until the troops were ashore, and I was perfectly willing to let it remain that way. He knew his business. There was never a moment of jealousy between the Navy and us at any time.

"I remember, the first night, Hewitt said, 'When are you going to get ashore, Mark? Because I'd like to get a little further away from here.' And I answered, 'Nothing doing. You're it. You stay here and maybe tomorrow I'll have enough room.' You know, you just don't put an army headquarters with all its paraphernalia in the front lines. I guess it was on the second day that I reluctantly put my headquarters almost right on the beach. That night, at eleven o'clock, German tanks came through my headquarters and we skinned right out of there and I established headquarters again over in the field. But the Navy stayed. They were subjected to heavy bombing, but they stayed. They did a fine, fine job.

"But it was touch and go. Back in the Army colleges, ·they always question you on the way you prepare a· hypothetical amphibious landing. That is, they want to know if you've prepared yourself so that if the enemy overwhelms you, the way they did the British at Dunkirk or Gallipoli, if you have alternate plans to make sure your ammunition and supplies don't fall into his hands. They want to know whether you are set up to destroy your stores.

"Well, you never know how hypothetical these things are until you get into a tight battle. At Salerno, next morning, I'd look out from our new headquarters in the field and I'd see some dust out in the distance. Through my field glasses, I could discern that they were tanks, but I didn't know who they belonged to. That's how touch and go this Salerno thing was. And, the more I thought about this demolition [of his ammunition and stores in case of a successful German counterattack], the more I thought it was the most ridiculous thing I'd ever heard of. How the hell would you do it? You just don't go up with a match to a pile as big as this room here and set it on fire. In fact, once you did decide to do it, your whole command would know you were getting ready to blow up the place and it would have a disastrous effect upon their morale. So, I remember saying one of those nights, 'The hell with *that* — that's one thing we'll kick out of the books. When I get back home I'll tell the colleges to forget *that* one!' "[2]

An English journalist at Salerno, Hugh Pond, offers a revealing description of Clark personally doing everything within his powers to convince his troops that no matter how strongly the Germans counterattacked, the invaders were on the beaches to stay: ". . . he drove off in his jeep along the dusty tracks just behind the forward trenches. He stopped and talked to hundreds of officers and men during the day; wherever he went, he noticed the fatigue of the troops and often the fatalistic air of defeat. Not many of the GI's understood the true situation and listened in wonder when the tall, gangling Army commander said: 'There mustn't be any doubt in your mind. We don't give another inch. This is it. Don't yield anything. We're here to stay.' "[3]

On one occasion, Clark saw a cloud of dust announcing the approach of a large number of tanks. Ascertaining that they were German, he used his jeep radio to call for a tank destroyer unit: a lieutenant general accepting the job of a junior officer because the situation demanded it. On another occasion, the rumor that the enemy was using poison gas threatened to demoralize a sector. Clark, driving up in his jeep, wearing no mask, was accepted by the troops as instant evidence that the rumor was false.[4]

Back at Supreme Headquarters, General Eisenhower interrupted his pacing of the floor to tell Harry Butcher that if the Salerno battle ended in disaster, he'd probably be "out."[5] This was not a callous announcement of self-interest. Ike was simply stating one of the immutable facts of military life: the personalization of command decision. There wasn't one headquarters officer unaware that Eisenhower was infinitely more concerned with the fate of Clark and his men than he was over his own career..

Although Clark secretly shared his friend's concern for the invasion force, he continued to hide it beautifully. A reporter from *Time* magazine, who was with Clark one day, watched him exercise tactical control. "On his long belly the General watched. 'Damned rear guard, holding up a whole division,' he said. 'Where are our troops?' He swung his binoculars north. 'Oh yes. I see three of them. Crossing an open field. Why the hell don't they take cover?' A few minutes later he crawled over to a slit-trench phone, talked to a regimental commander. 'Of course, your battalion commander knows more about the situation than I do,' he said smoothly. 'But maybe we ought to get in there fast and exploit this barrage.' Back at the outpost, he commented: 'We're going to attack in half an hour.' But he did not wait. He was off to other forward units, riding with one long leg astride a fender of his jeep."[6]

He gave official voice to his optimism on September 16 when, in a letter to all of the men in his command, he congratulated them on their advance in the face of determined German resistance and added again that "we are here to stay. Not one foot of ground will be given up." He concluded with the assurance that "we shall drive on relentlessly until our job is done."[7]

But, in a personal letter sent a week later to his wife (quoted here in part), he showed that his optimism was privately leavened by a sense of the cost:

September 22, 1943

My Dear Wife:

We had a real battle continuously. Now I sit writing in my field command post in a truck I have had made into a house and office on wheels.

I must blackout soon, for it is getting dark now and the air activity is intense. The earth trembles with the terrific bombing we are giving them. When the ackack goes, it is like a Fourth of July celebration.

Last night, after being all over the front all day in the thick dust and dirt, I went to the hospital to see the wounded. I stood in operating rooms so thick with ether you could cut it with a knife. I saw six men being operated on at the same time. Our medical profession certainly has done a magnificent job.

Our hospital has its nurses, and they mean so much to the wounded. They cheer them up. The nurses came in here the second day of the attack. They are the best soldiers we have, living in the dirt and dust, never complaining, working 24 hours a day.

I talked with many of the wounded. They never complain. All they want is to get back into the fighting. In my opinion, the Germans will never be able to stop the Fifth Army.

Lovingly,
Wayne[8]

Clark's actions at the beachhead were solid and sustained. He was everything that a general should be, and as a result the seeds for a colorful and wholly admirable public image should have been sown. But again a fluke, like McNair's deafness, had an influence on his career. This time the result was not beneficial.

His orderly, deciding that the blanket order that no pets would be taken ashore did not apply to the commanding general, had put a tag around the neck of Clark's police dog which read: *This is General Clark's dog. She is going to Salerno.* The animal was brought onto the beach, where it became a serious nuisance.[9] Thereafter, comments about Clark's activities in the front lines would often be rejoined with: "Yeah, but did you hear about his dog?" It was a petty incident, yet it flawed his reputation, although he was totally unaware of his orderly's action. The incident was still being introduced in conversations as far away as the South Pacific by correspondents transferred from Europe after the fall of Rome.

Another, and more serious, source of hurt to Mark Clark's public personality also gathered strength at the beachhead. Among the many senior officers he had passed in his meteoric rise to one of the Army's highest positions of command was his former tactical instructor, Major General Fred Walker. Walker, in command of the 36th Division, which, with Clark's consent, had been assigned a pivotal role in the beachhead operation, reportedly began to refer to Clark as a "Boy Scout." Walker's bitterness was supposed to have been inspired by Clark's reneging on a promise to give him the first available corps command. When it was decided to replace Major General Ernest J. Dawley as the head of the American VI Corps, Clark tapped another old friend, Major General John P. Lucas, for the job.

Clark refuses to believe these stories. "Fred was my friend," he said. "Every time I went to this command post at Salerno to talk with him, there was always an atmosphere of deep friendship. As far as Luke taking VI Corps is concerned, Walker was never under consideration for the job. The only other time there was a corps vacancy was at the Anzio beachhead when I took Lucas out. But even there, there was no question that Truscott was the man for the job."[10]

An Air Corps officer asked that he not be identified because "those 36th Division men down in Texas are still so loyal to Walker that they'd skin me alive for saying this. But," he continued, "I never changed my mind about actively disliking Walker all the time I was with that outfit. It started when I first reported to him right after Sicily. My job was to coordinate the air effort with the plans of the 36th Division. The first time I met him he said that he hoped that the Air Corps would give the division in its Salerno landing better support than they had given any other unit to date, meaning that up till then the Air Corps had been pretty damn poor performers. As far as he was concerned, he said, the Air Corps was a complete nullity and did more to handicap the ground forces than it did to help them. He was a little guy, and he drew himself up to his full banty-rooster height when he said this. I was told later that he had been very much involved in Washington before the war in the fight that had been going on in the War Department between the proponents of air warfare and the old-line people who thought that air represented a momentary fad and would never amount to anything from a military standpoint.

"There was one advantage," the source concluded meditatively, "of serving under Fred Walker as an air officer. He never asked for any air and I could work out my own plans and my own programs."

Walker, who has written his own account of the Salerno battle, noted:

Clark became alarmed and ordered the Navy to be prepared to evacuate the 36th Division and attached troops from the beachhead. He never discussed his uneasiness with me, nor did he ever discuss with me the detailed dispositions of my troops and their missions. It is my opinion that his uneasiness, which unfortunately was transmitted to the Navy and the Pentagon, was due in great measure to his lack of knowledge of my detailed plans and dispositions for disposing of German tank attacks.

On another occasion during the same battle, Walker had this comment to make about Mark Clark's tactical concepts:

General Clark informed me this day that the Navy was going to bombard Altavilla. At the same time we were in a defensive position along La Cosa Creek. I did not see how the destruction of buildings and killing of civilians in Altavilla was going to help our situation. There were probably some German troops in the town, but they would know to take cover and protect themselves as soon as the shelling began. A very few of them might become casualties. The greater part of the German force could be expected to be on the high ground outside the town. After the bombardment it would still be occupied by German troops.[11]

In 1965, Walker, after reading a book concerning the Italian campaign, in which the following words appeared: ". . . and the dispatches from the front which described our division's brilliant maneuver mentioned only the division commander," wrote to the author of the book: "I wish they had. If you know General Clark, you must know that the 'brilliant maneuver' was made by 'General Clark's Fifth Army.' So far as I know, he never let any division or division commander's name be mentioned in his censored dispatches."[12]

Whatever the equities of the situation, the fact remains that the 36th, under Walker, had a fearfully hard time at Salerno. Even the usually reliable German communiqués of the period once described the 36th as being in "headlong flight." However, it later turned out to be a planned withdrawal to even lines with its British neighbor.[13]

There are few who will dispute that the Texans of the 36th, under Walker, were a leathery lot. One page, taken almost at random from the questionnaires completed by ex-members of the unit, is indicative of their attitude. Norman J. Beaty, of Dodd City, Texas, wrote, "Pfc. Tucker, who was a friend of mine, and I were hugging the ground about twenty yards apart during a bombardment at Salerno. I turned my head to one side and we were looking at each other right in the eye and I said, 'Tuck, is this rough enough for you?' He said, 'Heck no, remember the Inn back in Breckenridge?' That Inn was a salty honkytonk, and I do mean salty. A man could get killed there and not half try."[14]

« 2 »

In contrast to the American landing at Salerno, the secondary landing by the British on Italy's heel six days earlier was almost unopposed. The landing force, which consisted only of the British

1st Airborne Division, quickly secured two fine ports at Taranto and Brindisi and opened up the avenues of approach to the large airfields at Foggia. Opposing them, in the entire area between Taranto and Foggia, was only one low-strength German parachute division. Unfortunately, it was almost two weeks before the British received reinforcements, and by that time, the Germans had brought in sufficient strength to make it a contest.[15]

By the tenth of September, Kesselring had already mapped his defenses and scheduled his retirement positions if they should become necessary. Wondering at Montgomery's cautious advance, he protected his left flank by sending out elements of his 76th Panzer Corps and within a few more days began to launch his counterattacks, which, according to his diary, "might have led to a decisive German victory if Hitler had acceded to my very modest demands."[16]

On the 16th of September, elements of the British Eighth Army linked up with the American Fifth, and although Montgomery's moves may possibly have caused the Germans to discontinue their attempts to destroy the American bridgehead, it cannot be doubted that the help being offered by the English at this point was mostly psychological. Montgomery's chief of staff, Sir Francis ("Freddy") de Guingand, observed: "It must be remembered that the situation at Salerno was well in hand before we established any pressure in that neighborhood . . . [even though] we were all patting ourselves on the back at the time saying, 'We've done it again.' I now realize how very irritating this attitude must have been to the Americans and General Clark!"[17]

Clark agrees that Montgomery's support was far from robust in the early days of the invasion. "He had landed first," said Clark, speaking of Montgomery, "and he was coming up, well, I won't say 'leisurely' but it sure wasn't as fast as I had hoped. In the meantime, I was really having a rugged time and in the middle of it I kept getting these messages from Monty: 'Hold on — we're coming up' and then, later, 'Hold on — we've joined hands.' I remember sending one message back where I said, 'If we've joined hands, I haven't felt a thing yet.'

"And, all the time, the British Broadcasting Company was blasting out the information that Montgomery was saving Salerno, Montgomery's troops were doing so and so. Naturally, we began to wonder.

"Then one day, around the twenty-first, the head of our public relations section showed me a directive he had received from Alexander's headquarters, which was above me. This directive, after mentioning the towns and the organizations that could be identified, concluded with the instructions: 'First, play up the Eighth Army progress henceforth. Second, the Fifth Army is pushing the enemy back on his right flank.' "[18]

However, Clark was beginning to acquire the rudiments of diplomacy. Recognizing Montgomery as a potentially difficult ally, he greeted Sir Bernard at their first meeting with: "Monty, you're a battle-proven commander. I'd like to lean on you — ask your advice from time to time." Montgomery beamed at this and the two men became close friends, continuing their correspondence long after the war had ended.

After their initial conference had concluded, Clark accompanied Montgomery over to his jeep. As the abrasive Englishman prepared to swing himself in, he paused and asked, "Do you know Alexander well?"

"No," Clark admitted.

"Well, I do. From time to time you will get instructions from Alex that you won't understand. When you do, just tell him to go to hell."[19]

"The relationship between my Chief and Field Marshal Alexander was most interesting," Freddy de Guingand wrote. "They always worked well together — a good team — but there seemed to be perhaps a falling off towards the end of their time together. Each had different qualities. Alexander excelled at sitting back and getting the best out of Allies and the different Services. He was self-effacing and always generous in allowing his subordinates their full measure of reward and praise. He showed himself most able at dealing with the complex political problems that came his way. Montgomery concentrated all his energies on the battle and those things that went to win them. I know that both recognized each other's assets."[20]

General Sir Harold Rupert Leofric George Alexander, the third son of the fourth Earl of Caledon, has been described by Robert Murphy as "the ablest of the British generals in the Mediterranean theatre of war"[21] and by an English journalist as "the best type of British officer; fearless, handsome, immaculate in dress, and with great courtesy and charm of manner, he fitted exactly the American concept of a British general."[22]

During World War I, Alexander was a major at twenty-five and at twenty-six was a lieutenant colonel commanding a battalion. During his four years in the trenches, he was wounded twice and won several of Britain's highest awards for valor. After Hitler invaded Poland, Alexander took the First Division of the British Expeditionary Force to France and commanded the First Corps in Flanders.

He was the last man to leave the beaches at Dunkirk. As his troops were preparing to leave, an aide remarked, "Sir, it looks as if we will have to surrender." Alexander is supposed to have replied: "So it does. But I don't know the form for surrendering. So it seems we can't." The final sentence of the official dispatch describing the evacuation of Dunkirk said: "At midnight on Sunday, June 2, 1940, Major General Alexander and the senior naval officer made a tour of the beaches and harbor in a motorboat; being satisfied that no British troops were left on shore, they themselves left for England."[23]

There are other sources for intimate descriptions of Alexander. General Charles de Gaulle called him "a great leader, of lucid mind and firm character."[24] General Omar Bradley, describing him during the Tunisian campaign, said: "He not only showed the shrewd tactical judgment that was to make him the outstanding general's general of the European war, but he was easily able to comport the nationally minded and jealous Allied personalities of

(Right) *Montgomery and Sir Alan Brooke touring the Indian Division of the 8th Army in Italy, December 1943.* (Keystone)

(Below) *General Sir Harold Alexander shares a joke with American soldiers.* (UPI)

Major-General Lucian Truscott (right), of the 5th Army, studies maps during the early Anzio beachhead operation. (Keystone)

(Below right) *General Omar Bradley at a roadside command post.* (Keystone)

(Below) *General George Marshall Jr, Chief of Staff of the US Army.* (Keystone)

his command. By the fall of 1943, with Tunisia, Sicily, and now Salerno behind him, Alexander occupied a unique position in the Allied high command. He was our only Army Group commander and therefore our only experienced one. At the same time he had demonstrated an incomparable ability to fuse the efforts of two Allied armies into a single cohesive campaign. Had Alexander commanded the 21st Army Group in Europe, we could probably have avoided the petulance that later was to becloud our relationships with Montgomery. For in contrast to the rigid self-assurance of General Montgomery, Alexander brought to his command the reasonableness, patience, and modesty of a great soldier. In each successive Mediterranean campaign he had won the adulation of his American subordinates."[25]

During this period, the New York *Times* contained this excellent word portrait of Alexander, by Frank L. Kluckhohn:

Although he is 52, Alexander, with his athlete's figure and Grecian profile, bears a striking resemblance to the late John Barrymore in his prime. The general's close-cropped mustache — it tended to be bushy in earlier days — goes well with his regular features. In his favorite field uniform of breeches, high boots, jacket with red facings and cap with red band, this Irishman reminds one of a deadly, poised rapier. His outstanding feature, cold blue eyes, capable of freezing under stress, point to the steel in his character.

He has a fine smile, but when those hard eyes turn really cold his subordinates feel the inherent authority he possesses. His voice is soft and melodious until he wants to emphasize a point. Then it becomes clipped and brittle. A champion athlete who always has kept in tip-top shape, he moves with a light rhythm and balance that point to another facet of his character. Alexander never allows himself to be upset.

He does not have that extraordinary power to inspire the troops possessed by Montgomery and Patton, but he knows men, how to pick and handle them. He knows what they are capable of doing. This is the mark of all successful commanders. Once he has picked a man for a job, he backs him to the limit.[26]

Fanned by the almost unanimous agreement that Harold Alexander represented the best that the British Empire had to offer,

Winston Churchill's natural optimism reached new peaks. His physician, Lord Moran, reported in a September 7 entry: "Last night he talked of meeting Alex in Rome before long — the capture of Rome has fired his imagination, more than once he has spoken about Napoleon's Italian campaign."[27]

Alexander was not so sanguine. After the landing, he told a correspondent, "When we landed at Salerno, the idea was to drive straight across the Italian leg and trap those German divisions contained in southern Italy. We had expected a few Germans in the Salerno area, certainly not more than one division. We no sooner landed, however, than we found ourselves with a four-division front on our hands."[28]

What had appeared as a brilliant strategic maneuver in the planning sessions had been torn apart by political considerations. The armistice with the Italians, which was to have created such difficulties for the Germans that they might even have had to flee all the way northward to the Alps, produced nothing but an increased determination to hold on. "The armistice," Alexander observed, "was, for the Italians, merely a signal to return home."[29]

This wasn't quite fair. When Marshal Badoglio offered his country's armed services, saying that if given the equipment, eight to ten combat divisions could be made quickly available, his offer was summarily rejected by Alexander with the statement that "the plans for the Italian campaign are already minutely prepared in great detail and, as a consequence, the participation of Italian troops cannot be taken into consideration."[30]

The Italians received so much of this kind of treatment during this period that they might have been forgiven for wondering whether the Allied occupation was an unmixed blessing. It would have been an all too human reaction to refuse to replace the devil they knew with the devil they didn't, and reembrace the Germans. But the Fascist miasma had begun to lift from the Italian scene, and on September 23, Dr. Goebbels noted in his diary: "Pavolini is in Rome to build up the Fascist party and the Fascist militia. He isn't having much luck. In response to his first appeal for re-creating the Fascist militia, exactly fifteen men in the Italian capital reported! But one can see from it to what depths Fascism has already sunk in the public esteem."[31]

Among the few Americans who remained in Rome was a nun who kept a diary which she later published under the pseudonym "Jane Scrivener." Her comments provide a faithful reflection of life in Rome and the Vatican during those days.

In a September description of the reaction to Kesselring's declaration that disbanded Italian troops should reassemble in order to help the Germans drive their common enemy from Italian soil, she wrote: "All the Roman papers carried this proclamation. The Italians simply loathe the Germans, but the latter do not seem to have grasped the fact. German brutality to Italian soldiers when retreating in Russia and in Tunisia will never be forgotten in Italy, apart from their resentment on account of the Germans cutting down the Roman food supply while themselves living on what is left of the fat of the land."[32]

Admiral Maugeri, who later became chief of the general staff of the Italian navy, described the general reaction among the Romans:

During these early days, the state of mind of the civilian population of Rome and the rest of German-occupied Italy fluctuated wildly. The first reaction to the news of the Armistice and the Salerno landing was one of joy and exultation mingled with a profound sense of relief. This was heightened during the first day of the American invasion. Many expected the Allies to march triumphantly into Rome that same afternoon. Our happiness was only increased by seeing the panic and confusion of the Germans as they gave every indication of fleeing the city. By September 10, however, our raptures began to fade. The Allied armies had failed to materialize nor did the news bulletins offer much hope of their early appearance in the Eternal City. And with each passing hour, our erstwhile German friends seemed more reluctant to quit . . .

Naturally, as Italian hostility increased, the German grip grew tighter, harsher. Restrictions became more severe. Rationing of bread, flour, meat, oil, salt and sugar daily grew more stringent. Essential public services practically ceased. Trolleys operated only sporadically. Electric power and light was "zoned" — that is, for two nights in each week a different area of Rome was completely without it. Cooking gas was limited to only a few hours during the day. Gasoline for automobiles was impossible to obtain except at grotesque black market prices. A trip by car from Rome to Venice, crowded in a tiny baby Fiat or Lancia with three or four other passengers, cost something like 75,000 lire or about a thousand dollars. Train travel was almost out of the question unless you were a member of the military, had official sanction from the German authorities or "knew the right people."

Under these conditions, black markets flourished like the green bay tree. Meat practically disappeared altogether. The cost of such staples of our diet as pasta (spaghetti and macaroni) and potatoes soared to stratospheric heights, if you were lucky enough to get any. Eggs cost 30 and 40 cents apiece. A quart of milk was worth a dollar or more. To secure such luxuries, however, it was necessary to have "contacts" among the farmers in the countryside around the city. In Rome itself they were impossible to obtain except at fantastic prices. Even fruits and vegetables, which have always been plentiful in Italy, were impossibly expensive. Lemons, for example, cost 50 and 60 cents each.

All of these hardships, difficult as they were, were supportable; they were a sacrifice we were happy to make in order finally to be fighting on the side of the Allies and against the Germans. The various Nazi repressive measures employed against us were less easy to bear, however. The forced-labor drafts, for instance, and the dragnets. Throughout the period of the German occupation of Rome it was common practice for them to raid a restaurant, theater, café or even a church and drag off twenty, thirty òr forty men at random to the slave-labor battalions. Or various sections of the city would suddenly be surrounded by a dragnet of *Wehrmacht* or SS soldiers. All men caught within it were forced to submit to an on-the-spot check of their documents. Those whose "papers were not in order" were summarily carted off to prison or forced labor.[33]

On September 16, Jane Scrivener noted:

The Vatican City is "protected" by German troops, although they have made no attempt to occupy it. The idea seems to be that they are "protecting" it from the Allies. Two German paratroopers slouch in a dispirited manner near the colonnade of St. Peter's, carrying Tommy guns. They wear battle dress, that is helmets resembling tortoise-shell basins in colour and design, and short green-and-brown-streaked camouflage overalls on top of their summer uniforms of buff cotton. In bearing and outline they suggest penguins. Sometimes they stand in the colonnade, out of the hot sun, but they never go inside the white line which marks the boundary of the Vatican City. In fact, whether on or off duty, they are forbidden to enter it. Inside the Vatican City serious police measures have been taken and the commanders of the Vatican forces are very much on the qui vive. A large number of extra Palatine Guards have been taken on, the numbers of Swiss Guards and Gendarmes on duty have been doubled, and ten Noble Guards are on the watch night and day outside the Pope's private apartments. Many of the latter who lived in Rome have taken up their quarters in the Vatican so as to be within call. . . .

Of course spies of every shade and colour could easily make the little Vatican City their happy hunting ground unless precautions were taken. As a matter of fact the Library is closed, although one may keep one's card of admission for future use. There was a good deal too much talking in the Library lobby and courtyard, and a few spies and "agents provocateurs" did make their way in there under pretence of study. There might have been serious trouble had not both the spies and the imprudent talkers been firmly excluded.

Even to enter St. Peter's, lay folk have to show some sort of identification card; that is to say, when it is open. Sometimes they shut it altogether. . . .

Certainly the Germans, whatever their motive may be, are trying to make friends with the Vatican. Their Ambassador to the Holy See, Baron von Weiszäcker, is extremely courteous and shows every consideration to the Pope.[34]

Having been refused status as actual allies by Alexander, many elements of the Italian population went underground to join the Partisan bands in a systematic harassment of the Germans. Field Marshal Kesselring found them to be a serious annoyance, stating in his memoirs:

The first signs that cells of resistance against the German armed forces were being created first became apparent under the Badoglio government. . . .

After the defection of Italy the network of spies and saboteurs spread, extensive assistance being given amongst other things to escaping Allied prisoners of war, who, joining with Italian soldiers who had taken to the mountains, themselves helped to build the first guerilla groups. Among these latter, rascally elements were allowed to become a scourge to decent Italians. In the autumn and winter of 1943 isolated and not particularly dangerous bands, mostly composed of escaped prisoners of war, made their appearance in the rear of the Tenth Army, as a rule trying to fight their way across the front. . . .

The main feature of the Partisan organization in the early months was the absence of any kind of responsible leadership according to Article 1 of the Hague Convention on Land Warfare, although later on, when the names of a few leaders became known, things were not so bad in this respect.

In the course of months the following facts became increasingly evident to the German Command:

The highest responsible leaders of the Partisan movement were located at Allied headquarters; we therefore assumed that they composed a mixed control centre relying on both Italians and Allies, the mainspring of their activities being the intelligence officer, although they were increasingly under the eye of the operations branch. Sabotage and reconnaissance parties, often composed of criminal elements, communicated with general headquarters through Allied liaison officers, in so far as they did not act independently.[35]

General Alexander felt differently. In his memoirs, he recalled: "Although I cannot pretend that the partisans, despite their personal gallantry, were ever a serious problem to the Germans, they played their part in the Allied cause. In particular, I should like to put on record my appreciation of the help given to our escaping prisoners of war by the good and simple people of Italy. Although their government had surrendered, they were still under enemy domination; and were able to render assistance only at great risk to themselves."[36]

And so passed the month of September 1943 in Italy.

CHAPTER V

OCTOBER 1–DECEMBER 20, 1943

. . . an Army Commander is a pretty lonesome fellow in combat.
— MARK CLARK[1]

AT this point, the unavoidable question is: Why didn't they stop here? According to all the strategic concepts which had been discussed and agreed upon by the Combined Chiefs of Staff, the Allied goals for this particular campaign had been met. The airbases around Foggia were large enough to support strikes against almost any part of occupied Europe. The restored port at Naples eliminated the possibility of Axis domination of the Mediterranean.

But the Allies did not stop because, apparently, there was a period of vacuum in the planning. Not until the Teheran meeting of Roosevelt, Churchill, and Stalin at the end of November would there be any further development of a strategic concept.

Eisenhower was wary of this interim period. He felt that if the Germans were to be separated from the Allied attackers by a buffer zone of inactivity — a point beyond which each army withdrew and waited — Kesselring would use his time to prepare defenses and Hitler would feel that he could safely divert a large part of the German force in Italy to both the Russian front and the potential invasion sites in Normandy.[2]

The Combined Chiefs accepted Ike's reasoning. Although they replaced a sizable portion of his combat-hardened troops with inexperienced divisions, he was given permission to maintain his attack.[3]

There are two reasons why this particular course of action was destined to become the deadly stalemate which, through the years, has tainted any discussion of the Italian campaign. The first was that Eisenhower did not have command of the air arm of the assault. His jurisdiction dealt solely with ground actions, and therefore he could only stand by as the Fifteenth Strategic Air

Force consumed 300,000 tons of shipping to build up the Foggia airbases during the most critical weeks of the campaign. And, since both the Fifth Army and Eighth Army were still being influenced by Montgomery's concept that before an attack can be mounted there must be an overwhelming superiority in men and materiel, it meant that the Allies were almost immobile at this point.[4]

The second reason for the stalemate was beyond the power of any man. The bone-chilling Italian winter had begun with grim speed, giving the attacking force only the alternates of snow-covered mountains and freezing mud. Efficient transport became a joke and personal comfort only a memory.

There were now only eleven Allied divisions facing between twenty and twenty-five first class German divisions. Kesselring had been promoted by Hitler to Commander in Chief South with two armies at his disposal: the Tenth, which he used to contain the Allied advance, and the Fourteenth, which was deployed north of Rome in readiness for possibly another Allied landing farther up the coast. He did not know, of course, that Eisenhower had so few ships that it was all he could do to keep his present forces supplied with the bare minimum needed to continue the campaign. Allied preparation and planning emphasis had now shifted to Operation OVERLORD.

Given this margin to breathe, Kesselring proceeded to burrow his defense along what came to be known as the "Winter Line," and, further, to make every yard between the line and the Allied positions a costly purchase for Clark and Montgomery.

By mid-November, German bullets and Italian frostbite had convinced the Allied generals that it was time to pause and reorganize. It was the beginning of the dreadful stalemate.

« 2 »

Although his post is a coveted one, a corps commander rarely finds it possible to achieve anything more than a fleeting identification with the troops who are his responsibility. Since the army system is essentially patriarchal, this makes the corps commander somewhat like a man who is suddenly given a brood of children and told, "Be a good father to them." They *may* turn out well, but if they do it is because their real fathers, the commanders who trained them, did their jobs properly.

And this is by no means a purely American phenomenon. One of the German corps commanders, General Frido von Senger und Etterlin, made this estimate of the job: "For a divisional commander it is an easy matter, and also essential, to visit his battalion commanders during a big action, but it is not quite so easy for a corps commander, especially if he has more than six divisions under him. But the front line begins with the battalion commander, for he is both the battle commander of a very mixed unit and the leader of the assault force.

"The corps commander's contacts are made more difficult by the fact that his divisions are constantly being changed round, so that the troops cannot exactly regard him as a 'father.' His solicitude for them is intangible, unless he occasionally shows himself to the troops."[5]

The point is important enough to be emphasized. In combat, a corps is not a fixed group. It is simply a headquarters unit of a few hundred (or, occasionally, a few thousand) enlisted men and officers whose job it is to harness and direct the efforts of the combat units temporarily placed under their control in a given military operation.

The fact that the American II Corps achieved a fine combat record in North Africa, Sicily, and Italy under Patton, Bradley, and finally under Major General Geoffrey Keyes, is a comment upon the abilities of those commanders and their staffs. With the use of only a dash of imagination, it might be said that under Patton it was a daring unit, prone to wide-ranging attacks. Under Bradley it was an organization of sober professionalism, and under Geoffrey Keyes it became a faithful mirror of his almost businesslike approach to warfare and his willingness to throw away the book when the situation seemed solvable only by unorthodoxy.

Keyes was a West Point graduate.[6] Although a traditionalist and the son, grandson, and brother of many other Army officers, he selected a junior officer, Robert Porter, to help him run the outfit under the almost empty title "Deputy Chief of Staff for Operations." As high brass is reckoned, such a job is equivalent to office boy. With II Corps, it came to describe the man who was the commanding general's right hand.

Keyes was and is a devout Roman Catholic. He attended Mass every morning and his men took comfort in the act because, as one of them explained, "a man that religious won't hold human life cheaply. He thinks before he orders an attack." Yet Keyes, when he met with the Pope in Rome, exhibited little awe. He spoke to the Pontiff as a fellow high executive in almost familiar terms.[7]

He was a cavalryman with an instinctive taste for the use of armor, so much so that Patton was later to describe his direction of a provisional corps as "a classic sample of the proper use of armor and I also believe that historical research will reveal that General Keyes' Corps moved faster against heavier resistance and over worse roads than did the Germans during their famous blitz."[8]

Keyes was the general, and not Clark as popular belief has it, who ordered the 36th Division to go back and back and back again for their bloody beating at the Rapido River.[9]

General Eisenhower once described him as a man who had everything but a sense of humor. When Keyes was given command of II Corps, Eisenhower sent him a letter which, in part, said:

But I do have a word of suggestion along a line that would possibly never occur to you, nor possibly to your immediate senior. It is this: Don't be afraid to show pleasant reactions in your contacts with your subordinates. Be quick to give credit and, wherever possible, shove a bit of the limelight on to a Division Commander where you could easily have absorbed it all yourself. Every commander is made, in the long run, by his subordinates. We are all intensely human, and war is a drama, not a game of chess, so a wide grin, particularly in trying situations, is often worth a battalion. Mere efficiency on your part will sometimes not be enough! An informal, but always a sincere expression of commendation — even if given in an offhand manner — is sometimes called for even when the particular subordinate may have been guilty of some mistake. You do not need to be told that I am not advocating that you court popularity. Such a habit is fatal. I am merely talking about honest, open-handed, pleasant readiness to give the subordinate more than his full share of the credit for any and every success and to sustain him in reverses.

A wide grin, far from being merely evidence of idiocy, can be deliberately used to further the purposes of the Commander.[10]

This gravity, against which Eisenhower cautioned, sometimes led people to underestimate or misunderstand Geoffrey Keyes. When the First Special Service Force, an improbable group that came to be known as the "Devil's Brigade," was assigned to his command, he tried to forewarn them the German military ability was not to be underrated.

The Forcemen were unaccustomed to this kind of talk. Their leader, Colonel Robert T. Frederick, had won their affection by his wild courage but rarely spoke to them unless it was a command for action. At Keyes's words, they shifted their feet uneasily in the ranks and one of them muttered out of the corner of his mouth to another, "Bullshit, what's he trying to do, scare us?"[11]

Keyes had not been trying to scare anyone. War, to him, was a deadly serious experience and he was trying to tell the brigade that unmanageable bravery was no military virtue.

"Geoff Keyes came to the II Corps," recalls Robert van de Velde, "at the end of the Sicilian campaign during which everyone had developed a tremendous admiration for Omar Bradley. The summer was bright, the weather was good, and everything made for extremely high morale. Then the word came that General Bradley was being transferred to England and an immediate pall of gloom fell over almost all of the officers and quite a few of the enlisted men. This unknown fellow Geoffrey Keyes was coming in, and I think one of the things which depressed us almost as much as losing Bradley was that the unknown was a protégé of Patton, and most of us intensely disliked George Patton.

"In a few months, though, Geoff Keyes won us over by his modesty and plain ability. By the time of Cassino [January, 1944] he had our admiration as an extremely able and valiant commander. I considered it a privilege to have served with him all the way up to Austria.

"It was amazing to us that a man who was as close a friend — actually, a lifelong friend — to Georgie Patton could be so terribly different. Patton was a flamboyant, boisterous, profane kind of a leader. In all those years, I don't believe that anyone heard Geoff Keyes utter a single swear word, not even hell or damn. And yet, in his own way, he was every bit as great a leader as Patton was.

"It's impossible, for example, to imagine Keyes telling an anecdote such as the one Patton mentioned during a visit to our headquarters. In talking about his trip to the Holy Land, he said, in that squeaky voice of his, 'Gentlemen, I just can't express my emotions — but as I stood there on Mount Calvary, I just said to myself: George Patton, you old son-of-a-bitch, here you are where Jesus Christ stood!'

"General Keyes was a man of medium height, slender. Today, he is well past seventy, but he's as erect as ever. He was a man of deep thought and deep emotion and was, essentially, a gentle man. I think Geoff Keyes really suffered every time he ordered an operation that he knew might cause the death of some of his troops."[12]

The other officers who served in II Corps recall Keyes with something approaching adulation. The very junior intelligence officer whose job it was to brief the commander on the daily situation recalls: "He made it easy on a person like myself to do my job because he gave me respect."[13] Another junior recalled the time that a lieutenant colonel began patronizing some of his staff because they were not West Pointers. "Keyes heard about it," the man said, "and had the guy transferred out within twenty-four hours."[14]

Major General James W. Holsinger, a II Corps staff officer during that period, said: "Keyes had a little trick which impressed me; at staff meetings he would ask the intelligence and the operations sections their estimate of the way the situation would develop in forty-eight hours. It was amazing how quickly the G–2 and the G–3 began reaching a high percentage of accuracy in their forecasts. Keyes did this on the theory that it would take the troops forty-eight hours to react to a decision made at Corps level, so, therefore, staff officers ought to have a proficiency in anticipating the effects of their decisions. It worked, too."[15]

Another staff officer who became a major general, John Willems, said: "I thought Keyes to be outstanding because he was so sound and so continuously right in his judgments, and because he was almost invariably able to determine how an action would go. He liked to be out among his troops, and this was the only trouble he gave his staff — we had to get his decisions before he'd head out on the road in that jeep of his. But once he gave a decision, he'd rarely change it. He didn't have to, because it was always thought out to the last detail, and was always based on logic, not emotion. You could always gamble on any decision he gave us as being *the* decision."[16]

When General Bradley went to England, he took many II Corps officers with him. This left Keyes to staff his headquarters largely with men of his own choice. A methodical man, he carefully investigated the backgrounds and abilities of key people before he appointed them. As a result, there was little shuffling of jobs after II Corps opened operations in Italy. These staff men were generally in the image of Keyes. For example, after the way to Rome seemed open, an intelligence officer sent out a summary which began, "The enemy is routed. The road to Rome is open." Mercer Walter, the intelligence chief, sent it back with a note saying, "You can't use a word like 'routed' on the Germans. They're far from routed. We don't want to give any false impressions."

An operations officer, talking about the moral level of the headquarters group, said, "I don't know whether or not they had any inclination to be running around, but I do know that we were kept so goddamn busy, that it just seems as if there were very few sexual adventures. One time a full colonel came over and brought a mistress with him. In some mysterious way the news got around, and the next thing we heard that, although he was a West Pointer, he was relieved and sent home, demoted to his permanent rank.

"It's hard to believe, I know, when I describe the II Corps men as such a somber breed, but by God they were. I can no more picture Bob Porter or Willems or any of them with mistresses than I can picture myself in that situation. I don't mean that we were prudes or anything like that; we were just a bunch of hard-working guys who were out to get a war over with. We weren't flag-wavers, but we did have an honest desire to help win a war for our country. It's a damned shame to admit it, but I can't recall too many other headquarters that I was attached to that had the same strength of motivation.

"Now that I think of it, it's hard to visualize how well Nic Malitch fitted in with a group like this. But he did. He and Bob Porter were all but inseparable. Almost every night they'd play chess together, and their closeness wasn't lost on the rest of us. Nic sometimes used his position with Porter to take advantage of certain situations.

"I remember one time three or four of us, Nic included, went into a fairly large town for dinner. Nic, with a very imperious manner, called the headwaiter over and told him that the wine he had served us was slop and fit only for the pigs. The man said it was the best he had. Nic didn't answer. He simply looked at the bottle there on the table in front of us for a minute and then he said almost conversationally, 'If you don't bring us good wine, the wine you used to give the Germans, I'm going to kill you.'

"As I said, Nic spoke quietly, but I tell you it was one of the most frightening moments of my life. None of us, especially the headwaiter, doubted for a moment that Nic would kill him almost as casually as he would take the cork off the bottle. The head-waiter, after a minute of staring at him like a bird would at a cat, . went down into the cellar and came back with some very good dust-covered bottles of wine."

This officer also recalled that "later that night when we went to our rooms, Nic came around knocking on our doors, asking if any of us wanted a woman. There were no takers."[17]

Ted Liese, another intelligence officer, offers further evidence of Malitch's cold-bloodedness: "In Africa," he recalls, "we didn't do too good in interrogations. We were always being very nice to everybody because, really, we didn't understand too much of what was going on. Nic wasn't. He didn't hesitate to shoot a prisoner if he thought it was necessary. In a number of cases, his technique was for the best. Nic was a cruel man. It didn't make any difference for him to use force, because he'd used it all his life. He was severely criticized, but he got the job done."[18]

Obviously, to the men of II Corps headquarters, who went about each day's activities as methodically as if they were manu-facturing business machines, the presence of Nic Malitch was an alien and sometimes disturbing thing.

The reason he was not only permitted but actually encouraged to become a key member of this group probably lies in the willingness of Geoffrey Keyes and Robert Porter to disregard their rigid West Point training in order to arrive at the right answer at the right time. This unorthodoxy was a rarer attribute among the British generals. One of the officers who was privy to the meetings between Eisenhower and Sir Alan Brooke and other members of that level once commented, "Ike used to get furious when we'd get back to our own offices. Brooke was a good man, but he was a fussy man. He'd always be lecturing Ike about what worked in the last war and Ike would storm to us later, 'Goddammit, we're fighting *this* war!' "[19]

Malitch was capable of turning up answers that helped with the day's fighting. He wasn't only fighting *this* war, he was fighting *today's* war, and this made him a welcome member of a headquarters dominated by the controlled impatience of Keyes and Porter.

General Porter explained how it was that Malitch left the 1st. Division in order to join II Corps:

"After the division had been ordered to England, I was transferred over to II Corps. At our first meeting, General Keyes asked me if I wanted to bring anyone with me from the Division. I demurred. He said, 'You surely have someone, haven't you?' After I demurred a second time, he chuckled and said, 'What about that Mad Russian?' So I said yes, I *would* like to bring him, but that he was a mixed blessing in that from time to time he might get the headquarters in difficulty because he had a way of knowing everything that was going on whether it was his own business or not. General Keyes said he'd take a chance on him if I wanted him. I ended up bringing Malitch as well as a young American who had been raised in Italy, whose father was an engineer with Firestone Rubber and had managed a plant in the Malayan area for a rubber company. This man became Malitch's driver. They made quite a pair. The young American was a talented boy, and under Malitch's tutelage, he developed a lot. Some of his development was good and some was not, so . . .

"When I made the recommendation to the commander of the 1st Division that Malitch should go with me, and told Malitch about it, tears came into his eyes. He had been afraid that he was going to be abandoned. I told him that he would have a wonderful time with the division in England. He said yes, but that he preferred Italy because England was very cold in the wintertime.

"Malitch was a fine intuitive bridge player. I normally played as his partner because I could understand when he was bluffing and when he was making psychological bids better than most. He also loved to play chess, and he played a splendid game. I found, though, that he could only play about one game a day. If he played more than that it became such a tug of war that everything was forgotten.

"In the corps headquarters, actually, I could not use Nic as well as I had in the past, so I asked our G–2, Mercer Walter, if he would keep him occupied. Mercer gave him a great deal of guidance and he returned by helping Mercer. Walter used him as a liaison with the OSS people, who had operatives behind the lines. Malitch also put people through the lines and then got supplies to them and helped bring back their reports. From time to time he asked permission to go behind the lines. I never would agree to this, feeling that he would be shot as a spy by the Germans."[20]

Robert van de Velde remembers Nic as "almost a caricature of a soldier of fortune. He had Old World polish and, at times, courtly manners — the real Russian aristocrat on the loose. He understood art, music, wines, and women, and was conceited to the point of arrogance. Almost, but not quite, because he had a strange facet of occasional humility that was quite attractive.

"He was perhaps the most perceptive forward observer that I met in all my time as an intelligence officer. We used to say that he could smell Germans before they even opened fire. I know that he could sit on a hill and listen to firing and come back with a quite accurate estimate of the strength that was opposing us. He had this intense instinct for combat on the local level, but his heart really was for grand strategy. He was a great one for standing in front of a map of Europe, making sweeping gestures to show how Stalin, Montgomery, and the others should move. By and large, he was usually right there, too.

"I think he was one of those born soldiers who come to glory in wartime, but is a complete misfit between wars. He had no sense of personal discipline.

"Nic was used primarily by the operations section, but during the times he got.in their hair, they shoved him off on us, in intelligence. He occasionally got in our hair, too, but there is no question that he earned his keep in many ways. He was absolutely fearless, would go anywhere on anybody's bidding, and the information that he brought back to either G–2 or G–3 was almost invariably accurate, whether it had to do with our own troops or the enemy's."[21]

Major General Mercer C. Walter, who was nominally Malitch's superior during this period, agreed: "Nic was not a military man. He would come and go, more or less as he wished. But he willingly accepted missions to visit certain places to find out what he could. He always operated on his own when he did this. All he needed to know is what we were interested in, and he would go and do his best to find out. He spoke many languages fluently and he helped us tremendously in the interrogation of civilians and military prisoners and anyone else that he thought could provide the information we needed."[22]

The chief of staff of II Corps, Major General John Willems, answered the question of whether Nic was a double agent by saying: "Well, I always suspected that he was working for other people besides us. But if he was, I think he was probably working for the French or possibly the British. He also might have been actually working for the Russians, too. In fact, it wouldn't surprise me if he wasn't working for *both* the French and the Russians, in addition to working for us. He was a typical Russian — ruthless, quite lacking in the sense of human kindness that we Western people would consider normal."[23]

Since the Italian theater was one of the few newsworthy arenas during this period, it was flooded with high-level visitors. Mark Clark once observed that Fifth Army headquarters was so busy showing VIP's around that it was a wonder they had any time left to fight a war.[24] Nic Malitch had his own way of dealing with the distinguished guests. He closed all conversations by describing to the important personalities exactly what he was doing and how he was doing it.

One delegation of Pentagon brass had heard that Captain Malitch was quite successful in interrogating prisoners of war. Nic was sent for and a rather prissy staff officer asked, "Captain Malitch, what are the psychological factors you weave into your interrogation?"

Nic answered, "Sir, it is very simple. I ask the person that I am interrogating a question. If he answers it truthfully, I ask him another question. But if he lies or refuses to answer, I stick a red-hot poker up his ass and after that he will always talk."

The conference concluded abruptly. Later, when General Keyes was asked by the group about his interrogator, a rare grin breaking over his face was the only answer.[25]

"Nic was one of the most resourceful and most unscrupulous characters I've ever run into," Keyes recalled long after the war had ended. "He was devoted to Porter, and the two were inseparable. He'd take any kind of a job — interpreter, scout, anything. He was very, very loyal to II Corps for taking him in. I don't think that some of his activities would have borne too close a scrutiny, but it was in a good cause."[26]

« 3 »

Among the visitors to the Mediterranean Theater of Operations in this late autumn of 1943 were three of the most important men in the world: President Franklin D. Roosevelt, Prime Minister Winston Churchill, and Marshal Josef Stalin. The "Big Three," as the world's press was now referring to them, met in Teheran in the last days of November 1943, in order to make a final determination of global strategy.

Prior to that conference, Roosevelt and Churchill, accompanied by their chief advisers, met in Cairo on November 22 to arrive at some private determinations.[27]

It is obvious that Churchill went with the firm hope of postponing the OVERLORD date and securing agreement to prosecute the war in Italy with increased vigor. Major General Sir John Kennedy, director of Britain's armies in the field under successive chiefs and vice chiefs of staff, and thus, at the center of British plans and policies, was quite revealing when he noted in his diary on October 28: "The P.M. has taken a strong line with the Americans on the Mediterranean versus OVERLORD strategy. As he says, it is no use planning for defeat in the field [i.e., withdrawing troops from Italy] in order to give temporary political satisfaction. All this will mean a meeting in the near future with the American Chiefs of Staff and, if we carry our point, a postponement of OVERLORD."[28]

Another entry by Sir John, dated three days later, testified to the sincerity of British belief in the validity of the Italian campaign: "That the Germans are resisting so strongly in Italy shows what importance they attach to keeping us off the Rome airfields. If we get our long-range bombers there soon, it will be a devastating blow, and may well bring about a complete collapse."[29]

Robert Sherwood accompanied Roosevelt to Cairo and agreed that the importance of this point was uppermost in Churchill's mind. "Churchill," he wrote, "urged that despite the heavy German reinforcements that had been sent to the front in Italy, the Allied campaign should be pushed more vigorously than ever, with a view to capturing Rome at the earliest possible date — for 'whoever holds Rome holds the title deeds of Italy.' He placed particular emphasis on the assurance that he had in no way relaxed his zeal for OVERLORD but he recommended that this major operation should not be such a 'tyrant' as to rule out every other activity in the Mediterranean."[30]

Roosevelt, unlike Churchill, did not consider himself a strategist of any great ability. He leaned heavily on Marshall and his other military advisers[31] whose opinion, needless to say, had not changed a bit. If Churchill were allowed his way, they believed, the Allies would find their strength so hopelessly dissipated in what they considered minor actions that OVERLORD would be destroyed. They honestly saw no way of bringing Germany to defeat without whipping her as soon as possible on her own land. They urged Roosevelt to postpone any further discussions until the meeting with Stalin at Teheran. Many of them subsequently have admitted that they expected the redoubtable Russians to support their position, and with the dice thus loaded, British resistance could be overcome once and for all.[32]

It fell to another Englishman, General Sir Leslie Hollis, finally to put an honest face on the conflict. He said: "America, a large country, adopted — like a large man — frontal tactics. They wanted quick and terrible hammer blows that would speedily finish the fight; in this case, a very early landing in Europe, and then on down through France into Germany, and so over with the war.

"Britain, a small country, with a long history of frequently successful engagements against opponents that could have overwhelmed her with their numbers, adopted — like a small man faced by a large enemy — more subtle tactics. Over the centuries we had established an Empire by a policy of small operations which could be consolidated. Frequently we have gone 'in at the back door.' For instance, we had beaten Napoleon by going through Spain. In Churchill's view (and mine) we could have destroyed Germany in the First War had the back door in Gallipoli been less ineptly opened."[33]

Thus, the meeting at Teheran became the decisive conference in the development of European strategy. This was the first time that the Big Three and their staffs met face to face. And, to the great relief of Marshall's group, Stalin threw his weight behind the American plan. He was strongly in favor of OVERLORD and stated unequivocally that any further actions in the Mediterranean should be limited to a thrust into southern France as a diversion when the OVERLORD landing was made.[34]

There are quite a few military and political historians who believe that Stalin had other reasons for this position. They consider that, confident at last of victory, he was thinking primarily about postwar positions in Europe.[35] Churchill had gone on record as favoring the use of Italian bases for a thrust up through the Balkans. If this were successfully accomplished, Yugoslavia, Turkey, and others might be induced to join the Allies as co-belligerents. This, of course, would have given England and America the opportunity to create a middle European bulwark against the westward spread of Communist influence.[36]

But, whatever the reasons, Stalin was for OVERLORD and mentioned that not only was he willing to assume a defensive role in Italy, he could even see merit in forgoing the capture of Rome if, by diverting the divisions from that battle, the invasion of southern France could be implemented.

Bristling, Churchill replied that the Allies would be no stronger if they pulled out of the advance on Rome, that after the city was taken, they would be in an even better position by having destroyed or mutilated ten or eleven German divisions, and, further, that the airfields north of Rome were required for the bombing of Germany. The Prime Minister concluded by saying: "It would be impossible for us to forgo the capture of Rome. To do so would be regarded on all sides as a crushing defeat, and the British Parliament would not tolerate the idea for a moment."[37]

The appeal was a strong one. Roosevelt, who had been acting as a mediator between Churchill and Stalin[38] rather than as the third equal voice of the team, was visibly moved. Perhaps Stalin was, too — but not to the point where it overcame his suspicion of British motives. All through the next day, he subjected Churchill and Sir Alan Brooke to repeated grillings, demanding each time that they go through the ritual of reaffirming their loyalty to the OVERLORD concept.[39]

For three days, Sir Alan and Churchill fought for their concepts. Convinced that the Americans were being strategically naïve and that Stalin was cynically determined to squander as many British and American lives as possible in the French theater, they felt that they had no option but to argue on.[40] Finally, they achieved a partial success. The Allies would go on to Rome and establish a defensible line just beyond.[41] In exchange, they conceded that OVERLORD would take place as planned, the only variance being that it might be postponed from May 1 to June 1 in order to coincide with the planned mounting of the Russian counteroffensive.

One more decision was reached in this area. It was agreed that the invasion of southern France (code-named "ANVIL") would also occur at this time and that Mark Clark would command it.[42]

The British were satisfied with this arrangement. Churchill and Brooke privately agreed that they had succeeded in averting what might have resulted in the worst disaster in British — and American — military history.[43]

The Americans were also pleased. The Italian campaign would now represent only a secondary effort and, as a result, would receive scant consideration in the allocation of men and materiel. They were also quite impressed with Marshal Stalin. Admiral William D. Leahy, who was one of President Roosevelt's key aides at the conference, has written: "The talk among ourselves as the meeting broke up was about Stalin. Most of us, before we met him, thought he was a bandit leader who had pushed himself up to the top of his government. That impression was wrong. We knew at once that we were dealing with a highly intelligent man who spoke well and was determined to get what he wanted for Russia. No professional soldier or sailor could find fault with that. The Marshal's approach to our mutual problems was direct, agreeable, and considerate of the viewpoints of his two colleagues — until one of them advanced some point that Stalin thought was detrimental to Soviet interest. Then he could be brutally blunt to the point of rudeness."[44]

Winston Churchill was not quite so charmed by Stalin. In a later conversation, he told Mark Clark, "One night I was sitting and having a drink with Stalin, and somebody knocks on the door and in comes his daughter. I was surprised to see what an attractive young lady she was, and what do you know, she walked right up and kissed that dirty bloke!"[45]

« 4 »

Although the meetings ended in general agreement, the differences of opinion had been so sharp that inevitably they were transmitted down through both the American and English chains of command.

One facet of the English military system was largely responsible for this — all major political and military decisions were made in London. The men around Churchill might quarrel with him, despair of his flashing moods, and grumble at his assumption of military expertise, but they were all absolutely loyal to him. Once a decision was reached, it became a unanimous one and its potential ramifications and extensions were carefully explained to every level of command. If a field commander ever attempted to follow his own inclinations, as General MacArthur did later in Korea, he was subject to instant replacement.

The American commanders had infinitely more autonomy. Mark Clark, in Italy, received little military and almost no political guidance. Robert Murphy, although specifically representing the President, had no status other than adviser. Clark and Eisenhower once mildly speculated as to what the hell Murphy was doing there with them, anyway.[46]

As a result of this naïveté, political mistakes generally followed in the wake of the American advance. In Sicily, members of the Mafia were put in key civil government positions on the theory that since they had been vigorously prosecuted by Mussolini's representatives, they must have been on the right side. In Italy, quite a few Fascists and innumerable Communists found comfortable employment with Allied commissions.[47]

But it must be remembered that at this stage of their development the American generals were not only unconcerned with political considerations, they seemed almost unaware that any existed. It is not surprising, therefore, that their British opposite numbers who began by criticizing this lack of sophistication in international affairs, later, as American forces and supplies loomed larger and larger over the English contribution, began also to criticize their military capacities.[48]

Some of the British comments in memoirs dealing with this period can be considered a guide to this tide of British opinion. On November 18, Montgomery, in writing to Sir Alan Brooke, mentioned blandly, "I fear . . . that the Fifth Army is absolutely whacked. So long . . . as the big idea is that everyone should 'combat' somebody all the time, then you don't get very far. My own observation leads me to the conclusion that Clark would be only too delighted to be given quiet advice as to how to fight his Army. I think he is a very decent chap and most cooperative; if he received good and clear guidance, he would do very well."[49]

About a week after the Teheran conference had been concluded, Lord Alanbrooke decided to see for himself how the war in Italy was going. Here are two diary entries for that period:

Monty strikes me as looking tired and definitely wants a rest and a change. I can see that he does not feel that Clark is gripping the show sufficiently. He called me into his caravan just before dinner and asked me how much importance we attached to an early capture of Rome, as he saw little hope of capturing it before March.

To my mind it is quite clear that there is no real plan for the capture of Rome beyond a thrust up the coast by Monty, and no longer any talk of a turn to the left by his forces towards Rome. The mountain roads are considered too difficult for any real chance of success based on such a swinging movement. I must now see during the next few days what hopes rest in the plans for the Fifth Army. Frankly, I am rather depressed from what I have heard and seen today . . .[50]

After lunch we motored out to the American Fifth Army H.Q. Camp, where Alex has a small camp also. We dined with Clark in his Mess. I had a long talk with him about the offensive on his front and do not feel very cheered up as to the prospects of the future from what I heard from him. He seems to be planning nothing but penny-pocket attacks and nothing sufficiently substantial.[51]

Similar criticisms were voiced by other generals, American as well as British. The biting discomfort of the Italian winter seemed to have caused disaffection among all ranks and all nationalities. Peppery Lucian Truscott, who was commanding the now veteran 3rd Division, when told about Clark's plan to renew the assault, entered in his diary: "A worse plan would be difficult to conceive." When the changing situation dictated its alteration, he wrote: "This plan was basically sound. However, it was to prove overly optimistic — a not uncommon failing among inexperienced higher commands and staffs."[52]

In turn, Clark felt that the British, notably at the crossing of the Volturno River, were hanging back, not quite putting out maximum effort, saying, in effect, "We've been taking quite a bit of punishment in this war for some time. Now it's your turn." This was an unfair statement which Clark hastened to correct after a November 16 meeting with Sir Ronald Adam, the adjutant general of the British Army. Sir Ronald told the General that the British were coming to the end of their manpower resources, and if they expected to hold their own after the war, or even to last out this war, they were forced to follow a rigid national policy of manpower conservation. As proof, the Englishman produced a series of secret reports which showed the replacements were so lacking that he was now breaking up one division every two months in order to supply men to other units in combat.[53] Clark, once described by Ernie Pyle as "a thoroughly honest man,"[54] never again permitted criticism on this point.

Sir Harold Alexander, blaming no one but the weather and the fighting conditions, said of this moment in history:

I and my commanders were determined to have Rome, and were not to be deterred by the German resolve to hold it; but Rome was not the end of the story. This side of Rome, and beyond it, the Allied armies were to be faced with a seemingly unending succession of difficulties of terrain — as Winston Churchill remarked, there was "always something else"; they were to be called upon to fight with resources always inadequate to their tasks; and they were to experience a "savage versatility" of climate without any parallel in northwest Europe. The axis of any advance northward invariably lay across natural obstacles of rivers or mountains; and, because German demolitions were so efficient and effective, a small rear guard could always put up a fierce battle while the main body went back at its leisure.

The line the Germans decided to hold, known as the "Winter

Line" — a misnomer, since it was not a line but a series of defended positions in depth — had been reconnoitered by them before the Italian surrender. Delaying positions could be held in front of it in order to gain time for the weather to deteriorate still further and to allow artificial defenses to be constructed to add to the natural strength of the whole position.[55]

As for the men in the lines, they had no better Boswell than Ernie Pyle. This frail and elderly reporter, who did not live out the war, shared the miseries of foxhole living with the soldiers. He earned their lifelong respect by sending home stories that told exactly what it was like to be a "doggie" in Italy:

Our troops were living in almost inconceivable misery. The fertile black valleys were knee-deep in mud. Thousands of the men had not been dry for weeks. Other thousands lay at night in the high mountains with the temperature below freezing and the thin snow sifting over them. They dug into the stones and slept in little chasms and behind rocks and in half-caves. They lived like men of prehistoric times, and a club would have become them more than a machine gun. How they survived the dreadful winter at all was beyond us who had the opportunity of drier beds in the warmer valley.

That the northward path was a tedious one was not the fault of our troops, nor of the direction either. It was the weather and the terrain and the weather again. If there had been no German fighting troops in Italy, if there had been merely German engineers to blow the bridges in the passes, if never a shot had been fired at all, our northward march would still have been slow. The country was so difficult that we formed a great deal of cavalry for use in the mountains. Each division had hundreds of horses and mules to carry supplies beyond the point where vehicles could go no farther. On beyond the mules' ability, mere men — American men — took it on their backs.

The front-line soldier I knew lived for months like an animal, and was a veteran in the cruel, fierce world of death. Everything was abnormal and unstable in his life. He was filthy dirty, ate if and when, slept on hard ground without cover.

Our men were going to get to Rome all right. There was no question about that. But the way was cruel. No one who had not seen that mud, those dark skies, those forbidding ridges and ghostlike clouds that unveiled and then quickly hid the enemy, had the right to be impatient with the progress along the road to Rome.[56]

Another perceptive view of the American soldier is supplied by Eric Sevareid:

Only at the front in times of crisis did one find grim purpose, selflessness, and a spirit of exaltation in the mutual high endeavor. A thousand times one asked himself why they were like this. They understood the war's meaning no more than the others — which is to say, hardly at all. Their country, their families were not in any way in mortal danger now, and yet they plodded on, fighting on in a way that the French had not done in 1940 when their country and loved ones were in peril. What motivated them? Surely it could be traced to the high school, the "team spirit," the conviction bred in their American homes that one did not let the team down. A pride in their outfits. The sheer American "pride in competence," for in the American tradition to be guilty of incompetence is the one unbearable disgrace. They did not hate the Germans, except at certain times and places, and only then because the Germans were killing their comrades. They did not hate the concept of Fascism because they did not understand it. But they struggled on, climbing the hills, wading the rivers until they dropped, and sometimes watching them die in ignorant glory, I had to fight and reason away sharp stabs of conscience: "What right have I to live and urge them on in behalf of my beliefs, these children who die not comprehending?" Common sense told one that in this direction lay only failure and the meaningless void, but reason did not always operate as one stood over a broken, sobbing boy. They had been right who said we were doing it as a matter of accepted routine. Yet, in all honesty, there had been no other choice.[57]

« 5 »

Mark Clark's personality now seemingly combined to turn him into a logical target for the general feeling of frustration. One general injected casually into a 1966 conversation: ". . . and, of course, Clark was publicity-prone. Everybody knew that." The general considered this as one of the immutable facts of life of the Italian campaign.[58]

Clark was panned for carrying his own photographers with him wherever he went, for insisting that all stories carry the dateline "With the Fifth Army" or, preferably, "with Mark Clark's Fifth Army," and for permitting his public relations officers to do everything short of deifying him.

A ranking officer of II Corps — not Keyes, who has never publicly criticized anyone — said, "I believe that many of the officers of II Corps intensely disliked Mark Clark. He had a personal arrogance about him that was terribly irritating. We all had the strong feeling that his plans and strategy were overly arbitrary.

"Of course, as things finally worked out, we had to acknowledge that he had some strategic skill. And, I must admit, there was the generally accepted belief that he was, personally, a very courageous man. He had no reluctance to being in front lines, studying the situation with the troops."[59]

"I think," said a former VI Corps officer, "that Clark's conceit was wrapped around him almost like a halo. He created that atmosphere, almost everywhere he went — even if he was just standing beside his jeep on a highway. He had bigger stars than most generals on his jeep. He was taller than most generals and stood out in a crowd, anyway. You had a feeling that here was a man who was conscious of himself every waking moment. I guess this is very subjective and very unfair, but it's the accumulation of little observations, the way he *strode* into our headquarters, ignoring everyone. Not that a general has to stop and shake hands with everybody, but you had the feeling that he was trying to convey a purpose so great that no one existed for him except the person whom he was walking towards — that he knew where he was going and no one was going to stop him. I thought that the way he got in and out of a jeep was a studied thing. Most of us came to the conclusion that the man was always acting a part."[60]

A combat infantryman, discussing Clark's habit of haunting the front lines, said, "Yeah, he'd be up there all right, peering through his binoculars at the Krauts, while his photographers snapped away. But just about the time the Germans had him zeroed in, he'd take off in his jeep and we'd catch the shellfire."[61]

Conversely, an operations officer remembers: "Another fellow and I one time wanted to get up on a high hill for observation purposes. Because the Germans had the hill zeroed in, we wormed our way up through the drainage ditches lining each side of the road. When we got to the top, congratulating each other on making it, who do we see but Mark Clark up there by himself, with only his aide who was in a ditch nearby, looking out over the valley at the situation and making notes on a clipboard. The only concession he had made to safety was to put his jeep's windshield down so that the glass wouldn't reflect in the sun. The man I was with whispered to me, 'How can one son-of-a-bitch be so brave?' "[62]

Sometimes it seems as if criticism of Mark Clark has taken on the aspect of a durable fad. A highly respected magazine writer once punctuated a luncheon conversation occurring twenty years after the war in Italy had ended with repeated four- and five-letter-word descriptions of Mark Clark, none of them even mildly approving. Later during the same lunch, the writer admitted that he had never met Clark and, in fact, hadn't been in Italy during the war. He was simply repeating what other journalists had told him — with vehemence.[63]

But a photojournalist who was actually with Clark during the days of his ascent to high rank, Eliot Elisofon of *Life*, said that he had found him a consistently decent man, free from pose, and apparently completely unconcerned with his scrapbook.[64] Robert van de Velde, certainly not an admirer, admitted that "one thing that puzzles me is the respect that Keyes and Porter had for Clark — so *something* must have escaped us."[65]

There were two unimpeachable sources in Italy for the judgment of a general's strengths and weaknesses: the *Stars and Stripes* and *Yank*. The men and women who wrote for these publications seriously assumed the responsibility of being the voice of the enlisted man. In addition to publishing first-class combat reports, they took immense pride in attacking inequities, military injustice, or unfairness, and in leaking the stuffing out of the shirts of some of the high brass. But, in the last analysis, they *were* under military control. If Mark Clark was as ferociously preoccupied with headlines as he has been reported, they would have been his first targets.

Bill Mauldin and Harry Sions worked for these two publications as sergeants. Sions was the managing editor of the Rome-based edition of *Yank* and after the war went on to become editorial director of *Holiday*. He is currently a senior editor of the publishing firm of Little, Brown and Company. Mauldin's cartoons from the *Stars and Stripes* are considered by many as the best source of comment available on the Italian campaign. Today, his syndicated editorial cartoons have made him one of the most respected social and political critics in the country. Both of these men would have been instantly aware of any pressure by Clark or his public relations officers. Both of these men were in a position to report grandstanding by the high brass, and their reputation is such that there is no doubt that if Mark Clark had tried to burnish his image or had become outrageously political while still in Italy, they would not only have reported it, they would have fought it. No matter what insignia they wore at any given period, Mauldin and Sions have always been thorough professionals. Here are their recollections and judgments:

In his book *Up Front,* written while he was still in Italy, Bill Mauldin said:

While the Italy edition of *Stars and Stripes* runs occasional pictures of General Mark Clark, who commands the Fifth Army in Italy, he gets no preference over anyone else. When Clark got Russia's highest foreign honor, the Order of Suvarov, he was given six lines of type on the last page of an eight-page edition. And he was probably surprised to get that much.[66]

In 1966, when asked to amplify this, Mauldin began by saying, "Well, even though I had lots of opportunities to get around, I was still a sergeant with the Army and only had the viewpoint of a sergeant. The fact that I'm a generation older doesn't make me any more of an expert than I was then. I'm really not competent to assess a general except in a subjective way."

When it was mentioned to him that lack of a close vantage point did not seem to keep anyone else from judging Clark and that, besides, the subjective viewpoint of a sergeant was exactly what was wanted, he continued: "I can tell you that there are two reasons for the criticism; the politicians were all afraid to be connected with him, and the newspapers disliked him because he had an eye for publicity.

"You're up against a sort of a consensus on this guy, but I can't join it. I'm not saying that he was a great man, and, since I'm not an armchair general, I can't judge him on strategy. But I think the Italian campaign was a nasty job to begin with, and I think he got saddled with it, but ended up doing it as well as anyone could. He had a rough job and there was no way of doing it gracefully. He probably took the rap for quite a few things and wasn't foxy enough to parlay himself out of it.

"He believed in letting *Stars and Stripes* alone. We were able to operate a free newspaper against the wishes of guys like Arthur Wilson, who commanded the rear echelon. I know that on at least one occasion and probably many others, Clark interceded for us, and although you can be cynical and say it's because he was courting us, well, you could also be cynical and say it about Eisenhower and a lot of other people. I don't care about the motive — all I know is that when Wilson was after us we needed a friend and we had one in Clark.

"One time he saved my bacon. The brass was really raising hell about one cartoon that I did and there was even talk of a court-martial. Clark heard about this and the way he resolved it was to call the editor of the *Stars and Stripes* and ask to have the original so he could put it up in his office. He sent his aide down after it, too. Well, of course, this was a very diplomatic way of saying, 'Let this guy alone,' and after that, they did. But he never spoke to me about it.

"I think the word for him is 'ambitious.' But what's wrong with that? You rarely meet a man who isn't. The only thing was, probably, that he was less than subtle about it. The worse thing I can say about him is that he was obtuse in some directions. He wasn't aware of the effect he created on some people. In other words, he lacked the politician's primary tool — he didn't have an antenna; he wasn't sensitive to other people's reactions. If he had had it, he would have known what people were saying about him, and he would have taken steps to do something about it.

"I remember a perfect illustration of this blindness to the reaction his words might have on other people. It was after he became overall commander in Italy and he was holding a press conference. He said, pointing to a map, 'Here's the Fifth Army over here with all this real estate, and there's the Eighth Army over there with just a little bit, and we're going to see if we can't give some of this real estate back to them.' You know, there were British correspondents as well as Americans at that conference, and he was supposed to be the Allied Commander, and it sounded just awfully condescending.

"I don't think you can make him out to be a great man, or anything of the sort. He was just a very human guy doing the best he could. He had his limitations. But I think that a lot of the criticism of him [occurred] because he was associated with a bad time."[67]

The soldiers might have coined the term "salty" specifically to describe Harry Sions. He is blunt, irascible, and direct. His judgments, although fair, are rarely charitable. When asked about the reaction of the newspaper correspondents, he answered: "They thought he was stupid because he talked mumbo-jumbo to them. He'd make a statement and then double-track backwards. He was formal and stilted in his communications and none of them ever got close to him. At least, that's the way it looked from where I stood. In fairness to him, however, I don't know of any pressure that he brought to curtail anything we did or said. As far as I know, he never tried to influence or suppress anything that ever appeared in *Yank.*

"As a matter of fact, we had much more pressure from the Air Corps than the Army. There was one guy, a colonel who later became a well-known broadcaster. I remember he called me up once and said he wanted a photographer and a correspondent to go to Sardinia because they were opening up an officers' club there. Well, you know, we were in the middle of a war and things were pretty hectic, so I asked, 'Are you serious?' He said yes and that he was going to send a plane to pick up my people. I said, 'Forget it.' He said, 'This is an order.' I told him, 'You can't order me, Colonel,' and he answered, 'We'll see about that, Sergeant.' Well, I made up my mind that I was going to go to General Clark about this. Clark was the head of the Fifth Army and this jerk wasn't. I was pretty sure Clark would back me up. That was his reputation.

"I guess the word 'stupid' is wrong to use to describe Clark. He was unsophisticated. Maybe unimaginative.

"One of the things that bothers me about the military mind is that many of them are so square. A lot of brass are easily corrupted by power. They develop a fantastic sense of their own importance. They read the reports and they start to believe that they really are these heroic figures that the newspapers are writing about. These guys get to feel that they are goddamned bloody Caesars because they get all the paraphernalia that goes with it.

"I don't know whether Clark handled it well or not. But as far as *Yank* is concerned, I have no complaints and, believe me, if I did I would yell pretty damn loud. He obviously realized that it was important to the morale of the soldiers that *Yank* and *Stars and Stripes* be unfettered. What we were being used as was a kind of an outlet for the GI's explosiveness. We knew it and it was all right with us. The GI had to beef somewhere and we were rightly used as the pressure vent. Clark realized this, so maybe he wasn't as stupid as the correspondents thought."[68]

When asked for his reaction to these observations, Mark Clark answered, "Well, first of all, there may have been some justification for some of these comments. In the early days of the campaign in Italy, all the reports seemed to deal only with the Eighth Army. Not that there's anything wrong with it, but the British wanted publicity for what they were doing, the French wanted it and so on for the other nationalities that were represented there. I wanted publicity for the Fifth Army. I thought we needed it for morale and that's what I told my public relations officers. By golly, the Fifth Army deserved publicity and it seemed to me that any public information officer, if he was worth his salt, would see that they got it.

"In a situation like this, there might have been a time when if we wanted to match what the radio was saying about 'Alexander and his troops,' I might have said, 'Well, for crying out loud, if you're going to mention names, well let's use mine.' But I'll tell you, there were many times that I made them cut my name out of a communiqué because I thought it was wrong.

"I may have been wrong sometimes. Maybe I did appear standoffish. But an army commander is a pretty lonesome fellow in combat. People don't come around to drop in on you. As a matter of fact, I brought over a classmate of mine to be on my staff. When they asked me what the hell I needed him for, I answered, 'I just wanted to make sure I had one man on my staff that can't ask me a question I can't answer.'

"These stories get started and they snowball. One time the War Department assigned me a Wac as a stenographer. I think they wanted it in order to help the recruiting drive they had on for these girls at the time. During a bombardment, once, we all — that is, my staff and I — followed standard procedure and hit the dirt. Some sergeant among them looked over and saw this Wac lying on her back and he hollered, 'Get the hell over on your face! What do you think this is, a Board of Directors' meeting?' And that story went all over Italy.

"I can't say I'm sorry about too much that happened in Italy, and I won't say that I ever felt sorry for myself that I had that particular spot. Frankly, I was grateful that I had been in the right place at the right time to get this high command. Of course, I realized it was a hell of a mission, sort of like being a guard on a football team while another guy gets the headlines for running ninety yards with the ball, but I didn't mind. I had no false ideas about the Italian campaign, but I never bemoaned the fact that I was stuck with it. I was doing a job I wanted to do as well as I knew how."[69]

« 6 »

By October 15, the Fifth Army had crossed the Volturno River. In another month, it had inched painfully a few miles forward to bog down in front of the vaunted "Winter Line" of the Germans. But it had become apparent that something more than a further headlong battering was in order. Something had to be done before Kesselring bled the Allies to death.

CHAPTER VI

DECEMBER 25, 1943–
JANUARY 25, 1944

. . . they have done it in other places at other times.
— LIEUTENANT GENERAL GEOFFREY KEYES[1]

AS Operation OVERLORD shifted into higher speeds, the standstill in Italy began to appear more forlorn than ever. General Eisenhower received word at his African headquarters that he was to leave for England to supervise the great force assembling there for the invasion of France.[2] He was replaced as Allied commander in the Mediterranean by Sir Henry Maitland Wilson, a good officer but incapable of the amiable informality which had helped Ike get maximum cooperation from the combined forces.[3]

Sir Bernard Montgomery also left for England. His place at the head of the Eighth Army was taken over by Lieutenant General Oliver Leese. General Alexander retained his position as Fifteenth Army Group commander and Mark Clark continued to lead the Fifth Army.

But these shifts did not indicate a lessening of Winston Churchill's interest in Italy. Obsessed by the conviction that if some radical change in tactical direction did not occur, "the Italian battle will stagnate and fester for another three months," he began to dust off an old plan of Alexander's which called for an amphibious landing behind the German lines and nearer to Rome.[4] With Churchill, at least as far as Italy was concerned, to think was to act. He informed President Roosevelt of his fears and concluded one exchange of messages on the sepulchral note, "If this opportunity is not grasped, we must expect the ruin of the Mediterranean campaign in 1944."[5]

It had become uncomfortably clear that the prospect of taking Rome by a quick march up the peninsula had been overly optimistic. The possibility that the Allies might not be able to hold on to their hard-won gains was beginning to be examined in some quiet corners.[6] It was obvious that the Germans were dug in so well and so deeply that nothing short of a Herculean offensive could sweep them further back; and, even if the Americans were to agree, the prospects for such an assault grew progressively dimmer with each huge gulp that OVERLORD took of available men and materiel. Thus, to the Prime Minister, another amphibious landing became a matter of urgent necessity.

His hopes centered about the sandy beaches of the Anzio-Nettuno area, located only thirty-five miles due south of Rome. A surprise landing in this area offered the only possibility of transforming the plodding Italian campaign into a swift war of movement where the superior mechanized Allied equipment could become a strong advantage.

Prewar Anzio was a sleepy little bathing resort just an hour by good highway from Rome. It is linked to another hamlet, Nettuno, by the green woodlands of the Borghese gardens. Behind the twin towns, after about twenty miles of level ground, the Colli Laziali, sometimes known as the Alban Hills, rise gracefully. These vineyard- and village-covered hills sweep upwards some three thousand feet, and from the peaks it is quite evident that whoever holds these heights holds the keys to Rome. There is no place for a defender to make a stand between the hills and the Eternal City.

The hills are flanked by two of the most famous highways in the world. Both the Via Appia and the Via Casilina reach from Rome to Italy's tip and both have been historical landmarks for thousands of years. The more famous of the two, the Appian Way, skirts the west side of the Colli Laziali on its way down the coast to Naples. On military maps, this route became known as Highway 7. Further inland, the Via Casilina, described by the Allies as Highway 6, flows through Valmontone, Frosinone, and a few other obscure places before it joins the Appian Way into an approach to Naples. The Byzantine general Belisarius, in A.D. 536, used this road in the first successful assault on Rome from the south.

Both roads are evidence of the marvelous engineering efficiency of the Romans. Laid almost as directly as we would a railroad, they were cut through hills and rocks and ran over fills of hollows and small glens, bridges over ravines, embankments across swamps. They became the broad approaches prized by both the attackers and defenders of Rome throughout the ages. The fight for Rome could be logically subtitled "The Fight to Control Routes 6 and 7."

On Christmas Day, the Prime Minister sent for Eisenhower to meet at Tunis with him and Alexander and the members of the Combined Chiefs of Staff in order to discuss the proposed landing. Privately convinced that the risks of the enterprise were so great that a minimum of four divisions should be employed in the venture, Churchill nevertheless asked for only half that number.[7]

Manpower was not the problem. The key to Churchill's modest request was his awareness that LST's — the landing craft which played so important a part in Allied planning throughout the early years of the war — were at a premium. America was producing almost all of these ships, which were still in such short supply that every planner tended to clutch the craft assigned to him with a miser's grip. The availability of the LST's often determined the success or failure of a mission, and as a matter of fact, the acquisition of even the minimum number requested by Churchill affected events in the Pacific, the Indian Ocean and the Mediterranean, and even the date of OVERLORD itself.

So Churchill, somewhat like a man importuning a banker for a loan which both sides know will act as only a stopgap, asked for only two divisions,[8] to be composed of British and American troops in order to equalize a possible sacrifice.

Almost the first question asked by Eisenhower at the meeting was, "Why am I here?" Ike reminded Churchill and the assembled chiefs that he was scheduled to leave for England within a week, and therefore strategy discussions would be more properly held with his successor. He was told that he had been asked to attend because the availability of landing craft would be a matter of direct concern to him as the commander of OVERLORD. It had become obvious to the planners that extra LST's were needed for the Anzio operation for at least two weeks longer than had been originally contemplated.

Eisenhower listened in silence as the British presented their theory that the threat of an amphibious landing in his rear would cause the German to weaken his main front to the point where the Fifth and Eighth Armies could make major advances up the peninsula. Finally, he answered: "You say you need two more weeks — you have it. But gentlemen, I think you're making a mistake. I don't think that the people who compare warfare to a chess game know what they are talking about. Just because you land at Anzio, that's no reason to believe that the German will predictably rush troops away from the main front in order to meet this threat. He hasn't been predictable so far, and there's no guarantee he's going to act the way you want him to now."

Eisenhower then entered the discussion of the tactics for the period after the landing. He felt strongly that if only two divisions landed and then struck for the high grounds of the Alban Hills behind Anzio, Kesselring could cut off and isolate them almost at his leisure. He concluded with the flat statement: "Yes, I'll give you two weeks, but you're going to need the ships for longer than that," referring by this to the length of time he considered necessary to build up and supply the landing force.[9]

Eisenhower's opinions did nothing to change the minds of Churchill and Alexander. Another participant in the conference, General Sir Leslie Hollis, was impressed not only by Eisenhower's thinking but even more by the fact that through "his genius for compromise and adaption, he reconciled both points of view. There would, after all, be a landing in Italy." Hollis also noted: "Eisenhower struck me as being impressive physically — alert and tireless — and also very quick to grasp a point that the others, his seniors, would like to argue about."[10]

Churchill had been ill with pneumonia during the preceding few weeks, but winning over Eisenhower to his side acted like a tonic on the old fighter. By using all of his considerable persuasive powers and charm, he was next able to convince President Roosevelt,[11] and, through him, the American planners, of the validity of the Anzio operation, which was code-named SHINGLE. D-Day was set for "as close to January 20 as possible."

The next order of business was to coordinate the movements of the Fifth Army and the Eighth Army in the peninsula so as to obtain full advantage from the seaborne attack. On January 8, an exhausted but happy Churchill wired Franklin D. Roosevelt that a series of subsidiary meetings had produced a unanimous accord on tactics. A few days later, Churchill left Africa to return to England where he would wait for the news of the landing's expected success.

The plan for the main thrust was quite simple. Clark now had the American II Corps, which included the 34th Division and the 36th Division, facing the center of the German's new defense, the Gustav Line. One of these divisions was scheduled to slant across the Garigliano River and the Rapido River and proceed up the Liri Valley. Two French divisions on one flank and the British X Corps on the other were to feint simultaneously and then, after the piercing of the center, go forward. The planners believed that Kesselring might be so torn between this thrust and the surprise Anzio invasion that, in his indecision, either or both attacks might succeed.[12] Intelligence officers estimated that the Germans would lay greater stress on the threat behind their lines and, as a result, the main body of the attacking force would have an almost free passage forward.[13]

From all available accounts, General Clark was enthusiastic about this plan,[14] but it must be remembered that everything else had failed. Something, *anything* new in the way of strategy was preferable to the slow inching which now engaged his troops. "Churchill, at first, wanted me to come down [to the conference]," Clark recalls, "but I sent word that it was just impossible for me to get away. I also sent word that I didn't want to get into Anzio unless I could go in with a minimum of three divisions. I went in, finally, with two, but only because British intelligence convinced me that it was enough. That wasn't the first time that British intelligence was wrong. In the beginning, they told us with our air-superiority and other advantages that we would walk right up through Italy. They told me the same kind of thing about Anzio — that we could go in on a shoestring and win. And they were wrong again."[15]

However, there were enough advantages to the Anzio concept for all the military commanders to become enthusiastic — even the 3rd Division's fine leader, Lucian Truscott, who, after studying the plans and just before the Navy thoroughly mangled a rehearsal for the operation,[16] had told Clark, "We are perfectly willing to undertake the operation if we are ordered to do so and we will maintain ourselves to the last round of ammunition. But if we do undertake it, you are going to destroy the best damned division in the United States Army, for there will be no survivors."[17]

The commanders of the American armored units were delighted. They saw only the flat sandy expanses of the beaches and felt that their tanks would have the chance to realize their capabilities for the first time in Italy. Up until then, Italy, with its mountains, hills, swamps, and rivers, had seemed more to them like one vast antitank ditch.[18]

Alexander's final instructions, as relayed by Mark Clark to the tank force, were "(a) to seize and secure a beachhead in the vicinity of Anzio, and (b) advance on the Colli Laziali."[19] Whether or not the second part of this directive meant that the VI Corps, which Clark had pulled out to make this invasion, was to secure a position on the Alban Hills or at some point *toward* the Alban Hills was purposely kept vague for reasons of flexibility.[20] In this way, Lucas, the VI Corps commander, would have maximum freedom to exploit the landing in the most promising manner. The American 3rd Division and the British First Division would comprise the corps.

It all looked good on paper. The logic of the move was unassailable to everyone, including Field Marshal Kesselring, who noted in his reports, "I did not believe that Alexander could be satisfied for much longer with the slow and costly way the Allied front was edging forward. Sooner or later, he must end it by landing, which, taking into account the enemy's systematic methods, could only be expected in the region of Rome. It was clear, furthermore, that such a landing would somehow be coupled with an offensive on the southern front."[21]

« 2 »

In the meantime, Clark was worried about Operation ANVIL. This was the code name given to the diversionary move into southern France scheduled for the time the invasion across the Channel into France was taking place.

While continuing to lead the Fifth Army, Clark had been given secret orders placing him also at the head of the Seventh Army, still in Sicily.[22] President Roosevelt, in Africa for the Teheran conference, had sent word to Clark that he would like to meet with him in Italy, but Clark, busy with the Salerno battle, had answered that he considered this an unsafe place and an unsafe time for a presidential visit.

"Then," Clark recalls, "he sent me another message that said, in part, 'If the exigencies of the battle will permit, will you meet me in Sicily?' I checked on what the hell 'exigencies' meant to make sure I understood it, and then I said they did, and I flew down to meet him in Sicily. That's the time he told me that I had been [officially] designated as the commander of the southern France thing, and at first I was pleased, but then after a few months of wearing two caps [commanding both the Fifth Army and the Seventh Army], it began to worry me sick. From time to time the people on my staff who were concerned with this ANVIL thing would bring me their plans and I was so busy with the fighting in Italy that I could hardly stand to look at them.

"As the days went by and the battle for Rome was raging, I'd get messages from him and Marshall, asking me when I was going to relinquish my Fifth Army and take over the Seventh. I finally sent a message to Marshall, saying that I just couldn't do it, that it's wrong, and for me to leave the main front here would be the biggest blunder in the world. After that, they agreed to put someone else in charge there.

"When I came to write my book [*Calculated Risk*] and I reached this part about the southern France thing, I went over to Columbia University to speak with Ike. We spent hours and hours over it in his office because I felt it had been wrong, just a shot in the dark. Ike didn't agree. So we finally worked out a chapter between the two of us that satisfied us both. I'd never publicly disagree with Ike. I appreciated that he didn't have anything to do with the overall strategy — that's the job of the Prime Ministers and Presidents — but any commander in battle wanted all the insurance he could get. That's why Ike believed in southern France. He thought it would help him get across the Channel."[23]

But although General Clark succeeded in disconnecting himself from Operation ANVIL, it was far from a dead plan. The following February, it again became the subject of a serious dispute between the American and British planners.

« 3 »

The preparations for the landing at Anzio were maturing into a series of crises. There were constant foul-ups in the matter of supplies, the rehearsal of the landing was an unmitigated disaster, and although elaborate preparations had been taken to mask the real destination of the invasion armada, it had become clear that the only one who was confident that the Germans would be fooled was Churchill, now serenely sailing back to England.

There were few planners, British or American, who did not privately fear that SHINGLE, instead of creating a successful diversion for the Fifth Army's main thrust, was doomed to become a parsimoniously mounted and isolated action. But the only voice raised in doubt belonged to Major General John Lucas, the fifty-four-year-old commander of the operation. Lucas, noting in his diary, "that the sacrificial lamb was entitled to one bleat" asked and was granted a postponement of D-Day from January 20 to 22.[24]

The rumbles of the potential catastrophe were so widespread that they even reached George Patton at his Sicilian headquarters. He flew over to Naples to wish his old friend good luck. He did it by saying: "John, there is no one in the Army I hate to see killed as much as you, but you can't get out of this alive. Of course, you might be badly wounded. No one *ever* blames a wounded general!"

Patton then turned to a nearby VI Corps staff officer and said, "Look here, if things get too tough, shoot the Old Man in the ass. But make sure you don't kill the old fellow!"[25]

The Allied air arms were kept busy throughout this period. During the first two weeks in January, all rail communications in southern Italy were systematically bombed in an effort to choke off the shipment of men and supplies into the area. After January 13, the enemy air bases in the same area became primary targets, and on January 19, in an effort to disguise the landing site, other seaports were hit with maximum force by medium and heavy bombers.

Despite Air Corps estimates, most of the bombing proved to be only of marginal help to the amphibious force bound for Anzio. The Germans kept enough railroad lines open to maintain supply, and, as later captured documents showed, Kesselring's plans for every logical invasion port in southern Italy included alternate routes for use in the event of air attacks.[26]

On January 21, the force set sail. The trip was uneventful. There was no sign that it had been spotted by the defenders. At 10:30 that night, Rear Admiral Frank J. Lowry's flagship, *Biscayne*, made a radio contact on Anzio lighthouse, and a few minutes past midnight she anchored four miles southeast of the town.

« 4 »

In the meantime, the Fifth Army began its new offensive, on January 12. The Free French Expeditionary Corps, under the direction of an able professional, Marshal Alphonse-Pierre Juin, drove ten miles through the German lines, knocked out one enemy position, penetrated a second, and took twelve hundred prisoners.

As commander of all the French forces in North Africa, Juin had reluctantly opposed the Allied invasion until ordered by Admiral Darlan to surrender his army. Then, in relief, he turned it over to be used by Eisenhower against the Germans in Tunisia. His men with him here in Italy were cut from the same tough cloth. While the British might occasionally pause for rest and refreshment and the Americans made jokes, the Frenchmen always fought like men possessed. The road through the Liri Valley was, to them, the pathway home. They made no jokes and rested only when absolute fatigue set in. In effect they said, "The hell with your plans and logistics and fancy strategy — just show us what you want done and we'll do it." Many of these men had gone through extraordinary adventures in order to enlist with the Free French. Some crossed the Pyrenees on foot, others made their way across part of Africa. All were united in the determination to wipe out the shameful subjugation of their country by the Boche.[27]

Eric Sevareid described it best:

These men had a cold, implacable hatred of the enemy that was almost frightening; they were driven by such a fierce desire to show the world and regain their pride that one knew at once they could be stopped only by death and that in victory they would show no mercy. They did not love Americans; they did not love the British; they were callous and cruel toward the Italians. Yet it was good to be among them now; it was a reassuring vindication of faith in these people. De Gaulle was now the unquestioned *chef*, although they scorned the "discussions" in the Algiers assembly and felt that action on their part was worth a million words in restoring France. As with the

Americans, their specific war aim was to get home again; for them home lay just ahead over the mountain range.[28]

General de Gaulle, who visited the French positions shortly after their opening drive, wrote that the drive had "left the French with a sense of victory; the enemy had not ceased to retreat before them . . . our men had discovered that for fighting in the mountainous country, which demands maximum effort and maneuverability, they had proved themselves without peer in the Allied camp."[29]

The British X Corps, on the other flank, achieved only weak gains before they were stopped cold, and the traumatic beating the Americans took at Rapido, in the middle of the line, later became the subject of a Congressional investigation. Although the battle to cross the Rapido River is now only a footnote in most World War II histories, to many Texans it is as memorable an event as the stand at the Alamo. It is almost indisputable that Mark Clark failed to become chief of staff of the American Army because so many Texans of the 36th Division were slaughtered on the banks of that obscure Italian river.[30]

General Clark had received formal instructions from Sir Harold Alexander to make as strong a thrust forward as possible in an attempt to draw the German reserve divisions away from the Anzio landing site. It was known that the Germans had several divisions in the Rome area, and if they were permitted to make contact with the amphibious force, in all probability Lucas and his men would be driven back into the sea.[31] Perhaps in a spirit of foreboding, Clark entered in his diary on January 20, ". . . it is essential that I make that attack [across the Rapido], fully expecting heavy losses, in order to hold all the German troops on my front and draw more to it, thereby clearing the way for SHINGLE."[32]

The troops at the Rapido were under the command of II Corps. General Keyes had two divisions that he could have used for this attack — the 34th and Walker's 36th.[33] The Texans were chosen for the job and began it after a period of heavy artillery bombardment so intense that one German soldier noted in his diary: "The artillery fire is driving me crazy. I am frightened as never before and cold. I am in need of someone to hold onto."[34]

On the night of January 20, the 36th approached a hairpin bend in the river, tight enough to permit the Germans on the opposite side to fire in their rear.[35] This was the spot selected for their attack and no unit commander had leeway to vary his instructions.[36] And then, until the night of the twenty-second, the Americans sent a stream of elements across which were systematically decimated by the well-dug-in German defenders. Despite a total of 1681 casualties, the three-day attack by the 36th failed to establish a bridgehead on the other side. But, at midnight on the twenty-second, General Lucas secured the beaches over at Anzio and suffered only 236 casualties in the next three days.[37]

Why was the 36th chosen for this attack?[38] There were few who believed that they had completely recovered from their considerable losses at Salerno and San Pietro. After the debacle, accusations leveled at Clark by certain correspondents and most of the troops ranged from incompetency to the wild statement that the selection of the target was evidence of a Regular Army officer's desire to rid himself of a National Guard outfit. Even after the war, the findings of the Congressional committee that the Division's report of 2128 casualties was inflated, that the action was necessary, and that the attack insured the success of the Anzio landing[39] were dismissed as a whitewash by the Texans and their many friendly observers.

Captain Nicholas Vladimir Malitch was one of the witnesses called by a board of inquiry that the army itself conducted after the battle. In Nic's opinion, "it was a mousetrap." An air support officer testified before the same board that "air" had not been requested by Walker for the assault, and, as a consequence, the officer had asked only that the Air Corps drop some smoke bombs in an attempt to conceal the attack from the enemy.[40] The officer recalls, ". . . and, unfortunately, the smoke did us about as much harm as it did good. It had the effect of blinding our own observers and, as a result, they couldn't direct our supporting artillery fire with any degree of accuracy."[41]

Among the many reports written by correspondents, "They'll Never Forget Mark Clark" by Sid Feder does the most complete job of describing the sentiments of the men of the 36th. It read in part:

"One of the most colossal blunders of World War Two," they [the men] called it. It was a futile heroic try. It cost some 2900 men [sic] in twenty hours, and it got nowhere.

[Their petition to Congress stated:] "The men of the 36th Division petition the Congress of the United States to investigate the Rapido River fiasco and take the necessary steps to correct a military system that will permit an inefficient and inexperienced officer, such as Gen. Mark Clark, in a high command to destroy the young manhood of this country . . . wastefully and uselessly."

Maj. Gen. Fred Walker, of Columbus, Ohio, commander of the 36th, combat veteran of World War I, pleaded against the crossing [concluded the correspondent]. He proposed that the 36th span the stream to the north and take the high ground above Cassino. His plea was unavailing.[42]

This side of the dispute received indirect support from General Truscott when, in his memoirs, he wrote that General Clark had earlier asked him if he would try to get his 3rd Division across. He had answered in the affirmative and then added, " 'But those attacks should be so powerful that every German gun would be [destroyed], for only two or three 88's would be able to destroy our bridges. I doubt our capability for making any such attacks.' The General agreed and there our conversation ended. However, these conditions were not fulfilled when the 36th Infantry Division made the attempt to cross the Rapido a few weeks later, and the attempt was a costly failure."[43]

Harold Bond, a junior officer in the 36th at the time, described the odds against the attack: "Protected in front by mine fields and barbed wire, these [enemy] emplacements were deeply dug. The best firing positions had been selected and defensive barrages had been planned. Sitting snugly under their heavily sandbagged roofs, the Germans had little to fear from our artillery fire. When the fire lifted to let our men go forward, the enemy soldiers had merely to resume their positions and shoot. At worst, they were only a little shaken by the bombardment. The Fifth Army had thrown the division headlong into one of the strongest defensive positions the Germans were ever to have in Italy."[44]

Time quoted a company officer as saying, "I had 184 men . . . 48 hours later I had 17. If that's not mass murder, I don't know what is."[45]

Other observers had other views. Will Lang, who was there, said, "The 36th Division, by that time, was not known as the best division in the Army. It was hardly the division to be assigned so tough and important a job. However, Keyes and Clark were caught between the devil and the deep blue sea. Every other division besides the 36th had been in the line for a hell of a long while — not big pitched battles, but the little things where manpower is just whittled down day by day. Their strengths were weakened almost to the point of complete exhaustion. The big question was whether or not the 36th, even though it was the freshest division, was ready to take on a job like that."[46]

Fred Sheehan wrote in his book *Anzio — Epic of Bravery:*

Clark had his faults, as most men have, but the 36th Division's difficulties in January 1944 were their own and could not rightfully be charged against him. They were handed a difficult but not impossible assignment, and failed. Clark's mistake may have lain in choosing the 36th for the role.

A Congressional board of inquiry headed by Representative Andrew J. May, the chairman of the House Committee on Military Affairs, ferreted out the facts of the Rapido River crossing. Clark's role was that of a middleman; the operation had been ordered by Fifteenth Army Group commander General Alexander both to score a breach in the Gustav Line and to serve as a divisionary movement to cover the amphibious landings at Anzio. The board also learned that the river crossing was far from impossible, that the British just a few days before had staged a successful crossing of the Garigliano, which is fed by the Rapido, only a few miles downstream from the point where the 36th attempted its crossing. Too, the 34th Division successfully crossed the Rapido under equal if not more difficult conditions further upstream several days later.[47]

To Fred Majdalany, author of *Cassino — Portrait of a Battle*, it was even more clear-cut; "It would appear," he wrote, "that this operation was badly mishandled by the Command and Staff of the 36th Division.[48] It is difficult to see how he [Clark] could possibly be blamed for the execution of an operation that was merely part of a larger design imposed on him from above. The operation was a difficult one, but not impossible."[49]

Where does the truth lie in the Rapido River disaster? It seems obvious from the above that there are few who are capable of a dispassionate view. Perhaps there is only one: General Geoffrey Keyes. His impartiality is best attested by the fact that he has never been the target of the bitterness of the survivors of the 36th, although he was squarely in the middle, between Clark and the division. And Clark, in turn, is quite willing to abide by Keyes's judgment, fully aware that the man who commanded II Corps is incapable of participating in a whitewash of so serious a matter.

"The plans were changed several times," Keyes said in 1966, "and then the weather entered into it. One time it was going to be the 1st Armored Division and then it rained and rained and rained, and then, of course, they couldn't spearhead anything. One time we were going to do it with the 45th and 3rd, then the 3rd and the 36th, and we ended up with the 36th and the 34th. That left us with the 36th in the valley and the 34th on the high ground opposite Cassino. Recognizing that the 36th had had the longest rest, we decided that they should make the main effort. It also depended on the British [X Corps] crossing one day ahead of us and getting the high ground. Otherwise, these people [the Germans] would be looking right down on top of us.

"Well, the night of the attack came and the British sent out a couple of advance parties, but the river had come up [fed by the rains] and they didn't get across. They ran into all kinds of fire and they came back and said, 'Well, we're through. We're not going to make this attack.'

"General Clark was put out by this, but he couldn't order them to do it, so he told me that he would have to go on with our attack, and what could *he* do, or anybody do, to make up for the failure of the British to get a foothold twenty-four hours ahead of time. So the attack started that night.

"On the day of the attack, I had all of the commanders up for a conference at the II Corps command post — General Rider [of the 34th], Walker, Frederick [of the First Special Service Force], and I've forgotten who else. Well, anyway, we discussed the thing and when I asked General Walker if he had any comments, he said, 'No, everything is all set and we'll take it — we'll do it.' So at that moment he had no protest, no criticism. He later claimed, I believe, that he pleaded and pleaded with us not to do that thing [direct that the attack be made] and intimated that being a cavalryman, I didn't know anything about infantry and that's why the thing had been fouled up.

"After the war, I talked to the German general who was in command there at the time, and he said that they really had that crossing covered. Well, those things seem as if it would be impossible for a man to get through there, but they have done it at other places and in other times."[50]

« 5 »

The landing at Anzio was spectacularly successful in its early stages, but quickly developed into one of the most dismal chapters of World War II. Adolf Hitler referred to it as "an abscess" and the Allied leaders rarely mentioned it without first offering a shamefaced defense. Winston Churchill's optimism turned into anger. He repeated his reaction to the execution of the SHINGLE plan on several occasions and in several versions, but always in the same scathing terms: "I thought we had flung a wildcat into the [Alban] hills but, instead, got a whale floundering on the beach."[51]

What happened is clear: VI Corps had surprised the Germans — the landing was almost unopposed. But instead of streaking for the high ground of the Alban Hills, General Lucas had ordered his troops to consolidate positions on the beachhead while he concerned himself with getting the maximum amount of supplies ashore. On the third day, the Germans rallied and VI Corps found itself beginning what turned out to be a four-month struggle to hold on to those few square miles of sand.

John Lucas, the mild and graying commander who seemed so much older than his fifty-four years that his troops referred to him as "Foxy Grandpa,"[52] has become the historical scapegoat for the stalemate that ensued. His caution and apparent indecision have been blamed for the loss of the thousands of extra lives that it cost to take Rome in June instead of January.

How fair is this indictment? A glance at the man and his private reactions to the Anzio adventure may provide a partial answer.

Lucas had gained considerable military stature as a divisional and corps commander in the United States. Early in 1943, General Marshall, feeling that Eisenhower would find the older man's mature good sense an attractive virtue in an associate, sent him to North Africa. When General Bradley left II Corps at the end of the Sicilian campaign, his position was taken by John Lucas. A month later, Lucas was transferred again, this time to an active combat command. Mark Clark, displeased with the performance of his VI Corps commander, Ernest J. Dawley, at Salerno, replaced him with Lucas, who for the next few months directed the mountain fighting north of Naples with such solid competence that he added the dimension of methodical organizer of battle to his reputation for levelheaded intelligence.

On his record, Lucas was a good choice to head the Anzio invasion. Mature, patient, and thoroughly experienced, everyone agreed that if anyone could bring it off, it would be "Old Luke." Everyone, that is, but Lucas himself. His diary for the period indicates a considerable amount of self-doubt and foreboding concerning the validity of the operation. He wrote: "I think too often of my men out in the mountains. I am far too tenderhearted ever to be a success at my chosen profession." And: "I am blessed in my subordinates. They do all the work and most of the thinking." He noted that his relations with Mark Clark would remain pleasant "as long as I win battles," that Clark "was not afraid to take desperate chances . . . but it doesn't seem to bother him much." Evidently he felt that only he saw that "a failure now would ruin Clark, probably kill me, and certainly prolong the war."

Lucas's bewilderment at seeming to be the only one of the ranking officers who felt that there were grave risks in the plan runs all through his notes for the period. When a British naval officer assured him that "the chances are seventy to thirty that by the time you reach Anzio, the Germans will be north of Rome," he entered in his diary, "Apparently everyone is in on the secret of the German intentions but me." He felt that his attacking force was too small, the supplies too limited, and that transport had been assigned to him on too short-term a basis. He was certain that these deficiencies would result in a bloody mess for which he would receive the blame. The thought never occurred to him that his superiors might also be having secret doubts; he viewed them as living in a sort of wonderland of buoyant hopes.

"I wish the higher levels were not so overoptimistic," he wrote. "The Fifth Army is attacking violently toward the Cassino line and has sucked in many German troops to the south and the high command seems to think that they will stay there. I don't see why. They can slow us up there and move against me at the same time." Another entry: "The general idea seems to be that the Germans are licked and are fleeing in disorder and nothing remains but to mop up. The only reason for such a belief is that we have recently been able to advance against them [the French at Cassino] with comparative ease. The Hun was pulled back a bit but I haven't seen the desperate fighting I have during the last four months without learning something. We are not (repeat not) in Rome yet."[53]

The only note of concern for his position was privately voiced by Mark Clark. In an attempt to assure Lucas of his confidence in him, he advised, "Don't stick your neck out as I did at Salerno."[54] Clark wanted to make Lucas feel that he was aware of his problems by talking man-to-man, but, instead, the older man chose to regard the words as a cautionary directive. Thus, Clark's ambiguously worded phrase in the official order to "advance on Colli Laziali," was construed by Lucas in its most conservative sense: he felt it meant "Go just so far as you think safe."

What everyone had overlooked, even during the most frenetic mutual reassurances that the move was going to be a good one, was that the landing would achieve complete surprise. Within forty-eight hours, almost fifty thousand men and five thousand vehicles had gone ashore in what an English journalist described as "an almost gentlemanly atmosphere."[55] Kesselring, confident that his series of alternate plans would be sufficient to guard him at almost any point, had withdrawn two Panzer divisions from the area on the previous day and moved them into the Cassino sector.[56]

It took too long for information like this to filter to Lucas. Allied Intelligence had accurately pinpointed the location of all major German forces in the area, but had overestimated the effect that landings would have on the German High Command and underrated Kesselring's capacity to counter the move. While Lucas continued to build up his force within a perimeter seven miles deep and fifteen miles wide, the German general first sent the bulk of his men smashing into the Fifth Army's offensive at the Cassino front and then pulled back enough forces to furnish his subordinate commander, General Eberhard von Mackensen, with six divisions — enough to contain the beachhead force until a counteroffensive could be mounted.[57]

In the meantime, the men on the beaches became understandably restive. The historians for one of the British units involved in the action later wrote:

> The delay and inaction caused unconcealed disquiet amongst the Battalion. Officers and men discussed it endlessly among themselves. It was about the only thing to do in the sodden, freezing woods. There was a sickening feeling of anticlimax . . . There were no Germans; what was stopping the Division? The men could not understand it, and the officers found it difficult to explain. The orthodox answers — the necessity of securing a firm base before advancing, the need for landing and accumulating supplies, the inadvisability of doing anything rash — all sounded very unconvincing. The 23rd was a completely wasted day spent unloading the lorries and reconnoitering possible or impossible counter-attacks in every direction and in all parts of the beachhead.[58]

Surprisingly enough, the men and officers who were to do the actual fighting seemed to be the only ones who grumbled at the lack of initiative. Both Clark and Alexander visited Lucas at the beachhead in the first few days and gave every evidence of satisfaction with the way Lucas was handling the operation.[59]

As a practical matter at the time of the landing, both sides were in the dark as to the actual tactical situation. It was simply a matter of misfortune for the Allies that Kesselring, an infinitely resourceful man, had guarded against his own confusion. He had received a misleading report from Admiral Canaris that no landing was to be expected in the Anzio area, and was concerned enough by the British X Corps's thrust over the Garigliano River in the beginning stages of the Fifth Army's offensive to bring down from Rome the two veteran divisions he had in reserve there. Yet he was still able to move like a boxer with a good punch in either fist. On one front he used his reserves to deny the British a bridgehead and his entrenched troops to keep the 36th from crossing the Rapido, and on the other, he was able to stall Lucas into immobility while he fed new troops from the north of Italy, France, and the Balkans into Eberhard von Mackensen's Fourteenth Army ringing the beachhead, which by January 25 contained elements of eight divisions and would within the next few days number more than seventy thousand men.

It was a gamble, it was an impressive display of military resourcefulness, and it worked — even though it left Rome denuded of German defenders.

On the other hand, Lucas had turned his back on the military precept that it is never wise to hedge a bet while taking a calculated risk. As a result, he was forced, until the day he died, to undergo the flood of armchair strategy which explained over and over again that if he had possessed only a bit of audacity, he could have cannonaded his force directly into undefended Rome.

And Rome *was* undefended. During those few first days that Kesselring and von Mackensen needed to fashion a tight cordon around the beachhead, the path to the Eternal City was undeniably clear. Kesselring later commented, ". . . the Allies had missed a uniquely favorable chance of capturing Rome."[60]

One of the clearest expositions of the condition of Rome during this period was given, after the war, to Allied interrogators by Lieutenant General Kurt Maelzer, the commandant of the city:

"The first hours after the landing were decisive for Rome. If the enemy [had] taken full advantage of the situation then offering itself to him, Rome would have fallen as a ripe fruit into his lap without notable losses.

"Three factors particularly propitious for him would have been [in] his favor.

"1. Two days prior to the landing, the 29 and 90 Pz Gren Divisions had been withdrawn from the areas south and north of Rome respectively to be committed with the 10th Army. Between Nettuno and Rome there were only remainders of units which would have been incapable of offering serious resistance to an enemy vigorously pushing forward with tanks.

"2. Rome was clear of any troop stations. In the city there were, except [for] the command staff, merely a few small, independent political and economic special staffs and two SS-Police battalions. The former were purely technical staffs and not subordinated to the Commandant. The latter were distributed throughout the city for the purpose of guarding the German offices and of blocking Rome. Their equipment and training was of little battle value and would never have constituted a serious danger for fighting troops. Add to this that the landing did not become known in Rome until the morning hours. Any organized assembling of the scattered police would have taken more than eight hours and would still have been only a half-measure. It was not taken into consideration at all.

"3. The third factor, and not the least essential one, was the attitude of Rome's population after the Allied landing became known. A large majority was pro-Allied. Any hour a coup was expected, and it would have required only a touch to make the populace intervene in favor of the Allies. But since neither on the first nor on the second day after the landing [did] anything happen on the part of the Allies and since it did not remain hidden to the Romans with what calmness on the German side countermeasures were implemented, the attitude quickly reverted to the contrary. Receiving the announcement that there would be no change on the German side concerning the status of the 'open city,' the population regained its confidence in the German leadership and life in Rome returned to normal.

"That the Allies did not take advantage of this great chance has to date been incomprehensible to us. On account of the good connections with anti-German disposed Italians, it can hardly be assumed that the Allies lacked information on these facts. A reason for this failure, therefore, can apparently be found only in the principle of the Allies, always demonstrated, of 100 per cent security."[61]

Other Germans in key positions held the same opinion of their vulnerability. Colonel General Eugene Dollman, the secret police representative of Himmler and Hitler in Rome, said, "An energetic thrust of a column of American tanks and a popular uprising within the city would have enabled the enemy to take Rome within 24 hours."[62] Lieutenant General Siegfried Westphal, the chief of staff to Kesselring, said, "The road to Rome was open. No one could have stopped a bold advance guard entering the Holy City. The breathtaking situation continued for the first two days after the landing. It was only then that German counter-measures were effective."[63]

Information secured by Peter Tompkins, the OSS chief of operations in the city, is in agreement. His operatives, in a report that must be considered authoritative, informed him that there were no more than fifteen hundred Germans in the city, during and immediately following the time of the Anzio landings.[64]

As for the reaction among the Italians, the Irish priest J. Patrick Carroll-Abbing reported that at first "the news spread through the capital like a brush fire. There was wild exultation. The Germans whom I met seemed to be on the verge of panic. Within 24 hours the Allies would be in Rome."[65]

This is what everyone thought. But the joy and enthusiasm of the Romans were short-lived. Admiral Maugeri describes how it ebbed into frustration: "The panic and hysteria that seized Rome during the first twenty-four hours was fantastic. On January 22, billets and barracks were being emptied in a feverish, headlong rush. Overnight, the proud warriors of the Master Race were transformed into a frightened gang of Flying Dutchmen.[66]

"By the morning of January 25, it was plain: the Anglo-Americans had once more missed the bus. Pursuing their customary procedure, the Germans had stiffened. Swiftly, skillfully, they swung into action, regrouping, reorganizing, reinforcing. And when they saw the Allied assault was to be limited to Anzio they felt much more comfortable and secure. As well they might.[67]

"Starting on the morning of January 25 I saw one German unit after another roll down the Via Impero on their way to the bridgehead. Day after day I saw long convoys loaded with troops, ammo and supplies. I saw long columns of artillery, 88's, howitzers, Long Toms. I saw Tiger tanks and armored cars. I saw medical units, field hospitals and battalion aid stations. The Nazis were digging in at Anzio. They were going to make a fight of it. They were pulling units out of the North and rushing them to the beachhead. They could well afford to; obviously, the Allies were not going to strike anywhere else."[68]

« 6 »

Most owners of major league baseball teams swear by the rule that the only course that makes sense when their hitters don't score and their pitchers continue to lose is to fire the manager. This doesn't add any more steam to a fast ball or power to a bat, but it does have the effect of making the fans feel that something is being done. And this, evidently, is why Lucas was fired approximately a month after his stalled VI Corps began to burrow into foxholes by the Tyrrhenian Sea.

It took sustained prodding by Alexander to accomplish the dismissal. Sir Harold wired Sir Alan Brooke to "consult" about it with Eisenhower and Churchill, and the consultation ended with the chief of the Imperial General Staff snapping at his Prime Minister: "Can't you, for once, trust your commanders to organize their Command for themselves without interfering and upsetting all the chain and sequence of command?" This had been prompted by Churchill's embroidery of the matter of Lucas's replacement with the idea that Alexander go into the beachhead in his stead.[69]

Churchill had an unquenchable determination to look affirmatively upon Anzio. Deeply disappointed when the landings failed to produce immediate dramatic results, he nevertheless wrote in a letter to Field Marshal Dill, his representative in Washington, "It is a great advantage that the enemy should come in strength and fight in South Italy, thus being drawn far from other battlefields. Moreover, we have a great need to keep continually engaging them, and even a battle of attrition is better than standing by and watching the Russians fight. We should also learn a good many lessons about how not to do it which will be valuable in OVER-LORD."[70] It is fairly certain that Churchill would not have been disappointed if Sir John had used this letter as a basis for his discussions with the American faction on the Combined Chiefs of Staff.

At any rate, Lucas was fired. Alexander gave as his reasons for demanding the ouster that Lucas had adjusted his mind to an opposed landing and, when it had not occurred, was incapable of the flexibility that a younger man might have demonstrated. Alexander felt that Lucas, in addition to the handicap of advanced age (he was two years older than Sir Harold), was, perhaps, physically exhausted.[71] Afterwards, Clark admitted that he might have made a mistake in waiting so long to make the move, but he just couldn't bring himself to put this stain on his old friend's record.[72]

In his memoirs, Alexander suggests that Clark ordered the ouster for other than purely military reasons: "His [General Lucas's] appointment, of course, was entirely an American affair and it would have been quite inappropriate for me to intervene. However, at the last I brought myself to remark to Mark Clark: 'You know, the position is serious. We may be pushed back into the sea. That would be very bad for both of us — and you would certainly be relieved of your command.' This gentle injunction, I am glad to say, impelled action."[73]

There is no question that General Lucas *was* mentally and physically tired after the Anzio landing. Whether or not a victory would have acted as a tonic is only speculation at this point, and the fact remains that the morale of the fighting men at the beaches and the public at home reading about them had been severely affected. So Clark and Alexander took the only positive step available to them at the moment — they fired their manager.

But the new commander of VI Corps refused to join in the chorus that was damning Lucas at the top of its voice. Although he could have enhanced his own stature by helping paint the picture as dark as possible, Major General Lucian K. Truscott said:

I suppose that arm chair strategists will always labour under the delusion that there was a "fleeting opportunity" at Anzio during which some Napoleonic figure would have charged over the Colli

Laziali, played havoc with the German line of communications and galloped on into Rome. Any such concept betrays lack of comprehension of the military problem involved. It was necessary to occupy the Corps Beachhead Line to prevent the enemy from interfering with the beaches. Otherwise, enemy artillery and armoured detachments operating against the flanks could have cut us off from the beach and prevented the unloading of troops, supplies, and equipment. As it was, the Corps Beachhead Line was barely distant enough to prevent direct artillery fire on the beaches.

On January 24th, my division, with three Ranger battalions and the 504th Parachute Regiment attached, was extended on the Corps Beachhead Line over a front of twenty miles . . . Two brigade groups of the British 1st Division held a front of more than seven miles . . . We were in contact with German detachments with tanks and self-propelled artillery everywhere along the front. We knew that the attempt to cross the Rapido River had ended in failure. Under such conditions, any reckless drive to seize the Colli Laziali with means then available in the beachhead could only have ended in disaster and might well have resulted in destruction of the entire force.[74]

After the battle, General Marshall observed, "For every mile of advance, there were seven or more miles to be added to the perimeter,"[75] and the most superficial calculation will show that Lucas just didn't have the necessary supply base to ignore General Marshall's equation.

General Alexander later wrote in this memoirs: "It is of interest to consider what our position would have been if the fresh German divisions had found us stretched out from Anzio to the Alban Hills. Could we have maintained our bridgehead intact on such a wide perimeter with the troops at our disposal? We had no more than two divisions. And it would have been disastrous to our ultimate operations if Anzio had been wiped out."[76]

Even in the face of these considered opinions that Lucas acted properly under the circumstances, there are quite a few authorities, including many of the men who were fighting or writing in Italy at the time who felt that if George Patton or Geoff Keyes had been in command, VI Corps would have struck immediately for the high ground.

Since General Patton is dead, the only source for a definitive answer to this supposition is his close friend and fellow commander, General Keyes. "There wouldn't have been any question about it if General Patton was there," Keyes said afterwards. "Not long afterwards, he came down to Italy to visit me and he said the same thing — that Johnny Lucas should have kept on-going.

"Well, he didn't know then, and neither did I, that Lucas had these instructions which limited him, and that they were written down in black and white.

"General Lucas told me: 'If they wanted me to read beyond their instructions, or if they changed their points of view and wanted to do something else, they could have told me. Alexander, Clark, [General Jacob] Devers — they were all there breathing down my neck and not one of them said to keep going, or to do this, that or the other thing until it was all over. Then they said, "Oh my, Lucas hasn't done a thing!" '

"It's a lot easier to be a sideline quarterback — the pressure isn't on you, you're not worn out, no one's kicking you in the shins. It doesn't make any difference if you guess wrong — you can change that right away and guess again. But the fellow down there doing it — he can't."[77]

There is only one comment to add: by the time a man arrives at the rank of general, his capabilities and weaknesses are no strangers to the record. He becomes a readily identifiable piece of equipment, and he should no more be blamed for acting in an expected manner than a rifle should be blamed for not exceeding the range for which it was engineered. General Lucas was a well-known commodity. He was a methodical and careful man, and when he was picked to lead the Anzio landing, a methodical and careful operation should have been expected. His role as the historical scapegoat for this key move in the march on Rome is unfairly awarded.

If there is any blame, it should not be placed upon Lucas, who acted scrupulously within his own frame of reference in the execution of the orders given him, or upon Clark, who showed his belief in the validity of the original concept by refusing to fire Lucas for almost a month after it was demanded. Alexander was the superior officer on the scene. There was no reason for Sir Harold to "request" Clark to make the dismissal; he was at the beachhead during the time of the confusion and indecision and, as commanding officer, it was incumbent upon him to *order* the changes he felt necessary in order to achieve victory in the size he wanted.[78]

It is fair to add that Clark's month-long delay in removing Lucas ought to provide a conclusive answer to the charges that he was an opportunist. A man with his eyes fixed only on the main chance would not have allowed considerations of friendship or theoretical concepts to interfere with the speedy identification of a sacrificial goat.

« 7 »

And so began the second deadly stalemate of the Italian campaign. Within a few months, the German broadcaster "Axis Sally" felt justified in describing the Anzio beachhead as "the largest self-supporting prisoner-of-war camp in the world."

CHAPTER VII

FEBRUARY–MAY 1944

It is strange to walk through a battlefield in the dead of night and know that two armies are facing each other in the blackness. Tens of thousands of young men are looking up at the stars and wondering whether those same stars are shining over their homes. Young men are poised to kill and yet their hearts are not filled with hatred. There is only bitterness and fatigue and an unspoken longing for home.
— MSGR. J. PATRICK CARROLL-ABBING[1]

« 1 »

BILL MAULDIN was in trouble. His habit of dipping his pen in acid when describing some of the activities of the rear-area high brass had so outraged the deputy theater commander that an order came down forbidding the distribution of any more of his cartoons. The next step seemed to be the court-martial of Sergeant William Mauldin — an event that had been long and eagerly urged by many of his past subjects.

And then the newly appointed commander of VI Corps bumped into Mauldin at the Anzio beachhead. Major General Lucian Truscott's first question was: "How's your battle with the rear echelon progressing?"

Grinning in relief at the implied approval, the baby-faced Mauldin answered that he had nothing against the rear echelon, only some of its generals.

Truscott had a raspy, impatient voice which made even his commendations sound like criticism, but there was no mistaking his warning to the would-be censors when he sent Mauldin on his way, saying: "When you start drawing pictures that don't get a few complaints, then you'd better quit, because you won't be doing anybody any good!"[2]

This is what Mauldin wanted to hear. It's what every GI on the beachhead wanted to hear in mid-February when thoughts of a further offensive had faded into the need to defend a narrow foothold against what promised to be an explosive counterattack by superior numbers. The men who told each other about Truscott's pat on the sergeant's back understood that they were now commanded by a man who regarded them as something more than the elements of a nasty military problem.

This ability to appear as something other than a remote figure-head is a generous bonus for a general. Patton had it, but it bounced back in his face when his men began to contrast the dashing public cavalryman with the privately petty martinet who subjected them to childish and unreasonable discipline during their rest periods away from the battle lines. They knew that he had slapped, or otherwise vented hysterical tantrums on, not one soldier in a hospital, but several. After the first flush of his entry into world-wide headlines,[3] they generally followed the mention of his swashbuckling nickname, "Blood and Guts Patton," with the sourly muttered rejoinder "Yeah, our blood and his guts."

Clark never had it. Basically a considerate man who showed a continuing respect for his soldiers, he never became more than a name to the average GI. He made many appearances during the fighting, but since he was often surrounded by a phalanx of photographers and correspondents, he rarely assumed any identity but Commanding General to the soldiers in the ranks.

Once he had his picture taken while eating K rations with a rifleman. After the photographers had finished, he handed his food over to the soldier, saying, "Here son, eat this." The General honestly thought that the extra ration would be appreciated. But the story that raced through the beachhead depicted a pompous brass hat who felt that the only time he needed to eat the same food as his men was when the flashbulbs were popping.

Here again Clark was hurt by an inability to communicate his basic warmth. Few gave him good marks for arranging a system of rotation to rest camps for combat troops, but everyone repeated with relish the story of the spurned box of rations. Episodes like this personified in the Commanding General of the Fifth Army the frustration and discomfort of fighting in Italy.[4]

But Truscott avoided this. The men who saw and lived with him generally understood him as a human being of likable dimensions. A former Oklahoma schoolteacher, he had received his commission in an officers' training camp in 1917. One of the few ranking generals who had not graduated from West Point, he

advanced rapidly to positions of command by virtue of exceptional ability. General Eisenhower first met him as a lieutenant
colonel and marked him as an able man who accomplished everything assigned him in a superior manner. Eisenhower thought
Truscott had the qualifications to be an Army commander, and
later considered the possibility of using him to fill the first
vacancy that might occur among the trio of senior generals scheduled to lead the armies of the OVERLORD invasion.

Physically, Truscott was a craggy, impressive man, possessing
what one English journalist described as "a rather theatrical
profile." He gave the impression of toughness. His mind and his
voice were quick. His dress was on the theatrical side, since he
generally wore a highly varnished helmet, a white scarf around
his neck, faded riding breeches, and boots.

In the beginning of the war, Truscott had been assigned to Lord
Mountbatten's combined operations staff in England. The ranking
American officer on the Dieppe raid, he later put his experience to
good use in training the first Rangers in England.[5] As commanding officer of the 3rd Division, he had honed that unit into what
was generally considered one of the very best of the American
fighting units. His selection as the new commander of VI Corps
was inevitable in light of his reputation as one of the army's better
tacticians. Winston Churchill quickly accepted him as the new
leader of the beachhead forces[6] and became his enthusiastic
admirer.

But it took more than a new leader to change the prevailing
military situation at Anzio. Although the staff officers of VI Corps
now moved with fresh determination and direction, the Germans
were still in the commanding position. Their long-range guns,
mounted in the hills ringing the flat tableland of the beachhead,
pounded the Allies unmercifully. Clark filled his limited space
with as many additional troops as he dared, but this number was
always limited by the danger of presenting a concentrated target
to the guns above. The beachhead force of three and one-half
divisions was so thoroughly exposed that they would certainly

have been obliterated by the five German divisions facing them
had it not been for the artillery support of the ships in the harbor
and the command of the skies enjoyed by the vastly superior
Allied air units.[7]

The men of the beachhead hung on. In spite of a series of
vicious counterattacks (one of which, on February 19, established
the high-water mark of German strength in Italy), the VI Corps
fought their way through February and then settled down to
containment for the next few months. The generally dismal picture was brightened only by the antics of Brigadier General
Robert Frederick's redoubtable First Special Service Force. His
sixteen hundred fighters guarded almost one-third of the perimeter
and, while doing so, found time to steal horses, chickens, wine,
and other booty from the Nazis a few miles away. It was here that
they perfected their technique of gliding black-faced through the
lines at night, slitting the throats of the Germans that they found,
and leaving a sticker posted on each dead man's helmet which
read "You May Be Next!"

One platoon actually took over a village located well behind
von Mackensen's forward wall and established a burlesque city
government which became a legend at Anzio. The Canadians and
Americans who made the hamlet their home during these weeks
occupied themselves by going out on patrols at night and farming
the adjacent territory during the day.[8]

« 2 »

As the high-velocity attacks and counterattacks at Anzio slackened
into pulsations of probes and counterprobes,[9] the activities of the
German and Allied soldiers facing each other along a line bisect-
ing the trunk of the Italian peninsula again took the spotlight. This
was the Gustav Line. It was anchored on one of the finest defensive
positions in all of Europe; the historic Benedictine Abbey of
Monte Cassino.

Built by St. Benedict in A.D. 529 upon the crown of a hill

soaring 1715 feet above sea level, the Abbey was a huge structure two hundred yards long, filled with what were considered irreplaceable treasures by those who loved art and history. But in February 1944, its reputation as one of the glories of the world was eclipsed by the question of whether it was a legitimate military objective. It seemed to tower like a huge observation post over the entire battleground.

The battle to breach the line at Monte Cassino lasted from February to May.[10] As we have seen, the first phase ended with terrible hurt to the 36th Division as it failed to get across the Rapido River in a flanking movement just south of the Abbey. The British X Corps had gained an important bridgehead on the Allied left flank, near the coast, but had lost almost four thousand men among its three divisions before being stopped by the rugged terrain and the apparently immovable defensive position held by four German divisions. The American 34th Division, losing twenty-two hundred men in the process, succeeded in driving a small breach in the line just north of the center, and on the extreme right flank the French, with only two divisions to cover one of the widest sectors of the front, had advanced and consolidated a position in the mountains after suffering twenty-five hundred casualties.

It was important that the Allies capture the series of peaks which furnished observation points for the defenders. The need for this may seem obscure to most laymen, but battles are often fought for observation. Victory generally goes to the holder of the high ground, and this is why the Italian campaign largely became a struggle up one hill or another for the Allied forces.

Because this first phase of the battle had gotten off to a bad start with the debacle at the Rapido, the movements, up until February 12, gave the appearance of a series of uncoordinated thrusts. Every Allied element paid dearly for minimal gains, since the Germans, possessing almost unlimited mobility, were able to face each attack in strength. When this pattern became apparent, Clark found himself relying increasingly on his artillery. A Russian observation party visiting the front during this period was shocked at what they considered an extravagant waste of materiel. Conditioned by the need to get maximum results from the expenditure of limited stores of ammunition on their own front, they criticized the American policy of keeping every large and small gun spewing fire night and day.[11] In truth, Clark had no other choice. He had too few divisions to have succeeded in any of the attempts against the Gustav Line. The strength of the German defensive positions doubled the efficiency of their soldiers, and had Clark ordered an increase in the tempo of frontal attacks, the epithet "Butcher," so dear to the second-guesser, would have been irrevocably pinned upon him by many more than the 36th Division.

However, the Russians were partially right. The bombing and shelling were largely ineffective. Almost every report of the period mentions that during even the most concentrated shelling periods, the Germans played cards and otherwise imperturbably went about their daily business in deep underground chambers and bastions protected by reinforced steel and concrete, alternate layers of railroad ties, stone and earth.[12]

Kesselring manned these positions with some of the best units in the Nazi army. Colonel General von Vietinghoff-Scheel, in overall command of the situation as head of the Tenth Army, was an old and expert Prussian infantryman who was once described by a VI Corps intelligence report as "the most capable officer on this front and the driving power behind Kesselring."[13] General Frido von Senger und Etterlin, whose employment of the 14th Panzer Corps in the defense of Cassino has become recognized as a strategic classic, was the commander on the scene.

Thus, almost impregnable positions were manned by soldiers whose toughness and efficiency were later described by General Alexander in terms that approached awe. He noted, "I doubt if there are any other troops in the world who could have stood up to it [the continued bombing and shelling] and then gone on fighting with the ferocity they have." On one occasion, while visiting an Allied hospital for the wounded, he asked whether there were any

German soldiers in the ward. While he was being conducted to where they lay, one of them, spying him, barked, "Achtung — Herr General!" At this, the wounded men all stiffened to attention in their beds, arms outstretched stiffly over the sheets. He later recalled that he felt that they would have remained in this position indefinitely if he hadn't given the order to "carry on."[14]

Even against odds like these, the men of II Corps showed their awareness that no matter how many tons of explosive poured down from the sky or thundered from the big and small guns on the ground, the infantryman had to bull his way onto the scene before a victory could be realized. Twice during the first week in February, men and tanks battled their way into the outskirts of Cassino itself. Once a platoon of the 135th Infantry Regiment fought up Monastery Hill to the very walls of the Abbey before being thrown back.

The only answer seemed to lie in augmented manpower. The colorful Sir Bernard Freyberg, commanding the New Zealand Corps (which consisted of the 2nd New Zealand Division, the 4th Indian Division and the British 78th Division) began, on February 11, to relieve II Corps.

A word about these striking additions to the battle line is in order. The Indian unit was composed of volunteers from among the most martial groups in that subcontinent. They were men who enjoyed everything about soldiering, and as a result, achieved an almost matchless proficiency as a fighting force. The New Zealanders, at the other end of the line when it came to spit-and-polish, were recklessly brave and independent men whose unconcern with standard forms of discipline became one of the most durable legends of World War II. On one occasion, a senior British general on an inspection tour mentioned to their commander, "Your people don't salute very much, do they?" Freyberg shrugged and answered, "You should try waving to them. They always wave back."[15]

Lieutenant General Sir Bernard Freyberg, V.C., was one of the few senior field commanders of the First World War to hold an active field command in the Second. He was, in effect, a law unto himself. Responsible only to his own government for his activities, he represented to Alexander and Clark a major problem in diplomacy. On paper he could be commanded, in practice he was only asked, and therefore he had almost the status of an autonomous ally.[16]

His introduction to II Corps had come just a few weeks before Alexander detached his group from the Eighth Army and assigned them to the Fifth. Colonel Robert Porter was in charge of headquarters while General Keyes was forward picking out a target for the 34th Division on the slope of the hill which looked over to the Abbey. Porter received a call from one of his guards that "a strange man without any insignia, wearing a big camel's hair overcoat and a funny black beret, is asking for General Keyes." The MP went on to say that the stranger had a funny accent that was neither British nor American, but seemed to know what he was doing.

"It had been a tough day," Porter recalls. "One of our best battalion commanders had just been killed in the minefields in front of Cassino and things generally weren't going our way. Our communications were not too good and the situation was discouraging. I told the MP to send the man up, and when he arrived it turned out to be Freyberg. We had a cup of tea together and I told him about the situation, and I guess I did sound a bit pessimistic. When he left, he put his arm around my shoulder and said, 'Porter, don't worry, the New Zealand Corps is coming to help.' That's the way we found out that the Fifteenth Army Group had released the New Zealand Corps to the Fifth Army."[17]

Geoffrey Keyes picks up the thread: "General Clark told me during the second or third assault we were making up to the hills with the 34th, 'If you don't make it this time, you're going to miss the boat, because I'm going to bring the New Zealanders and Freyberg in — he'll do it.'

"Well, Freyberg came up and stayed there two months and he didn't get any further than we had. He took several beatings because he decided to climb right up the front of the hill that the monastery was on. But he just got trapped from every side. These fellows were hanging on with their fingers and toes to the side of the hill with no support or supply or anything else. Nothing. Then he launched his air attack in front of all the big brass. [He] destroyed the monastery and the town but then waited too long for his assault to take off. He waited until after dark, and by that time the Germans had come right back in there and occupied every rock and he never made an inch."[18]

There are at least a half a dozen excellent books which deal with the battle for Monte Cassino. Depending upon the views of the author, they either condemn Mark Clark for ordering the destruction by bombing of the historic Abbey or commiserate with him for having been forced into it by the demands of Freyberg.

In his own book, *Calculated Risk,* Clark states quite emphatically that he was opposed to the move. He describes at great length his conviction that the Abbey was not a legitimate military target because there was not a shred of proof that the Germans were using it for observation purposes. He makes it quite clear he feels that he was forced into the move by Freyberg's demands.[19]

This position has made Clark a further target for criticism. Some of the German generals who discuss the subject in their memoirs seem to believe that since Clark was the commander on the scene, he presents a sorry picture of himself by attempting to shift the responsibility onto the shoulders of a subordinate.[20]

It may be so. It also may be a very human thing to refuse to take the blame for a wantonly destructive act when, as a matter of hard truth, the senseless decision was made and demanded by a third party who was almost unanimously considered as an independent force. Unquestionably, in the chain of command, Freyberg was below Clark, but the situation differed from Alexander's earlier unwillingness to order Clark to remove Lucas at Anzio. The wiping out of the Abbey was an act of historic vandalism which transcended military protocol. Clark did not want the Abbey bombed. He told Freyberg this, and further pointed out that once the edifice was reduced to rubble, the Germans would find it even easier to defend than the original building. But Freyberg was adamant. That this was the unvarnished situation can be attested to by the air support officer of II Corps at the time. Charged with the setting of the bomb safety line before Cassino, this officer had an unobstructed view of the factors which resulted in the commission of one of the most serious mistakes of the campaign.

He recalls: "II Corps left a small force of about a battalion remaining close to the Abbey in that part of the front that was being taken over by General Freyberg and the New Zealand troops. As corps air officer, I was responsible for setting the bomb safety line, which meant I had to draw a line far enough in front so that the Air Corps would not bomb them. I placed this in such a fashion that the Abbey of Monte Cassino was included *within* the bomb safety line.

"General Freyberg was insisting that the air attack take place on the Abbey, but in order to do this, it became necessary to change the bomb safety line. In an absence of a direct order from the corps commander, I was the only one authorized to make this change. But I had received word from General Keyes that he and Clark felt that, come hell or high water, I should stick to what I thought would be the best safety line and that I would receive their entire support. As a consequence, whenever Freyberg demanded the bombing, General Keyes would reply that he felt it wasn't safe to bomb the Abbey so long as his troops were up there. As I understand it, he told Freyberg that the corps air officer would not move his bomb safety line while our officers and men were in that particular position 'unless I give him a direct and written order, which I am not about to do. I have considerable confidence in my G–3 Air and I will not give him an order to move his bomb safety line.'

"Terrific pressure was brought on me to change my position during this period. The G–3 Air from Army Group came down along with quite a few of the other high brass. I was told that the

President of the United States and the Prime Minister of Great Britain wanted that Abbey bombed and here an obscure captain like me was holding it up. But so long as Clark and Keyes were tacitly encouraging me to hold on, I refused to change the line.

"Finally, even they had to give in. II Corps elements in front of the Abbey were relieved in a few days by New Zealand troops, and this permitted Freyberg to set his own bomb line.

"I was standing with General Keyes watching the scene when the bombing started. The first stick of our bombs fell squarely on the New Zealanders."[21]

This was February 15, 1944. Approximately 576 tons of high explosive were dropped on the Abbey by 225 Allied bombers, and after the planes departed, the massed Allied artillery completed the ruin by churning the rubble for hours afterward. A great monument had been destroyed.

The attack which followed was repulsed almost as easily as the ones which took place while the building was still intact. The Indians and the New Zealanders found that the Germans now felt free to use the ruins as a defensive base and, in short order, had established such fine positions that they were able to turn back the onslaught with comparative ease.

Later Clark was to discover that the Vatican had ordered an exhaustive investigation of the alleged German occupation of the Abbey. It yielded the conclusion that the defenders had refrained from using the Abbey as an observation post. And when it had become apparent that the building would be bombed, the Germans had helped the Benedictines remove many of the art treasures to a protected location. Needless to say, the incident made fine grist for the propaganda mill of Dr. Goebbels. Motion pictures had been taken showing German Army trucks transporting the works of art to safety.[22]

After the massive shelling, Father Carroll-Abbing ventured from a hiding place to drive away from Cassino. He describes the first nights: "Along the deeply rutted road which once passed through rich farmlands and now traversed a barren waste dotted with craters and barbed wire and the snarled stumps of trees, came two small figures. At first they were two specks in the distance, but as they drew near I saw that they were children; a boy and a girl, holding each other by the hand as little children do. Their clothes were filthy; their faces and legs fouled by mud; their eyes swollen by excessive tears. Now they smiled, a vacant smile that put a chill into one's heart. Seemingly unconscious of my presence, they meekly took their place beside me in the car."[23]

Is it any wonder that Harold Tittman, the American chargé d'affaires in the Vatican, later remarked: "The bombing of Monte Cassino caused considerable anti-Allied feeling both within the Vatican and throughout Rome"?[24]

« 3 »

Harold Tittman was not the only American in Rome disturbed by the by-products of the Allied effort to reach the city. The jaunty OSS agent Major Peter Tompkins was now worried about the effect of the almost regular morning bombardment of the city's outskirts. The sight of dead and dying civilians being rushed in ambulances, and sometimes horsedrawn carts, to the hospitals, of private homes in flames or powdery ruins as a result of misses on the marshaling yards, and the terror of innocent civilians caught in the streets during a raid, made him wonder if the missions were particularly well advised. He noted in his diary that "they miss the target so often, and sometimes by quite some distance, and the people of Rome are angry, and it creates a wave of hatred and bad feeling which isn't worth the candle — especially as I still don't believe that the rail yards and stations of Rome are an effective target, when they could interrupt traffic more effectively, and with no loss of civilian lives (and prestige) outside the city."[25]

The bombing was not the only reason for the growing skepticism of the Roman citizens. While the VI Corps was landing on the Anzio beachhead, the resistance forces in Rome received a radio message from the Allied command which read: "The hour has arrived for Rome and all Italians to fight in every possible way and with all forces. Sabotage the enemy . . . block his roads of retreat, destroy his communications to the last wire, strike against him everywhere, continuing the fight indefatigably without thought of political questions until our troops have arrived. Notify all bands and parties."[26]

A one-sided slaughter would have followed if the anti-Fascists, the Communists, and all the other clandestine splinter parties engaging in the underground struggle to dominate the politics of post-occupation Italy had surfaced in response to this poorly advised call to arms. The Germans would have lopped each identifiable head as soon as they had reasserted their mastery of the city. It was a close call and its effects were not lost upon the members of each of the competing groups temporarily bound together in the loose junta known as the CLN (*Comitato di Liberazione Nazionale* — the National Liberation Committee). Each group secretly resolved to rely even more heavily upon its own counsel and resources in the future and to evaluate carefully the new promises of Allied military and political spokesmen.[27]

The Italian-language broadcasts from America which described in glowing terms the democratic way of life were dismissed as hopeless platitudes and all Americans were considered naïve.[28] There were too many instances of their cynical manipulation by ex-Fascists. As for the British, their continued sponsorship of the King left the liberals with the pronounced feeling that Winston Churchill was infinitely more interested in creating a postwar sphere of power than he was in the emergence of an Italian democracy.[29]

By the most charitable construction, there *was* considerable naïveté among the Allies. It seemed as if they felt that all they had to do to abolish Fascism was to take military possession of an area, put signs on a street corner or proclaim from a balcony that Fascism was dead, and the effect of Mussolini's decades of domination would disappear. No one apparently took into account that when a system of government had endured as long as Fascism in Italy, it inevitably touched — and had adherents in — almost every family in the country. Thus, the middle and upper classes were forced into complicity and the poorer people, as always, in every time and war, suffered the most.

They saw opposing armies sweep over their farms, leaving hopeless bogs and pits where once there had been a few cherished acres. They saw their pitifully few possessions bombed into splinters and their families mangled as an unintended and unlamented by-product of a struggle between two strange titans.

And the Allied soldiers, like soldiers everywhere, were young and strong and almost totally unaware of the degradation that holds hands with the need to cadge goodwill from strangers.

They saw young Italian children offering to pimp for young girls who would perform any service for a can of food and fathers and mothers who suffered any indignity which permitted them to hold their family together for another day, and the twenty-year-old soldiers became convinced that the Italians were dirty, thieving, whoring sycophants.

Bill Mauldin's book *Up Front* in its original draft was severely critical of the Italians. He was reflecting the general view held by the average GI. But Harry Sions and other friends on *Yank* and *Stars and Stripes* tried to persuade him to soften judgments. Afterwards, Sions said, "It was typical of GI attitudes, but I expected that Mauldin would have been a bit more knowledgeable. I was wrong, of course. Not that he has any malice in him — he's a decent and generous man — but when he got into the army he was just a kid, maybe eighteen years old. He had no way of knowing. He had to mature. Years later, he saw me and said, 'You were right. I shouldn't have written about the Italian people that way.' But Mauldin was young. All of the soldiers were young. They thought the Italians were dirty because that was their nature. But some of us realized it was because they had no soap."[30]

There was no question that the heart of the average soldier was touched by the plight of the very young and the very old. They gave generously of their own rations to these groups, but Italian manhood was almost unanimously dismissed as inferior. As fighters, the Italians were considered to be bad jokes by both the Allied and German soldiers. This is one of the unfairest reactions of all. There are few who surpass in bravery the Italians when they believe in a cause. Not many of those who demean Italian valor realize the immense courage it took to be a Partisan in Rome, where even the suspicion of identification meant an instant death sentence, or the amount of raw decency involved in hiding a refugee from the Nazis in one's home. Yet many thousands of Italians unhesitatingly exposed themselves to torture and death for just these reasons.

The Italians were criticized for their lackluster fighting spirit by Kesselring and other Germans while the divisions of Mussolini were still arrayed alongside them.[31] But the Germans never had the sensitivity to realize how deeply they were loathed by most Italians.

The Italians wanted to fight alongside the Allies after the surrender, but Sir Harold Alexander peremptorily refused. Only on one occasion were they permitted to field a fighting unit, and when the episode ended in disaster, Allied commanders treated it as a typical Italian performance. But Robert Porter, who was there at the time, recalls: "We had gotten word from Fifth Army that all that was left of the Italian troops in Libya were joining us and that it was important that they be used as early as possible. It was an odd outfit. The officers were assembled from all over Italy, the men in the same way. After some prompting from Fifth Army, we decided that they should be attached to the 36th Division and make a limited-objective attack against Mount Luongo, which was a long narrow spine about a mile in length and a half-mile in width. It's a sort of an island sitting right in the middle of the valley and both sides of it were in American hands. Our intelligence indicated that there were only one or two companies of an engineer battalion holding this hill, so it looked like an easy victory which would give a morale boost to the Italians.

"But, apparently, someone in the Italian unit talked. When the attack was made, the engineers were gone and a Panzer division was waiting for them on the forward slopes of Mount Luongo within two hundred yards of their line of departure. The Germans held their artillery until they got very close and then as their big guns went off, they charged out of their foxholes at the Italians. The Italians broke and ran. What was to have been a morale boost turned into a fiasco.

"The sad thing about this was that the Italians were actually a fine group. But they had been thrown together so rapidly that the junior officers did not know the men in their platoons, the company officers did not know the platoon leaders, and so on. No one knew who to depend on and it turned into a really bad failure."[32]

After this rout by a superior and waiting force, there were no more directives from higher commands for the employment of Italian troops. But this didn't keep the Italians from fighting. Robert Capa, one of the war's fine photojournalists, described entering a schoolhouse after the Allied tide had swept past Naples: "I entered the school and was met by the sweet, sickly smell of flowers and the dead. In the room were twenty primitive coffins, not well enough covered with flowers and too small to hide the dirty little feet of children—children old enough to fight the Germans and to be killed, but just a little too old to fit in children's coffins. These children of Naples had stolen rifles and bullets and had fought the Germans for fourteen days . . ."[33]

In Rome, despite the growing disenchantment with Allied activities, there was no discernible tendency to offer help or comfort to the Germans. Later, Kesselring remarked, "I loved the Italians too much. Now I hate them,"[34] but this ambivalence had not yet caused him to seriously question his welcome in this country. He had Rome plastered with signs which alternately cajoled and ordered all able-bodied Italian men to join the German army "to throw back the invader," and instead of responding, the men of Rome went underground. Women conducted most of the business activities, ran the errands, and delivered messages for their sons and husbands, who remained in hiding rather than run the risk of being snatched by the Nazis to fill their thinning army ranks. Admiral Maugeri observed, "The Eternal City became the eternally feminine city."[35]

Activity in the Via Tasso shifted into high gear. The name of this street near Santa Croce quickly became a synonym for all the systematic horrors of the Gestapo interrogation system. The Germans located their prison in a sealed five-story apartment building there, and although it was officially described as a "temporary" station, Jane Scrivener wrote in her diary that "in reality it is a place whence very few return and when they do so they are often broken men. Those who do not return are either tortured to death or shot. Names of accomplices and confederates are forced from the victims unless they have superhuman endurance. When they die, their families are often not told, for mental cruelty as well as physical is brought to a fine art by the Germans."[36]

It was fatally easy for a Roman to find himself in the Via Tasso. There were placards everywhere which described the punishments that Kesselring deemed appropriate for certain infractions. Death was the automatic sentence for being found harboring or helping or making contacts with an escaped prisoner of war, for owning a radio transmitter, for looting in evacuated areas, and for desertion from work or otherwise not fulfilling what the Nazis considered to be labor obligations. Life imprisonment was meted out automatically when a Roman was found circulating news derogatory to the Axis forces or taking photographs out of doors. Minor infractions received lesser penalties; only twenty years' imprisonment was meted out to those found guilty of not acquainting the authorities with a change of address.

And yet, even though systematically tortured and oppressed by the Germans, rebuffed and held in contempt by the Allies, the Italians fought on in small Partisan bands or, quite often, as individuals. A captured German directive of the period warned all regiments to view the Italians with suspicion. The order went on to say that "there are treacherous Italian elements in the vicinity of our positions to use these [stolen] weapons. Hence, all trains and regimental supply dumps are to be constantly and strictly guarded, especially weapons, munitions and explosives."[37]

By March, the junta of resistance parties had agreed on a strategy that was intended to weaken the German lines of communications to the fronts at Cassino and Anzio. By systematic acts of sabotage, the leaders of the CLN hoped to divert to the outskirts of Rome the movement of reinforcements and supplies that was now going through the heart of the city. Further, they attempted to discourage the Germans from holding the city, by creating a zone of intense hostility. Most of them believed that when the Allies arrived, the Germans would engage them in street-by-street combat. It was felt that if this came to pass, it would mean the end of everything beautiful and treasured in Rome.

This was a very real fear. Although the Vatican and the Germans and the Badoglio government had declared Rome to be an open city, the parties really essential to such an agreement had never formally acquiesced in it.[38] While Kesselring continued to proclaim his belief in the validity of this status, there is irrefutable evidence that the city was treated by his forces as a vital link in their supply line.[39] Every train and vehicle route that ran through the city was crowded with men and supplies on their way to the front or with troops being shifted to another sector. As for the Allies, their position was unmistakable; they would treat the city as a sanctuary whenever the Germans withdrew their military goods, men, and headquarters from its environs.[40]

Kesselring's reaction to the Italians' failure to return his often-professed love for them was one of anger. The edicts bearing his signature carried increasingly stringent penalties for Partisan activity. He issued restrictions so severe that even riding a bicycle became an offense demanding heavy punishment.[41] It was his assumption that the leaders of the Partisan movement were located at Allied headquarters and that the "criminals" who made up these bands were directed almost solely by Allied intelligence officers. Later, in his memoirs, he described the Partisans in terms which contained an almost emotional reaction to their activities:

> The Partisan war was a complete violation of international law and contradicted every principle of clean soldierly fighting . . . Their "patriotic" mission combined with [their] vicious instincts left few loopholes for compunction. In small groups or singly, they ran amok without restraint, doing their nefarious work everywhere . . .
> In consequence, there was considerable irritation on our side, for the German soldier in the infested areas could not help seeing in every civilian of either sex a fanatical assassin or expecting to be fired at from every house. The whole population had in any case helped in or connived at elaborating a warning system which placed every German soldier's life in danger."[42]

There exists no better testimony to the willingness of the Italian people to fight when they have something they believe worth fighting for. Unfortunately, too many historical chronicles have dismissed the entire Partisan movement as being Communist-dominated and therefore incapable of true patriotism. Unquestionably, there were many Communists in the movements.[43] Toward the end of the war, the Partisan bands became almost completely Communist-dominated, but it should be remembered that during the days before Rome fell, few of those who risked torture and death by joining in the harassment of the Germans felt themselves to be anything but good Italians. Political labels were undeniably important, but the Partisans' first loyalties were almost invariably to their country.[44]

One of the most shocking events of the period took place on March 23. A small band of Partisans, determining that a detachment of German police troops marched each day at the same time down the same street in the heart of Rome, planted a bomb which exploded on schedule, killing thirty-two men. There are some who claim that this act of sabotage was executed by the Communists to provoke savage penalties against the entire population of Rome. Following in the wake of the reprisals, the Communists could

achieve nationwide identity as the preeminent fighting force opposing the Nazis.[45]

It has never been proven that the bombing was the sole work of
the leftists. But there has never been any question that when the
bomb went off, the Germans lost no time in shucking the mask of
benevolence which they sometimes assumed in Rome.

General Kurt Maelzer, the habitual drunkard who commanded
the German troops in the city and who loved to hear himself
described as the "King of Rome," was the first to react. He
immediately ordered the slaughter of every person living on the
Via Rasella, the street on which the explosion had taken place.
Dissuaded from this step by Eitel F. Mollhaussen, the head of the
German Embassy, he referred the matter to Berlin. Hitler and
Himmler promptly directed that every able-bodied male in Rome
be deported to labor camps in Germany. Kesselring convinced
them that this would represent an intolerable burden on his rail
and supply system and then reduced the punishment; he issued an
order over his signature that ten Romans should be executed for
every German soldier who died.

This created a problem. There simply weren't enough prisoners
at the moment in the Via Tasso to meet this quota. So the conscien-
tious officers charged with the discharge of this sentence made up
the difference with Jews, criminals and ordinary Romans who
were merely suspected of harboring anti-Fascist sentiments. In
an excess of zeal, the jailers had rounded up three hundred and
thirty-five instead of the three hundred and twenty called for by
Kesselring. The only difference this made was to the associates of
Obersturmbannfuehrer Kappler, the officer who supervised the
roundup and, later, the execution. They felt that Kappler had
invited criticism by including the unauthorized fifteen hostages in
his bag. At any rate, the sentence was carried out. Kappler, with a
detachment of men, herded the Romans into one of the Fosse
Ardeatine caves, gunned them to death according to a system he
had efficiently worked out the night before, covered the bodies

with lime, and then sealed the tunnel leading to the charnel chamber with a blast of dynamite.

After the slaughter of the three hundred and thirty-five civilians took place, two orders were issued by the German High Command. The first, which appeared in Rome's newspapers on March 25, said:

On the afternoon of March 23, criminal elements committed acts of violence by means of bombs against a German column passing through Via Rasella. In consequence, thirty-two members of the German police were killed and a number of them wounded.

This brutally violent act was committed by Communists of Badoglio's party. Investigations are being made as to the [possibility of the] crime being caused by Anglo-American influence.

The German High Command is determined to crush the activities of these villainous bandits. No one will be allowed to sabotage the renewed Italo-German cooperation. The Command has ordered that, for every German who was murdered, ten of Badoglio's Communists shall be shot. This order has already been executed."[46]

The other order was a communiqué to the troops which, after describing the bombing of March, forgot that part of the statement to the civilians about "renewed Italo-German cooperation" in order to warn that "Partisans and sabotage activity of anti-Nazi elements must be expected in all parts of Italy. The formation of Partisan groups is to be neutralized by continual supervision of the civilian population . . . and . . . mutinous happenings must be reported by quickest possible means. In such cases [we] will act with remorseless severity. Commanders, all grades, must counteract the characteristic blind faith of the German soldier in the civil population of foreign countries. It must be hammered into every man that every civilian may be either an agent or a saboteur, who uses the trusting nature of the German soldier to do him harm."[47]

After the war ended, Kesselring was tried by a war crimes court for his part in this massacre. In defense, he said that he had acted humanely by scaling down Hitler's demand that all Italian males be deported to labor camps and that, further, the Ardeatine reprisal was an act that was sanctioned by international law. The court refused to accept this defense and sentenced him to death. Kesselring found this "incomprehensible." He said after the verdict had been announced that he had not committed any reprisal on his own but that his responsibility had been "relieved by Hitler's order." He concluded these comments by declaring that he had "tried to achieve a deterrent effect" to force compliance with international law and that such an effort should have been regarded by the court "as an honest effort to exercise humanity."[48]

Later his sentence was first commuted to life imprisonment and then cut to twenty-one years. Finally, in 1952, it was canceled altogether. After his release he returned to Munich, where he died in 1960 at the age of seventy-four.

There is no record that Pope Pius XII ever encouraged the activities of the Partisans. He too felt that they were Communist-dominated at worst and, at best, so wild in nature that they constituted an undigestible element to the Church. He was considered fearful of the new situation in which Fascism had fallen and the Communists were seemingly emerging as the only governmental group strong enough to take over the reins.

The record is clear. The Pope viewed Communism as a more baneful force than Nazism, and this is the pump which has generated all of the controversy over the conduct of Pius XII during World War II.[49]

Eugenio Pacelli was so complex a man that it becomes an easy matter to read support for almost any personal position into his actions. He was a consummate diplomat, conditioned to subtlety and indirection by a lifetime of movement in international affairs. He was also a mystic and each day retreated within himself for an hour of prayers and contemplation. He radiated glacial self-assurance, but in 1955 he was terribly hurt by the general skepticism which followed his announcement that Jesus Christ had appeared before him during one of his hours of solitude.[50]

He apparently had a sense of humor. One story about him might have been apocryphal, but it would not have been so widely repeated if there had not been some basis for believability. Claire Boothe Luce had just been appointed Ambassador to Italy. A recent convert to Catholicism, the lady was both enthusiastic and exhaustive in her first meeting with the Pontiff. He finally took advantage of one of her rare pauses for breath to observe, "But Mrs. Luce, I *am* a Catholic."

Sometimes he could be quite pragmatic. Shortly after Eugenio Pacelli became Pius XII in 1939 at the age of sixty-three, he issued a proclamation warning the 375,000,000 Catholics throughout the world that "the Vatican's sole protection is its moral authority." There were many who saw this statement as a reflection of insights gained as a papal nuncio in Germany.

He radiated the conviction that he represented all of mankind. When a delegation of II Corps officers visited him after Rome fell, he blessed them, saying, "Even if you are not of my belief, you are still my children."[51] On another occasion, he mournfully intoned in a proclamation, "My children are killing each other."

And yet there is no evidence to indicate that he extended this belief of universality to the Communists. One of his milder statements on this head was: "It is not possible to be a Communist and a Catholic."[52]

His great fear of this group is undoubtedly the reason why he kept silent after the massacre of March 23. He believed the ambushing of the police detachment to be totally leftist in origin and his subsequent lack of comment was interpreted to mean that he feared that Fascism was giving way to Communism as the ruler of Italy.[53] There is reason to believe that he felt a certain amount of disapproval for Roosevelt and Churchill because of their commitment to the entente with Josef Stalin.

But, like many other leaders, he helped the cause that he detested by overstating its vitality. Vatican diplomats studded every report to Britain and America with estimates of Communist strength, most of which were later shown to be seriously exaggerated.[54] Documentary evidence amassed since the war discloses that at this point the Communists of Italy were weak and disorganized. Almost twenty years of repression by the Fascists had left the party with only a few thousand members. A document prepared by the Roman Communists themselves on March 2, 1944, confessed that the party's total membership, in a city of two million, was less than three thousand.[55] Vatican notes on this subject to the U.S. Department of State sometimes approached hyperbole. The inference drawn by many of the people with access to these reports was that the Pope and his cardinals were doubtful of their position in an Italy turned anti-Fascist.

Those who disapprove of Pius XII have interpreted his silence after the slaughter in the Ardeatine Caves and his belated condemnation of the Fascist regime to mean that he found Hitler's Germany to be the least of several evils. They draw further strength from the reports and correspondence of Ernst Weizsäcker, the German ambassador to the Vatican during these years, which uniformly report a favorable Vatican attitude toward German courses of action.[56] But here, too, they lose sight of the Pope's amazing subtlety. The connotations of the term "fine Italian hand" would not be inappropriately applied to Pius XII. In light of the documents which have been made public to date, it is evident to anyone who approaches the situation objectively that Weizsäcker was encouraged to read approval into equivocal actions and further, as only a lukewarm Nazi, he was prone to report what Berlin wanted most to hear.[57]

The truth remains that up until the day Rome fell, the Vatican was an island of weakness surrounded by Nazi strength. Worldwide opinion was the only force that really manned its walls, and Hitler had never been noted for his sensitivity to public opinion. Obviously, the Vatican felt itself to be in a precarious position. Whether or not a papal pronouncement would have dissuaded the Nazis from any of their prosecutions is debatable. In its logical extension, the question really becomes one of whether the Catholic hierarchy represents a temporal or a spiritual power. Those who see it as a purely mystical force regard the silence of Pius XII as a grievous act of omission. Those who consider the Curia as a more tangible entity of course think that the Vatican, having bought German protection, was compelled to close its eyes to acts of Nazi brutality in the Holy City and elsewhere.

It is unfortunate that a matter as important as this has been so widely judged within emotional frames. Devout Catholics and dedicated anti-Communists face anti-Church elements and ultra-liberals angrily across a gulf. Neither side seems capable of dispassionately evaluating the record. But what, actually, did happen? Did the Pope, while doing everything he thought possible, believe that there was too little that was possible?

The accumulated entries seem to indicate that Pius's evaluation of the limited extent of papal influence was correct. The priests of Holland, for example, were more outspoken than the clergy in other countries occupied by the Nazis. They showed consistent courage in opposing the genocidal acts of Hitler's agents. But in Holland, seventy-nine per cent of all Jews were deported to concentration camps — the highest percentage recorded in all of the countries that came under German domination.[58] On one occasion, Pope Pius sent his nuncio to Berlin to plead with Hitler for the Jews. The interview ended with Hitler smashing a glass at the nuncio's feet.[59] Pius felt he could not speak out without exciting even more harm to the people for whom he would plead. The weight of the evidence indicates that there was considerable basis for this belief.

But as a private individual, Pius conducted himself in a fashion that unmistakably indicated the direction of his sympathies. When the Germans demanded a ransom in gold for Rome's Jews, he had a score of priceless relics melted down to help the community make up that sum. He spent the entire fortune he had inherited as a Pacelli in order to help the Jews escape to freedom in other parts of the world.[60] Pinhas Lapide, an Israeli who at one time was a consul in Milan, has written: "The Pope deserves a memorial forest in the Judean Hills with 860,000 trees, [which is] the number of Jewish lives saved through his efforts."[61]

Harry Sions once published a lengthy article dealing with the help offered the Jews of Rome by the Vatican and the general population. It is his impression that "the Pope helped many to escape deportation and death. In the Vatican and in many other Church buildings, Jews were hidden until they could be smuggled out of the city. The Italian people generally did this, and it took so much courage to do it that I honestly don't know where they found it all. Remember, being found harboring a Jew meant an automatic death sentence. But thousands of people, both priests and ordinary citizens, risked it time and time again. I think it's a sign of deep ignorance when I hear someone criticize the Italians for lack of guts."[62]

The extent to which this help was offered by the Vatican, not only to the Jews but to almost anyone hiding from the Nazis, is described at length in Major Sam Derry's book *The Rome Escape Line*. Derry, a British officer who escaped becoming a prisoner of war by finding refuge within the Vatican's walls, became the head of the British Organization in Rome for Assisting Allied Escaped Prisoners of War. The mission of Derry's group was to keep the constantly growing number of escapees out of enemy hands, and in this he was aided by the Church and certain lay Italian organizations. His activities involved finding places for the soldiers and airmen to live and making sure that they had enough food, clothing, and medical supplies while waiting for the opportunity to get back to their own armies.

It was a remarkably successful enterprise. Even though there were literally thousands of Romans involved, it was never halted. Once it was temporarily curtailed after a leading Fascist newspaper printed an indignant article about British officers brazenly sitting around eating first-class meals in fashionable restaurants while the poor had difficulty in getting enough food to keep alive. In one attempt to break up the ring, the Germans began sending out informers dressed as priests, under the theory that all Allied soldiers were convinced that members of the clergy were auto-matic sources of aid for them.

After a while the Vatican became concerned at the number of Allied airmen and infantrymen within its properties, fearing that the Germans might consider this as vitiating the provisions of the Lateran Treaty which guaranteed the sanctity of Vatican property. The Swiss Guards were informed that they must keep a more vigilant watch over the gates; however, the ground rules did not substantially change. Major Derry mentions a long list of priests who were delighted to escort the escapees into the grounds at opportune times and places.

As the spring wore on, the Rome Escape Line became even more active. Anzio had enlarged the numbers of arrivals who were to be processed for transfer, generally to Switzerland. The only complaint Derry had during those busy days was the attitude of the American bomber crews. Sometimes they arrived in groups of six or seven expecting that the best hotel in Rome would be taken over for their reception.[63]

« 4 »

The Allied forces were still preparing themselves to shake loose from the Anzio beachhead and to break through the strong German positions stitched through the peninsula, and on the evening of March 6, Kesselring's chief of staff, Siegfried Westphal, the youngest general in the German army, was admitted to Adolf Hitler's presence at Berchtesgaden. The purpose of his visit was to plead with the Fuehrer to reconsider the decree that the Anzio "abscess" should be attacked until either the Allies were swept into the sea or the last German had died in the attempt. For three hours Westphal desperately tried to make his point that Army Group simply did not possess the manpower to make another major assault on the beachhead. In return Hitler told him, "I will do my best to bring about a speedy solution," implying that there were still resources that might bring about the victory which the realists among the High Command would have considered a miracle.

Westphal left, realizing that he had failed to convince his leader of the hopelessness of Kesselring's prospects. As he packed to return to Italy, he was visited by Field Marshal Keitel, who told him, "You're lucky. If we fools had said half as much, the Fuehrer would have had us hanged."[64]

Evidently Westphal's chief, Albert Kesselring, was not disposed to accept this as an unanswerable order. James Byrnes, the South Carolina statesman who functioned as "assistant president" to Franklin D. Roosevelt, noted in his papers: "On March 11, the Allied Commander-in-Chief in Italy, Field Marshal Alexander, learned through [the OSS] that General Kesselring and several German staff officers were willing to meet in Switzerland to discuss the surrender of the German Army in Italy." This meeting was canceled when the Russians, learning about the proposed parley, insisted that the negotiations be stopped.[65]

The Russians caused further problems when they began their efforts to deal directly with the Badoglio government. It was not until Roosevelt bluntly reminded them that there had been an agreement to channel all such contacts through an Allied Control Commission that this source of friction was eliminated.[66]

The warm atmosphere of friendship so noticeable at earlier meetings between the Big Three was now thinning out. On April 23, 1944, Winston Churchill, in a note to his Minister of State, said, "You will remember that we are purging all of our secret establishments of Communists because we know they owe no allegiance to us or to our cause and will always betray secrets to the Soviet even while we are working together. The fact of the two Communists being on the French Committee requires extremely careful treatment of the question of imparting secret information to them."[67]

CHAPTER VIII

MAY 1944

The German Supreme Command should have foreseen that after the establishment of the Anzio-Nettuno beachhead, the spring offensive of the considerably reinforced Allied Army, which had been anticipated for weeks, would not be conducted along the pattern of separate battles adhered to before, but that the Allies, employing superior forces on both fronts, would launch a well-coordinated though not simultaneous attack in order to smash both German armies.

— COLONEL GENERAL HEINRICH VON VIETINGHOFF[1]

AND now, a few tiny cracks and fissures began to appear in what had seemed to be an unflawed German military machine. Up until this point in the campaign, Kesselring had moved his troops about the battlefield like a virtuoso, seldom performing a wasteful or ungraceful feint, capitalizing upon every example of Allied inexperience to run up a skein of defensive masterpieces. The competence he displayed in the early months of 1944 still enhances his name, and the memoirs of every Allied general refer to the Field Marshal's brilliance. But, like football coaches, generals are aware that their reputations do not suffer when their opponents are known for sustained ferocity.

An interesting picture emerges when the statements recorded by subordinate German commanders after the war are used as the measure of the events of the period. It becomes evident that the "brilliance" of Smiling Albert began to run dry on May 11. From this point until Rome fell, his improvisations were no longer impeccable.

For the first time, Alexander and Clark began to make their moves with the kind of deftness that good generals show when they are confident of their men and their plans. Alexander's strategy for the spring offensive, and the execution of it by the Fifth Army under Clark and the Eighth Army under Leese, resembled nothing so much as a perfectly functioning motor, each piston driving smoothly and precisely in turn. And as the war in Italy went on, the legend of Kesselring's invincibility began to show signs of wear.

It started with a successful deception.[2] By leading Kesselring to expect another Anzio-type landing in his rear, Alexander forced the German to weaken his front lines. Then, quietly, Alexander began to shift his units into positions of maximum efficiency for the big push. Clark was given a sector running from the seacoast inland to the Liri River. His Fifth Army now became composed of seven American, four French,[3] and two British divisions. Five and a half of these divisions operated out of Anzio under the command of General Truscott. His other commanders were General Keyes and the Frenchman Alphonse-Pierre Juin. The Eighth Army on the right under Sir Oliver Leese continued the line through Cassino and extended on up into the mountains. The Allies now had twenty-eight divisions facing twenty-three German divisions.

On May first, Alexander met with Clark and Leese to co-ordinate the planning for the offensive. The commander of the Army Group stressed at the conference that his primary aim was to destroy the German Army and to pursue northward whatever was left of it. The taking of Rome would be only incidental to that drive. Both subordinates agreed, but there is reason to believe that each had mental reservations about treating the capture of Rome as a by-product.[4] Rome was more than another point on the map; it was the great and shining prize of the campaign, and whoever took it could expect to have it linked firmly with his name in the years ahead. This reservation became the subject for quietly bitter recriminations in the postwar world. No matter how casually the attempt is made to establish that "we really didn't care about Rome," the fact remains that everyone wanted it; the Americans, British, French, and almost every other one of the twenty-six nationalities under Alexander's command strained toward the prize.[5]

There is no greater testament to Alexander's ability as a commander than his harnessing of these diverse forces. During this period, in addition to British and American units, he also counted under his banner troops identified as New Zealand, South African, Canadian, Indian, Singhalese, Basuto, Swazi, Bechuana, Mauritian, Rodriguez Islander, Caribbean, Cypriot French, Polish,

Nepalese, Belgian, Greek, Brazilian, Syro-Lebanese, Jewish, Yugoslav, and Italian.[6]

The problems presented by such an extensive array of nationalities were described by Mark Clark during a discussion of the complexities of his own command. "I had many national groups in the Fifth Army," he recalled, "many of whom had different objectives, but this, I guess, is to be expected of any nation. But they also had different equipment and different languages, which made it difficult for me to shift them around. The Germans didn't have this problem. They could take a unit out of one division and put it in another without too much difficulty. We couldn't. My God, the troubles that were involved in just moving a division from one point on the front to another! If the roads were muddy and the trucks of one country had worn ruts in them, then another country following with trucks of a different gauge would invariably get fouled up and find it difficult to move. Many of them had different kinds of ammunition, so we were limited in the number of ammunition dumps we could put around. Sometimes the units insisted on using only their own equipment — like their own phones, and then communication with them became a terribly difficult thing. The German didn't have that. He had flexibility."[7]

Kesselring had other advantages in addition to flexibility. The Allied superiority in manpower on May 11 was more than nullified by the mountainous terrain which intensified the edge always held by a well-entrenched defender.

There was no question that Alexander and the Allies stood to lose heavily if the attack failed. As a matter of fact, the situation was so ambiguous a few weeks before the Allied offensive was scheduled to begin that Clark was spirited back to America to explain to the leaders of Congress and to President Roosevelt exactly what steps were contemplated.[8]

Clark's wife, "as fluttery as a schoolgirl," was permitted to meet him at the airport. Because it was felt that if his presence in Washington became known, the Germans would suspect that dra-

matic moves were about to take place, she remained hidden away
in the car that was to take him to General Marshall's home in
nearby Fort Myer. Mrs. Clark was shocked at the strain in the face
of her husband, as he came to the car. "He looked so thin and
tired," she recalled. "I had never seen him look like that before."[9] The intense concentration on the continuing problems of
the campaign, which many staff officers had construed as arrogance, had almost changed Mark Clark into a stranger to his wife.

The morning after his arrival, Clark asked General Marshall if
he might contact his mother. Marshall permitted this, but stipulated that it should be only by letter. Clark sat at Marshall's desk
and scribbled a note which Marshall made him read aloud in
order to make certain that military security had not been breached.

After several days of discussions with Marshall and Roosevelt,
Clark met with Congressional leaders at a small Washington
restaurant taken over for the night and guarded by a detachment
of military police. While all the guests ate oysters, throwing the
shells in a bowl in the center of the table, Clark described how he
intended to take Rome.

The discussion was a successful one. Clark's plans were endorsed by all. The possibility that he might be withdrawn from the
campaign in order to head the invasion of southern France received little attention because now there was a tacit agreement not
to weaken the Italian effort. Everyone was aware that Eisenhower
would begin his cross-Channel invasion of France within a few
months, but the American military establishment had bought the
British concept that the attack should be a one-front affair, at
least in its beginning stages. Clark was evidently not the only
American leader who wanted Rome.

It should be noted, however, that Alexander's strategy was
designed to offer maximum assistance to OVERLORD. By forcing
Kesselring to commit everything he had to offset the proposed
attack, Alexander intended to make it impossible for the German
commanders in France to draw upon Italy for reserves.

« 2 »

Alexander's plan was impressively simple. The Fifth Army and the Eighth Army in the trunk of the peninsula were to smash the Gustav Line now being held by the German Tenth under von Vietinghoff. As the Germans went backward, Truscott's force, now almost an army in size, would drive out of the beachhead, then turn at a right angle to trap the retreating Germans before they could reach the high ground of the Alban Hills and link up with von Mackensen's Fourteenth.

In order to gain the three-to-one superiority that Alexander felt he needed to achieve the breakthrough, it was essential to make the Germans believe that, at last, he regarded their Cassino defense as impregnable. As a matter of fact, on March 15, after another intense bombardment, Freyberg and his New Zealanders had made one more attempt to get through and had again been thrown back. The Germans, succumbing to the insidious "they shall not pass" mystique which often weakens the judgment of a defensive force, were sure that they had finally convinced the Allies that further efforts should be made elsewhere.

To encourage this belief, Alexander inaugurated a cover plan which gave every appearance of constituting the preparations for another amphibious landing, this time ostensibly at Civitavecchia, a port on the Tyrrhenian Sea about as far north of Rome as Anzio is south. This would force Kesselring to keep reserves well away from the point where the attack was actually to be delivered.

To achieve credibility for this elaborate scheme, the 36th Division was sent back to the Naples area to take a well-publicized refresher course in amphibious training. All roads leading to the training area were marked with the Maple Leaf insignia of the Canadian troops and several detachments from Canada actually participated in the exercises to make it seem as if it were going to be a joint operation. Allied aircraft repeatedly flew observation missions over the beaches of Civitavecchia.

While this bustle was going on, Alexander completed the night-time switching of the Eighth Army to the Cassino front. Strict silence and camouflage discipline was maintained. After a motorized unit left an area, its place was filled by dummy tanks and trucks so that enemy air reconnaissance would report an undisturbed status. When the Polish Corps found that the ban on daylight movement was impossible to maintain because of the amount of work involved in its move into Cassino, the road leading to divisional headquarters was shielded from the view of the monastery by miles of camouflage screens erected along the roadway.

The fire from Allied guns was reduced to a desultory tempo. Artillery exchanges became sporadic and were generally employed only during those nighttime periods when the enemy's attention had to be diverted from such quiet efforts as the repairing of the approaches to the Rapido River. The only noticeable Allied activity throughout the period stretching between the last failure to take Cassino on March 24 to the time in May when the attack kicked off was the increased naval activity in the ports of Salerno and Naples. And here it was logical for German intelligence to assume that the activity was preparatory to the expected amphibious landing.

The plan worked perfectly.[10] As late as the second day of the offensive, Kesselring was still under the misapprehension that only six Allied divisions were opposing the four that he considered ample for the defense of Cassino. In fact, there were thirteen poised to shatter the German belief that they could hold the heights for as long as they wished. The Germans felt comfortable and secure. Behind the Gustav Line, they had built another defense known as the Hitler Line. A third defensive belt in the Alban Hills was being constructed as a form of insurance. When completed, it would be named the Caesar Line. In the event that the Allies ever breached the first two bastions, the high hills of the Colli Laziali would afford the Germans a favorable arena in which to make the last-ditch stand before Rome.[11] In effect,

Kesselring saw these three interlocked lines of defense as a braking mechanism. By holding each position until the last moment, then extricating his troops and falling back to the next line, he felt he could dissipate the momentum of expected future offensives before they could develop into strategic break- throughs.[12]

As for the proposed landing, Kesselring simply could not see any source from which Alexander might draw enough men and materiel to mount it in any greater strength than was used in the sketchy initial assault at Anzio. He assumed that he would contain the landing with the same techniques that had worked so well in January.[13]

Only one element of Alexander's plan remained to be settled: the matter of timing. After many conversations with staff and subordinate commanders, it was decided that on May 11 the Fifth Army and Eighth Army offensives on the southern front would start up the Liri Valley and then head across the mountain ranges to link up with the beachhead forces, who would break out as soon as the situation became favorable enough. The direction taken by the beachhead forces later became the basis of the controversy which clouded the relationship between Alexander and Clark.

Fifth Army was assigned the primary job of driving up the coast toward Anzio. Clark determined that Highway 7, which alone ran along the coast, represented a road to suicide unless the formidable Aurunci Mountains which towered over it were also taken.[14] Thereupon he decided to do what the Germans had considered to be so impractical that they had made only scanty plans for a defense: he included the mountains in his scheme of attack and then drew a route through them for the French under Juin.

The Allies were ready. Enemy intelligence might report the front as somnolent, but as one company commander noted in his log, "As D-Day approached, the air was so thick with tension it could have been sliced."

The Germans were not ready. In addition to being taken in by mock preparations for an amphibious landing, they grossly underestimated the strength and the fighting capacity of the French Expeditionary Corps, they overrated the mountains as barriers, and they so completely failed to forecast the timing of the offensive that when the Allied attack began, the chief of staff of Army Group C, the Tenth Army commander, and the 14th Panzer Corps's commanding officer and chief of staff were all back in Germany on leave.[15]

« 3 »

The long stalemate on the southern front ended abruptly at 11 P.M. on May 11. One thousand big guns stretching across the peninsula from Cassino past the coastline to a naval flotilla at sea began a relentless pounding away at German positions. During the next twenty-four hours, nearly 174,000 shells poured down on Kesselring's armies.

The Allied Air Force took off at dawn. During the previous month, they had been systematically seeking out and destroying rail, communication, and supply systems. Now they stepped up their tempo, flying fifteen hundred sorties in support of the advancing infantrymen.

And none advanced faster or further than the French during the first week of fighting. The most significant penetration of the Gustav Line was made by the Goumiers, the Colonial troops under Marshal Juin. One of the Allies' greatest handicaps in Italy was the lack of troops specially trained in mountain warfare. But now they were here. The Goumes and the French divisions which made up the French Expeditionary Corps were hard and seasoned mountain fighters who regarded this type of terrain as an opportunity rather than an obstacle. Unexpectedly vaulting into the hills, they overran all the German positions in their path. In three days, they had traveled six miles through this terrain, engulfing the key massif, Mount Majo, and had fought their way to the heights overlooking the Liri Valley while destroying seventy per cent of the combat strength of the German 71st Division.[16] This created the leverage needed to loosen the Gustav Line. The path was eased for the British troops to outflank Cassino and press up the valley. The American II Corps also felt the relaxation of the German pressure as they charged forward on the left near the coast.

At all times, the French stayed in the van. They created military history as they swept from massif to massif. American engineers, after surveying the territory during the days of stalemate, had considered the route impossible to supply. The French thought differently. They said that the mules could be led in the path of the foot soldiers and, in what amounted to a logistical miracle, made good their estimate. Later, General Westphal was to describe Marshal Juin's offensive as a major surprise because of its aggressive daring. Clark is on record as regarding it as the assault that broke the way into Rome.[17]

Ironically, the plan was not a new one. Although Alexander and Clark and finally Juin each in turn regarded it as a fresh concept, it had first occurred to Geoffrey Keyes while studying in Paris before the war. During this period, he had traveled the famous battlefields of Europe. When he came to Cassino, he put himself in the place of Hannibal, who had been trying to bring his Carthaginian legions up from the south to the gates of Rome and, like the Allies, had foundered at the sector dominated by the hills overlooking the Rapido River. Keyes had concluded at that time that troops could come from the south only if Cassino could be outflanked in almost exactly the same spot that the French now made their breakthrough. Keyes had submitted this plan in the early days of the campaign to Fifth Army, who then passed it over to the British. But the Eighth Army categorically rejected it as "a tactical monstrosity."[18]

There were others besides Clark and Alexander who took pride in the explosive progress of the French through the mountains. General de Gaulle, visiting the front at this time, noted that Clark "made a good impression on me . . . because he remained simple and direct in the exercise of his command. There was all the more merit in this because among the American generals, he was the first to command an army in the Western theatre and his country was therefore eager for his success."[19]

De Gaulle, whom the Allied infantrymen generally referred to as "Big Charley," proudly described the accomplishments of his countrymen: "The French Army in Italy achieved precisely what its leader had planned . . . after years of humiliation and dissension, what a magnificent spectacle the troops . . . offered us!"[20] The French troops themselves were unconcerned with this kind of rhetoric. One of their captains said it all when he simply told a correspondent, "It's hard to explain a man's emotions when he is fighting to get back home. Our men would go through hell to do it."[21]

Zeke Cook, a *Newsweek* reporter with the French forces, sent back his description of Juin's men during one phase of the battle: "Up the road rumbled American M–4 tanks and trucks full of French infantry with rifles slung on their backs. Aboard jeeps, their officers are reckless as New York taxi drivers, weaving in and out of the column, heedless of shell pockets in the road. Bound for the rear come ammunition carriers and jeeps with the wounded on stretchers placed crosswise, their covering sheets billowing in the wind. Farther back they are transferred to ambulances driven by pert Frenchwomen who can navigate the roughest roads of Italy."[22]

"Those damned Frenchmen," said General Vietinghoff. "We will exhaust them yet. I wish we could say we had done it already!" But in spite of their exasperation, the Germans found no way to contain this thrust. Instead, they found it necessary to draw to this front the bulk of their reserves, including some formations from in front of both the II Corps and the Eighth Army. It took a series of urgent pleas by Vietinghoff finally to persuade Kesselring to release enough reserves to help try to block the path to II Corps.[23]

After eight days, the French had almost completely destroyed the right wing of the German Tenth Army. Like a spring flood they had gushed over the land. The three divisions and the Goumiers who made up the French Expeditionary Corps, commanded by officers of exceptional ability, had left the broken Gustav Line behind them and were now threatening to turn the Hitler Line — a threat so imminent that the Germans, in an effort to disconnect their Fuehrer's name from certain defeat, hastily renamed this secondary defense the "Dora Line."

In the meantime, on their left, the II Corps fought its way through the lines to take Itri, a small but strategic town on Highway 7 located a few miles northwest of the coastal town of Formia. This permitted Clark to release the 36th Division from its reserve status and begin preparations for shipment to Anzio, where it would participate in Truscott's coming offensive.

After the seizure of Formia, Robert Porter recalls that the move forward "actually became a battle of engineers repairing broken bridges and a problem in logistics. We had two infantry divisions [the 85th and the 88th], Corps headquarters and Corps artillery using this one road, the old Appian Way, and there was a great deal of competition to get forward. At Terracina, up ahead, the road went through a narrow wall of rock that had been cut out by hand against the sea many centuries ago. The Germans had blown up the road in several places in front of this aperture and this made it difficult to get through. Once, General Keyes, getting impatient, went up to see what was taking so long to put the road in shape so we could get around Terracina. He got to about three hundred yards in front of the city's walls and found only one of our bulldozers at work. The operator would make one pass around the turn in the road before he apparently became visible to the enemy's machine guns, which would open up on him. The driver would wait about ten minutes and make another quick sortie, pushing a load of dirt in front of him. He was all by himself in this hot dirty place. General Keyes worked his way up the mountain side of the dugway and called the operator to get off his vehicle and tell him what the situation was. The man did, brushing off his dirty uniform and swearing a blue streak as he came to General Keyes. After saluting, he said that the goddam Heinies were interfering with his road but he was getting forward as fast as possible. It dawned on the General that this man was taking on the entire rear guard of the German army in Terracina all by himself. Keyes lost no time in getting some infantry up to clear out the area and, later that night, personally pinned a Silver Star on the brave man."[24]

Captain Nic Malitch was one of the busiest officers in II Corps during this period. The highly fluid situation made knowledge of enemy dispositions more vital than ever, and Nic, sleeping only in snatches, continuously interrogated prisoners and Italians suspected of having information of enemy movements. Occasionally his sense of urgency, sharpened by fatigue, led him into acting even more brutally than usual. During one interrogation of a civilian suspected of flashing signals to the enemy, he so frightened the man that in an effort to save his life he not only confessed to his own guilt, but also implicated his family. After the confession, Malitch told him, "You know, you are a most worthless bastard. Anyone who would blame the members of his family for what he has done does not deserve to live. But I have given you my word I will not kill you." He then turned to a sergeant standing by and added, "But Sergeant, you have given no such word. Kill him immediately!"[25]

By the morning of the twenty-fifth, the 85th Division had taken Terracina, the last sizable city on the road to Anzio.

On the right flank, the Eighth Army had entrusted the capture of Monte Cassino to the Polish Corps. The Poles, like the French, were men each of whom had endured great difficulty in reaching the front lines. Escaping from their ravaged country, or from the prisoner-of-war camps in Germany and Russia, they had little hope that the world they had known could be restored. The families of many of them had been put to death and their country was suffering from an even more desperate fate than occupation — the prospect of obliteration. There were few in the Polish ranks

(Above) *US Generals Mark Clark and Geoffrey Keyes study a battle map on an Italian mountain top, November 1944.* (Below) *The British Generals in Italy:* (left to right) *General Alexander, Lt-General Allfrey and General Sir Alan Brooke, visiting the 8th Army.* (Keystone)

(Left) *General Frido von Senger und Etterlin –
Commander of the 17th Panzer Division.*
(Wiener Library)

(Below) *Lt-General Heidrich and Field
Marshal Kesselring discussing strategy during
the campaign.* (Keystone)

who were not convinced that after their enemy Germany had been defeated, another agonizing struggle with their "ally" Russia remained. These were men who had lost everything but implacable hatred. For them this campaign was a crusade and the intensity of their emotion sometimes passed beyond the understanding of the British soldiers who fought alongside them.

Their commander, Lieutenant General Wladyslaw Anders, had begged for this chance to fight in Italy. When General Maitland Wilson had asked how the corps would be reinforced in the event of casualties, Anders replied that reinforcements would join from the front lines. "We have no country behind us," he said, "to get our reserves from, but we know that at the first news of Poles fighting on the Continent, all Poles, above all those who have been conscripted by force into the German Army, will join us!"[26]

In a day of bitter fighting, much of it in hand-to-hand combat, the Poles and the British XIII Corps broke the enemy's northern defensive ring. On the morning of May 18, a patrol of the 12th Podolski Lancers wiped out the last thirty German soldiers in the ruins. Before noon, the Polish flag flew above the ruins of the once impregnable monastery. Now, all of the German defenders in the valley below Monte Cassino found that their positions had become untenable. Their commander drew them back to defend the Hitler-Dora Line, but this became another movement into peril. The position was already in danger of being outflanked from the south by the triumphant advance of the French and the II Corps on its flank.

Alexander had considered the Liri Valley the best route to Rome, but this is where the British had found the going the toughest. The German positions confronting them were the most solid in the entire line of attack, and as a result, the Eighth Army could make little headway in the opening stages. Sir Oliver Leese found himself the object of severe criticism because the slowness of his troops increased the vulnerability of the French flank adjoining them. The faster the French went, the more exposed they became as the British failed to keep pace. But it should be emphasized that the British had been given the hardest part of the assignment. Their success depended almost completely on the threat of envelopment becoming so strong to the Germans that they would be forced to pull back. Proof of the British desire to press the attack is that the XIII Corps alone suffered four thousand casualties in these first few days.

Finally, and slowly, the British attack ground forward. Its advance contained none of the slash of the French movement, nor was it highlighted by dramatic spectacles like the stolid advance of the Poles up the mountainside in the face of withering fire. But nevertheless, it was productive. It soon became apparent that the British drive could crunch on through the Hitler Line as it was now doing through the Gustav defenses. Winston Churchill, evidently feeling that this lack of color might give rise (as it did) to comments that the British were allowing the French and others to carry the weight of the battle, sent this message to General Alexander on May 23:

Your battle seems to be approaching its climax, and all thoughts here are with you. Owing to the enemy pivoting backwards on his left, the advances of the French and the Americans are naturally filling the headlines. Your well-deserved message to the Poles also gained them great prominence.

At Cabinet yesterday some queries were made as to whether the part played by the British troops was receiving proportionate notice. They have been up against the stiffest and most unyielding parts of the line. We do not want anything said that is not justified, but reading the current press one might well doubt if we were making any serious contribution. I know of course what the facts are, but the public may be upset. Could you therefore bring them a little more into the communiqués, presuming of course you think that such mentions are deserved?[27]

In answer, Alexander next day sent off a telegram in which he barely hid his jubilation. The message presents the clearest possible picture of the ending of the frustration in southern Italy:

Herewith some interesting and pleasant facts. My usual daily report to C.I.G.'s follows through normal channels.

The Gustav Line, which the enemy has been preparing all winter, and which was guarded by Rapido River, was penetrated by both armies in the initial assault, and the enemy was driven out of it in first week of battle. Cassino, which was an almost impregnable fortress, was turned by a brilliant pincers movement, which ended by isolating it from the battlefield.

The much-vaunted Adolf Hitler Line, fortified by wire, mines, and concrete and steel pillboxes, has been smashed on the front of Eighth Army.

The beachhead enabled us to position a strong force on the German rear flanks, which is now in operation to complete another larger pincers maneuver. The deepest penetration up to date is a distance of thirty-eight miles as the crow flies.

In the Anzio sector the Americans have advanced four thousand yards through heavily prepared fixed defenses, and have surrounded Cisterna.

We have taken over ten thousand prisoners and killed and wounded a large number of enemy, of which figures are not yet available. Owing to extent of battlefield and rate of advance, it has not been possible yet to check the materiel captured, but it includes not less than a hundred guns of various types and a great deal of ammunition and other equipment. Much mechanical transport has been destroyed and damaged by our air forces, who claim at least a hundred vehicles destroyed today.

Of German divisions that have been engaged, the 71st and 94th Infantry Divisions have been destroyed as fighting formations. The 1st Parachute Division, 90th Panzer Grenadier Division, and 15th Panzer Grenadier Division have lost the greater part of their effective strength. Heavy losses have been inflicted on 26th Panzer Grenadier Division, 715th and 362nd Infantry Divisions; 576th Regiment, 305th and 131st Regiments, 44th Division, have also been practically wiped out. All enemy reserves, including a division which was believed to have been north of Rome, have been drawn into the battle, and there are strong indications that the Hermann Goering Division, which was in O.K.W. Reserve, is on its way south to try to stem the tide, though this cannot be referred to in public, as this division has not yet been identified in the fighting.

Cooperation between the two armies and Allied Air Forces has been quite excellent. British, American, French, Canadian, New Zealand, Indian, and Polish troops have all been engaged in fighting. British troops have played a conspicuous part in very bitter fighting, especially for the crossings over the Rapido River and in turning Cassino from the south. I will see that they have their share of publicity in the communiqués. British and American Air Forces have combined in both the close and more distant support of both armies. Allied naval forces are cooperating by bombardment and by the movement of troops and stores by sea. It is, and will continue to be, in every sense an Allied battle.

Finally, we have freed five hundred square miles of Italy from the grip of the German aggressor in under a fortnight.[28]

« 4 »

At last Truscott began his final preparations to get away from the resort beach which had turned into a prison for his VI Corps. The offensive would not be an easy one. Although von Mackensen's five and a half divisions were outnumbered by the seven divisions that Clark had assembled within the narrow perimeter, the advantage of holding the high ground still remained with the Germans.

But there were three other factors which gave the Allies the edge in the situation: command of the air; the advantage of surprise, because the Germans did not know when the attack would take place; and, finally, the fact that Truscott had infected his men with his fighting spirit.

D-Day at Anzio was set for 6 A.M. May 23. Because the linking of the Anzio forces with the main body of the Fifth Army had become a concern which had haunted Mark Clark for months, he could not resist the impulse to be on hand when the jumpoff came. He spent the hours before dawn sitting with Truscott in an artillery observation post just behind the line of departure. Neither man said much. It had rained during the night, but now the stars suggested that the day would be clear. The artillery batteries on both sides were almost silent and there was no sign that more than 150,000 Allied soldiers were crouched in the darkness waiting to explode into the enemy lines.

At 5:45, the big land- and naval-based guns broke into one thundering roar that continued for forty minutes. The enemy's lines were lit by walls of fire as the shells crashed down upon them. Then, suddenly, the shelling stopped and swarms of light and medium bombers flashed in the sky, their loads creating new geysers of earth and steel and smoke in the hillsides. As they banked and left, the signal was given. Like a pack of famished hunting dogs, the men of VI Corps bolted for the hills which had contained them for so long. The tanks of the 1st Armored Division lumbered alongside them in as many clattering waves as Colonel Hamilton H. Howze, the division's reserve commander, could space in the time allotted.

The attack was sudden and vicious, and it gained complete surprise for the Americans who made up the majority of the assault force. Although the German infantry recovered quickly, the preliminary bombing had torn their communications systems apart and all defensive actions could be described only as local and piecemeal — an impotent condition in the face of an attack as well coordinated as this had been.[29]

By noon, Bob Frederick's mixed force of Canadians and Americans had cut Highway 7 and were racing inland toward Cisterna, where the Germans had concentrated the bulk of their strength. By evening, the 1st Armored Division had smashed the enemy's main line of resistance by crossing the Cisterna-Campolene railroad. All other units had reached their initial objectives, and the Germans, although still holding together, were going backwards. General von Mackensen tried to get permission to pull his left flank out of the area and back to the Lepini Mountains, but this was refused by Kesselring.

The next day VI Corps troops encircled Cisterna. Although the Germans mounted a dozen counterattacks in tank formations, they were beaten back each time. The following morning, Cisterna and a thousand German prisoners fell into the hands of the 3rd Division. The ring around the beachhead had finally been cracked by the men whom a German radio spokesman in Sweden described as "farmers from Texas and Alabama, broad-shouldered and strong . . . who fight well, particularly in hand-to-hand battles."[30]

The 36th Division, arriving at Anzio the day before the breakout, supplied the broad-shouldered "Texans" referred to in this report. One of them, W. A. Garrard, learned about the chaos behind the German lines in a particularly vivid manner: "My squad and I were eating our K rations during a break in the fighting on the second day," he recalls, "when all of a sudden we heard a plane coming down. It was one of ours and it looked like it was going to come right down on top of us. It crashed a little way away from us and then I heard somebody holler, 'There he is!' and we saw the pilot coming down in this parachute. At first he thought we were Germans, but when we ran up to him and started hugging him, he got mighty happy. He told us that he had been out knocking over trucks and motorcycles and other vehicles when he had caught a shell from a German flakwagon. Before he caught it, he said, it had been like shooting fish in a barrel. Every road behind the lines was clogged with German vehicles of every kind. He said that his outfit had been flying for two days with almost no rest in between missions, that the Air Corps was doing everything they could to hit everything in sight."[31]

At 7:31 A.M. a II Corps engineer lieutenant named Francis Xavier Buckley was driving his jeep northwards from Terracina along a coastal road. Stopped by a blown-up bridge, he and the enlisted man accompanying him got out to walk. They had only taken a few steps when they saw a platoon of Allied soldiers approaching them. A captain from Hawaii named Ben Souza growled at them, "Where the hell do you think you're going?"

"I'm trying to make contact with Anzio forces," answered Buckley.

"Boy," said Captain Souza, "you've made it!"[32]

The quick linking of the II Corps and VI Corps had caught everyone by surprise. Even Mark Clark, who was rarely found far away from any scene of dramatic action, didn't get to the broken little bridge before 10:30. He was so delighted that he could only beam as the two task forces formally shook hands for the benefit of the photographers and correspondents. "It's a great day for the Fifth Army," he kept telling everyone around him.

« 5 »

A few miles away in Rome, the news seemed too good to be believed. Admiral Maugeri wrote, "Those were feverish, exciting, delirious days during that month of May 1944! Under the pile-driver blows of the Allied attack, the German resistance crumbled each day, each hour, minute, and second. Yet, painfully remembering Salerno and Anzio, we dared not hope, we dared not even dream of victory."[33]

The heavily censored Roman newspapers carried headlines that proclaimed German and Fascist "victories" and reports that the Allied forces were being decimated. But no one mistook the steadily growing list of captured towns being announced by the British Broadcasting Corporation as a prelude to another rabbit coming out of Kesselring's cap. The Germans were simply making too many pleas for civilian help in a "last-ditch" defense.[34]

Peter Tompkins discovered that his OSS operation had become one of the most popular organizations in the city. Everyone seemed to be telling everyone else about it and, he recalls, "I found myself confronted with a wealth of offers of help. Everyone who had the slightest suspicion of the existence of the organization now wanted to join it. With the Allied occupation of Rome imminent, Italians whose cooperation had not been conspicuous in the past were falling over themselves in the scramble to offer their services to anybody with the slightest claim to be an enemy of Germany."[35]

Not everyone was jubilant. Some were more frightened of the Germans now than they had ever been in the past. Rumors swept the city to the effect that the Gestapo was making a house-to-house canvass, shooting on sight all who were suspected of being Allied sympathizers. It was widely believed that the Germans would use the civilian population as a vent for the frustration and impotent anger generated by their inability to contain Alexander's forces anywhere for any length of time.

Jane Scrivener made several somber diary entries which reflected this feeling: ". . . and all the time the Allies are nearing Rome; joy at their approach is balanced by dread of German savagery. As I write, it is getting on to midnight, and the streets are strangely quiet; there is no sound but 'halt!' occasionally shouted at a passing vehicle, followed by the screech of brakes. Hope rises as the Allies progress. We have waited for over eight months, but now every added hour seems interminable."[36]

« 6 »

This was the moment when the military life of Sir Harold Alexander should have reached up and touched its zenith. And this is the way future generations will probably regard the last few weeks in May and the first week in June 1944. The squabbling and the politically inspired misunderstandings of the generals will be footnotes at best, and all that will be remembered and studied is how he employed the light sure touch of a master surgeon in opening Rome to his armies.

For the first time he had all the troops, materiel, and supplies that he needed. His subordinate commanders were first-class men. Clark had become a seasoned veteran, judging the terrain's potential with far more accuracy than the Germans opposing him and achieving maximum efficiency by shifting his forces with split-second precision. Oliver Leese was proving to be a tenacious bulldog as his men slowly but methodically ground up the bulk of the German strength. Juin and Anders were inspirational leaders at the head of inspired men, and the corps commanders were acknowledgedly capable of commanding armies of their own at any time and in any arena; Keyes had driven his II Corps sixty miles through the mountains in fourteen days to link up with Truscott, who by dispatching his men out of the beachhead like so many bazooka shells had cracked the backbone of German offensive power.

Alexander operated this machine faultlessly; two weeks after the offensive began, everything was working exactly as he had planned. The Gustav Line and the Hitler-Dora Line had been smashed. The German Tenth Army was in full retreat and it was obvious that it would be soon joined by the Fourteenth. Alexander outgeneraled Kesselring at every turn; every mistake that the German made was capitalized on by a quick Allied exploitation.

After the war, the German subordinate generals crowded Allied interrogation sessions with bitter criticisms of Kesselring's tactics during this period; they said he shared Adolf Hitler's ruinous disinclination to permit a backward step to the defending troops, so that the opportunity to make a successful stand at a stronger position invariably came too late. They accused him of handling his reserves in a grossly improper manner, committing them piecemeal in situations that were already lost, failing to estimate relative tactical strengths properly, and holding an overly optimistic view of the capabilities of his troops and the situations in which they found themselves. One thread runs through the transcripts in the National Archives: bitterness that he held too long to the belief that the Allies would continue making the same mistakes that had characterized the earlier battles. This is rooted in his subordinates' feeling that Kesselring's ego did not permit him to believe that he had any equals in Italy.[37]

Kesselring spent much of his postwar time defending himself from these charges. He declared that his generals were insubordinate, failed to advise him promptly of changes in the tactical situation, misunderstood on many occasions his defensive concepts, and too often exhibited a lack of command ability. He even chose the propaganda mill of Dr. Goebbels as a codefendant. Writing about the increase in Allied efficiency, he said:

I believe this development was due to a cardinal error of our German propaganda, which could not do enough to taunt the enemy for their lack of initiative, thereby goading them into a gradual change of operational principles. The method of cautious and calculated advance according to plan with limited objectives gave place to an inspirational strategy which was perfected through the months remaining till the end of the war. At that time I took energetic measures to put a stop to this foolish propaganda, but it had already been effective to our detriment.[38]

However, none of this should be construed to mean that the German army and its generals were in a state of collapse during the last two weeks of May. On the contrary, they fought with skill and tenacity, and to say that they exhibited any weakening of their superb fighting ability would diminish the record of Alexander and the Allied forces. Both sides fought well enough to win almost any campaign ever recorded. The difference was the generalship of Sir Harold Alexander.

These were his great days. But like everything else in the Italian campaign, a tarnish soon came upon them.

CHAPTER IX

MAY 28—JUNE 3, 1944

You see, we had been through this bitter winter at Cassino. I think it was the low point in the life of everyone who was there. Now, the prospect of taking Rome was like sunshine breaking out after four months of being locked in a kind of a dungeon. Even before Rome was captured, the jump-off attack was a tremendous psychological lift. Down to the lowest private there was a sort of a resurgence of spirit.

I remember the feelings of my fellow officers that by God we weren't going to let the British get there first! It was a landmark that we were sure we could attain and one that would go down in the history books.

— COLONEL ROBERT VAN DE VELDE[1]

« 1 »

THE argument had begun at the beachhead just before the breakout. During the first week in May, Alexander told Clark that as the
Army Group commander he reserved to himself the right to
determine the day and the direction of Truscott's attack.

Clark bridled at this. Although Alexander had spoken in the
tactful manner that had characterized all of his past discussions
with the Fifth Army commander, there was no question in Clark's
mind that he was now being told how to run his own business.[2] He
would have objected to this type of treatment under any circumstances, but with the scent of victory so unmistakably in the air,
he felt that there was something even more at stake — a suspicion
which grew in strength as Alexander began to outline his plan.

Briefly, the Englishman wanted the VI Corps to strike out
almost due east below the Alban Hills, cutting across both Route 6
and Route 7, which at approximately this point were beginning to
converge to their junction in Rome. The first goal of the VI Corps
would be Valmontone, a town through which all of the traffic on
Highway 6 must flow. Taking this goal, Alexander explained,
would mean that the escape route of the German Tenth Army
could be closed off. Then, as the British Eighth Army came up
through the Liri Valley, it would join with VI Corps and the trap
would be completed.[3]

Clark saw it another way. He told Alexander that he felt that
Truscott ought to be allowed flexibility of movement. Although
Lucas, given the same prerogative during the days when he
headed VI Corps, had failed to capitalize on the breaks, a differ-
ent course of action might be expected from a man like Truscott.
Clark said that he thought that the strength of the German

Fourteenth Army, which was facing the beachhead forces, presented no problem, because, as far as he could see, its commander, von Mackensen, had only one unit capable of causing trouble, the Hermann Goering Panzer Division. Further, he said, this plan did not contemplate the elimination of the Alban Hills as a site for the Germans to make a defensive stand. If they massed in those heights, a long and costly fight could be expected.[4] And, finally, Clark told his commanding officer, it was erroneous to believe that the only escape route that the Germans had was through Highway 6 at Valmontone; there were many more escape routes available in the area.[5]

What Clark *didn't* say was that a violent suspicion had suddenly flared within him. As the Englishman quietly and logically described the strategy involved, Clark became more certain with each moment that the plan represented nothing so much as a scheme to deprive his Fifth Army of the glory of capturing Rome.[6]

While Alexander reaffirmed the statement, which he had made on many previous occasions, that the only job for the Allied forces in Italy was to kill Germans, a man with Mark Clark's motivations could be expected to review the slowness of the British force as it came up the valley and, in this context, feel that perhaps he was being asked to use his French and American troops to help the Eighth Army do its job.

Literally hundreds of critiques have been written of the decision that Clark made. Some writers say that his actions constituted gross insubordination. Others say that he showed good judgment in reserving to himself the right to go after the prize of the campaign. Clark himself equivocates on the point. When asked for the reasons which moved him to disregard the spirit if not the exact letter of his orders from his superior, he answers that he believed the possession of the Alban Hills to be of paramount importance, that the Germans were by no means limited to Valmontone as an escape route, and he softens his evident belief that the English were not doing their share by saying, "You've got to remember that the longer troops fight, the more conservative they become — and the Eighth Army had been fighting for a hell of a long time."[7]

One need only glance back at the whole pattern of his conduct since the prewar days in Washington to realize that it would have been difficult for him to jeopardize the opportunity of taking Rome. But not even his most ardent detractors will claim that he was capable of ordering an action that he honestly felt wrong in order to gain further personal glory. Clark liked headlines, yet, as Robert Murphy remarked, "There were damned few of those generals who didn't."[8]

After the first meeting had ended with Alexander remaining adamant, Clark informed Truscott of his assignment but added that he should also develop alternate plans in case the battle should indicate a need for a change. Truscott complied. He produced four plans in which the emphasis was given to BUFFALO, the operation which embodied Alexander's directive.

However, by now Alexander knew Clark intimately. A few days later, the Englishman visited the beachhead to tell Truscott to forget about the development of alternatives and concentrate on taking Valmontone. When Truscott informed Clark of this conversation, Clark became angry.[9] He called Alexander and asked him to deal directly with him and to refrain from instructing his subordinates.

At a face-to-face meeting two days later, Clark repeated his conviction that the situation developing after the breakout might be hurt by a rigid operational concept. Alexander agreed that flexibility was a virtue, but restated his conviction that the VI Corps should drive east to Valmontone instead of north to Rome. He did not, however, issue a written order to this effect. The meeting ended with neither general having convinced the other of the validity of his position.

Finally, on May 20, an American general on the Army Group staff relayed an unequivocal order from Alexander to Clark: The VI Corps would attack toward Valmontone. Clark was shocked.

He now regarded Alexander's actions as high-handed interference. Recalling Alexander's frequent assertion that the Liri Valley was "the only way to Rome," he decided that his Fifth Army would no longer ease the way for Sir Oliver Leese. It was probably at this moment that he decided upon the method of straddling the issue in a way that would pay lip service to obedience but would not keep him from his prize.

On May 20, he moved to the beachhead to be with Truscott at the time of breakout. The next night, in the cellars of the Villa Borghese, which served as one of the command posts at Anzio, he met with the correspondents who were covering the attack. Standing in front of the huge war map, he detailed with sweeping gestures the progress in the south, and although he obviously could not breach military security by describing all of the phases of VI Corps's plans, the underlying note of his talk was the desirability of entering Rome. "We're going to take Rome," he assured the writers more than once during the night.

During this waiting period, the 36th Division arrived at Anzio. Clark lost no time in getting over to see Fred Walker. One of the men who was there at this meeting, Harold Bond, has written: "The army commander was determined to be the first to get to Rome. He seemed tense and excited as he explained these plans and delivered some curt instructions to our general [Walker]. Then, getting his caravan of jeeps in order, with his aides, his staff, and his photographer mounted, he pulled out of the camp with a rush, again leaving clouds of dust behind him."[10]

General Truscott noted in his memoirs that "Clark was fearful that the British were laying devious plans to be the first in Rome,"[11] and there is an abundance of other evidence that the commanding general was being dominated by the prospects of taking the city.

On the other hand, Ambassador Robert Murphy has since suggested that Mark Clark was not alone in the apprehension that the British were threatening to snatch away the victory which Roosevelt, Churchill, and Stalin had each described at separate

(Above) *Mussolini with Marshal Graziani and Pavelini (right), Secretary of the Italian Fascist Party. Graziani had just been appointed jointly by Hitler and Il Duce to command a new German-Italian army on the Italian front* (UPI). *Sprucely clad in new uniform, Mussolini (below) inspects a motorised division at Parma, northern Italy.* (Keystone)

'Rome Fell Today' – General Mark Clark at the triumphant climax of the Italian campaign. (UPI)

times as the campaign's plum. "There was a strong feeling," Murphy recalls, "that the British wanted to lead the procession into Rome just as Montgomery later wanted to capture Berlin. There's no doubt about that one — I think Alexander wanted to get into Rome first."[12]

There was one other reason why Clark assigned precedence to the taking of Rome over the capture of the bulk of the German forces in the area. On his April trip back home to meet with America's political and military leaders, he had been given the date for OVERLORD. He was aware that only a few weeks remained before the world's attention would be riveted on the beaches of France and that if Rome were captured after that time, the news would possess even less impact than that produced in the past few months by the fall of such obscure places as Gaeta and Terracina. Rome's value as a prize depended on timing. The fact that it would have been the first Axis capital to fall to the Allies would be meaningless to a world that considered the unmistakably looming cross-Channel invasion as the main event.

But ironically, while Clark gave and continues to give reasons for his decision which his critics consider to be only a transparent mask for his personal ambition, one of his chief adversaries in World War II saw sound military logic in his move. After the war, General Frido von Senger und Etterlin wrote:

We now know that the Allies were in two minds as to the best direction in which to launch the attack from their beachhead in order to be sure of destroying the German Tenth Army. That was bound to be the main object of the pursuit. Lord Alexander was particularly anxious to swing the forces in towards the locality of Valmontone, while his subordinate, General Mark Clark, commander of the U.S. Fifth Army, considered Rome to be the most important goal. While this latter viewpoint, like all strategic decisions, had a political basis, it also fitted in with the tactical concept of the parallel pursuit, which leads far into the rear of the evading opponent, thus forcing him to capitulate without any major battle.[13]

By "parallel pursuit" the German meant that by lancing northward through Rome, Clark would soon have been in a better
position to separate the retreating German Tenth Army and Fourteenth Army, a result that would have been tantamount to total
defeat of Kesselring's army group. On the other hand, von Senger
thought, in view of the British speed, that if Truscott went east in
full force, he would probably end up floundering in the difficult
terrain well beyond Valmontone before linking up with Oliver
Leese.[14] By this time, the majority of the Cassino defenders
would have escaped to the north.

Truscott broke out on May 23. It was an American enterprise in
that two British divisions from Anzio were attached directly to
Fifth Army. Clark felt that he could answer both Alexander's
demand and his own needs by splitting Truscott's force into two
prongs after a certain stage in the attack had been reached.

He talked with Truscott about it first. After VI Corps had
broken into the clear and just before the linkup with II Corps, he
asked his subordinate whether or not he considered it feasible to
have an alternate plan ready in case it looked as if the Germans
might escape through the Valmontone gap before the noose could
be drawn. Truscott said that he would do it, and that, further, it
seemed a logical precaution to take. He asked only that he be
given enough time to accomplish the complex logistics involved in
the change of principal directions.

The attack developed quickly into a dramatic success. On May
25, the day of the linkup, VI Corps also succeeded in taking the
key city of Cisterna along the route to Valmontone. Clark
promptly sent the word to Truscott to wheel the bulk of his forces
northward to Rome. Only a fraction of the corps would continue
on to Valmontone, but in this way the letter if not the spirit of
Alexander's order would be carried out.

Clark made certain that Alexander would have no opportunity
to interfere with this plan. He had his chief of staff, Major General
Albert Gruenther, inform the Army Group commander of the
tactical change a quarter of an hour after it began. Alexander,

confronted with a *fait accompli*, remained imperturbable. According to Gruenther, he seemed "well pleased with the entire situation" and instead of voicing disapproval added, "I am for any line which the army commander believes will offer a chance to continue his present success." Alexander then asked Gruenther whether Clark also intended to pursue the part of the attack extending toward Valmontone, and Gruenther assured him: "General Clark has the situation in mind and you can depend upon him to execute a vigorous plan with all the push in the world."[15]

Gruenther, reporting on the meeting to Clark, said that he could see absolutely no evidence of anger in Alexander's manner. In light of the subsequently published memoirs of the principals, it seems obvious that Sir Harold at this point was merely projecting his concept of the role of the Unflappable Englishman and that he was far from being as calm as he appeared to Gruenther. Later he wrote, "I had always assured General Clark in conversation that Rome would be entered by his army; and I can only assume that the immediate lure of Rome for its publicity value persuaded him to switch the direction of his advance."[16] For Sir Harold Alexander, whose military pronouncements even on the beaches of Dunkirk were consistently understated, this represents a rather grave indictment.

But the chief inspiration for the criticism which later followed Clark's conduct came from Lucian Truscott. Clark had always treated his junior with consideration and favor. He had always asked for, never ordered, Truscott's cooperation. When Clark was later elevated to Army Group commander, it was at his suggestion that Truscott replaced him as commanding general of the Fifth Army.[17] Yet Truscott's memoirs always constitute the primary arsenal when any writer or historian decides to take aim at Mark Clark.

Truscott wrote, "There has never been any doubt in my mind that had General Clark held loyally to General Alexander's instructions, had he not changed the direction of my attack on May 26th, the strategic objective of Anzio would have been accomplished in full. To be first in Rome was poor compensation for this lost opportunity." He described himself as "dumb-founded" when the order came to change directions and sought to characterize Clark as inept by asserting that "a more complicated plan would be difficult to conceive. It was practicable only because staff preparation was thorough and complete and it was carried out by well-trained and disciplined troops, and because enemy capabilities for interference were limited."[18] In effect, he assumed that Clark was saved from disaster only by the general superiority of VI Corps's performance, but Truscott evidently was unwilling to concede that Clark might have based his calculations upon it in the first place.

But the facts as disclosed by others who participated in the moment do not do Truscott much credit. To the Fifth Army operations officer, Brigadier General Donald W. Brann, who brought news of the plan to VI Corps, Truscott was quite enthusiastic. He said that he was confident that the weaker force would reach Valmontone by itself and that the only reservation he had concerned a proposed frontal attack on Velletri which was included in the scheme. This facet was deleted by Fifth Army planners and at 6 P.M., May 25, Truscott called Brann to say that he was entirely in accord and "I feel very strongly we should do this thing. We should do it tomorrow."[19]

That evening, at a meeting with his divisional commanders, Truscott enthusiastically presented the plan "as if it were his own," recalled one of the officers in attendance. "He told us that . . . the Boche is badly disorganized, has a hodgepodge of units and if we can drive as hard tomorrow as we have done in the last three days, a great victory is in our grasp!"[20] Still later that night, when Clark visited his command post, Truscott had no words of criticism. He was known to be an outspoken man. He was close enough to Clark to discuss freely the possibilities of any move, especially something so vital as a key attack. He chose instead to reserve his criticism of the plan for his postwar memoirs. It seems that there might be grounds for at least the suspicion that the place he was shortly to take in the race for Rome later affected the store of goodwill he had for his superior.

« 2 »

This backstage bickering was confined to the higher levels. Although the generals might squabble, the troops were aware that the cycles of frustration and stalemate they had endured since September were now giving way to something electrifyingly new: a victory so smashing in scope that it would be even past the abilities of their old tormentor, Albert Kesselring, to reassemble the broken parts into a new obstruction. The generals could not keep from thinking about the headlines that would announce the fall of Rome, but a sentence which appeared during these days in the morning report of an 88th Division unit most accurately mirrored the dominating sentiments of the anonymous infantrymen: "Every mile forward is a mile closer to home."[21]

The only question that apparently remained was who would actually capture the city. Which of the forces on the scene would thereafter be able to claim, "We were first in Rome"?

The record indicates that Clark wanted the honor for his friend, Lucian K. Truscott, Jr. "General Clark said at that time," recalls Geoffrey Keyes, "that the way he doped out the capture of Rome, VI Corps ought to get in first. He said that he felt that they were entitled to it, having withstood that hard seige at Anzio."[22]

It seemed by this time that II Corps was out of the picture. The IV Corps had been newly brought into being under the command of Major General Willis Crittenberger and Keyes had received orders to turn over his sector and troops to the fresh force.[23] As it now stood, VI Corps would push north on the side of the Alban Hills closest to the sea and into Rome; IV Corps and the French and the British on the right would blot up any remaining German pockets in the area around Rome.

At least this was Clark's plan. But it paid too little attention to the momentum supplied to the Germans by their past string of successes. Refusing to accept that total defeat was staring down the highway at him, Kesselring sent the tough Hermann Goering Panzer Division to Valmontone, where it effectively blocked the 3rd Division and the First Special Service Force which constituted the VI Corps element of attack to the east. Then he placed in the line before the VI Corps a new defensive force made up of whatever fragments he felt he could spare from the retreating Tenth and Fourteenth Armies. This ragtag collection fought a rearguard action skillful enough to stall the VI Corps while their regular units joined the stream running backwards through Rome.[24]

Kesselring's presence of mind was not shared by the German housekeeping organizations and the native Fascists in the city. The streets were crowded with marching columns, heading north, who no longer seemed quite so frightening. A fire broke out in the Pensione Jaccarino, the torture house of the Italian SS Battalion, and the Romans wondered whether it meant that the turncoats among them were destroying the evidence of their perfidy. The installations at two of Rome's airfields were mined and blown to smithereens. German wounded were being evacuated from the hospitals and German diplomats and journalists were leaving under the cover of these nights for safer bases in the north.

Clark was aware of these activities. The Partisans, Peter Tompkins's OSS organization, and others kept him apprised of the happenings in the city, but instead of heartening him, the news heightened his anxieties. The VI Corps, exhausted by almost two weeks of sustained hard driving and facing the larger part of the Fourteenth Army, was making slow progress in the fighting at the base of the Alban Hills. The 3rd Division and the Special Service Force which he had sent east to Valmontone were being blocked by the determined fight of the Hermann Goering Panzer Division. The IV Corps, which he had used to replace II Corps, was going nowhere, and on the right the French and the British elements were churning methodically forward, each passing hour bringing them closer to where either one of them might be in the logical position to swoop behind the fighting front and into the city.

Alexander, meeting with Clark during this period, offered with every appearance of helpfulness: "Wayne, if you can't do it, or if you feel that you're going to be tied down here, I'll direct the Eighth Army into Rome." Clark answered, "Well, you wait until I holler, because *we're* going to take it!"[25] After the meeting, he intensified the tempo of his troop-shuffling. General Keyes recalls, "There was a change there, every minute."[26]

And this was the moment when one of the most dramatic about-faces of the war took place. As much as he wanted to give the glory of capturing Rome to Truscott, Clark took back the troops he had given IV Corps, turned them over to Geoffrey Keyes and gave him a green light to go ahead into Rome.[27] He did this because Keyes had convinced him of a plan that Porter, Malitch, and the other planners had worked all night to evolve. Malitch had been a whirling mass of energy during these few days, making innumerable intelligence trips behind the German lines, fiercely interrogating every Italian and prisoner of war he could find, and generally radiating an unquenchable determination to get the raw material that Keyes, Porter, and the other leaders needed to convince Clark to let them make the bid for the prize they had worked so long to win.[28]

Robert Porter recalled the situation: "It didn't make General Keyes too happy to think that at this stage of the game that the IV Corps would replace us in the line. Actually, we were left with the band and a company of military police, and before we could really react to the order, they took these away from us, too. That left us with nothing but Corps headquarters. However, the roads were so jammed between Formia and Fondi and Terracina that before we could get any more orders, General Keyes put the Corps headquarters in a forward area and then flew down to Anzio to talk to General Clark about the maneuver.

"When he came back, he told us to go ahead. We worked all night, a planning team in almost every tent, getting together a proposal which would give us the 85th and the 88th divisions to move north on Valmontone, cutting Highway 6."[29]

The plan was based upon securing the heights above Valmontone, and then executing a wheel westward toward Rome over the Via Casilina. VI Corps would continue on its way west of the Alban Hills, getting into the city whenever it could.

Porter refrains from pointing out that the new proposal was, in large part, an idea conceived by Keyes and himself.[30] After it was complete, Porter was given the job of explaining the idea to the Fifth Army's chief operations officer, while Keyes went back to Clark to assert that the Germans were now in such a position that every Allied unit should be thrown into the line on the theory that the breakthrough could occur at any point.[31]

Clark bought Keyes's proposal. In addition to the 85th and 88th, he was given those elements of the 3rd Division now at Valmontone, the First Special Service Force, and a task force under Colonel Ham Howze from the 1st Armored Division. This extended the Fifth Army's flank far enough to the right to successfully pinch out the advancing French and English, who were still roughly twenty-five miles back on Highway 6 — a troop disposition that certainly enhanced the merits of the II Corps plan in Clark's eyes.

After the plan was approved, the officers who made up II Corps went into operation with smooth dispatch. They had been together for many months and each knew almost everyone else's capacity, because under Keyes there had been a relatively light turnover of personnel. Within twenty-four hours, they assumed control of the situation and, despite the choked road conditions, had taken over in what had been the French Corps zone of advance.

Valmontone fell, and on the next day the First Special Service Forces, the 3rd Division, and Task Force Howze were turned toward Rome. The 85th Division was moved over in front of VI Corps, to the considerable displeasure of Truscott and his staff, and the 88th began coiling for a leap to the city's gates.

The plan was intrinsically worthwhile. But beyond that, Clark since Anzio had shown increasing respect for Keyes's suggestions. Contrary to those who regarded him as an arrogant man, he was willing to listen to advice. Robert van de Velde recalls that occasionally when he and other members of the II Corps intelligence or operations sections found themselves in disagreement with the staff officers above them at Fifth Army, they took the problem to Keyes, who "in his quiet way, would force the issue up through the staff to Clark and often Clark would change or modify his estimates to conform to the convictions of the Corps Commander. Clark was always willing to listen to advice from what he considered was an authoritative source."

Van de Velde remembers Malitch clearly during these days. Even though the general atmosphere was frenetic, a telephone conversation he once overheard Nic holding with the motor pool reduced him to almost helpless laughter. Nic was roaring into the phone, "I mahst gat to de front!" Evidently the sergeant at the other end of the line couldn't hear him clearly, because he kept asking Nic to repeat. After a few minutes of this, Malitch fairly screamed: "EV-ERR-UNT, YOU SON OF A BITCH, I GOD TO GAT TO DE VRUNT!"[32]

Porter also testifies to the Russian's sense of urgency during this period: "Although I never cut Malitch in on the complete operational plan, I'd give him a specific problem and send him out to whatever area we were evaluating, and he always came back with a factual report which permitted us to then go ahead and dispose of reserves or to position the artillery to help our people get forward. Overall, he made a very fine contribution. He was a very objective and a very courageous man. He was very astute; he had a tactical judgment and sense that was greater than that possessed by many of our people. He really had a splendid military mind. In peacetime, he may have been a sort of a restless duck out of water, but in the confusion and stress of the battlefield, he was calmly objective."[33]

It was about this time that the 36th Division made the decisive break at Velletri through the German ring that was described in the first chapter of this book. The race to Rome was now on in earnest.

« 3 »

Preventing the Allies from encircling the city had become the job of the German Fourteenth Army. Straggler collecting points had been set up throughout the area, and men who had become detached from their organizations during the pullback were gathered here, formed into units, and sent to von Mackensen to help him fight the rearguard action that was supposed to delay Alexander's forces long enough for the Tenth Army to escape the closing noose.

These preparations did not go unnoticed in the city. The almost superstitious fear of hoping too much was now becoming diluted by the signs of a general German loss of confidence. Admiral Maugeri, taking his customary walk through the city on one of these evenings, was struck by

something strange, something different tonight. The traffic. It had mysteriously changed direction. When I had started out, it was rolling southward, as it had been for weeks and months before. Now it had reversed direction. At first, it had only been a few vehicles, a mere trickle; but now the trickle had become a steady stream and the stream a torrent. It was heading toward the Via Flaminia, toward the road to Civitavecchia, Florence, Bologna, and the safety of the North.

I stood watching for some time, fascinated, trembling with joy and excitement. There were artillery pieces of every size and caliber. There were trucks in endless procession, piled high with all sorts of vital equipment — machine-guns, searchlights, mortars, field kitchens, rifles, motorcycles, miscellaneous furniture, rations — and all of it tossed together in great haste and disorder. And piled on top of this materiel were hundreds upon hundreds of men who had once been soldiers, tired, dirty, grim, defeated. This, this was once the proud and invincible Wehrmacht, the greatest army since Napoleon's, the savage conquerors of Europe, now in full flight before the decadent democrats.[34]

Jane Scrivener's diary entry for June 1 read:

The Allies have taken Frosinone and Sora, both of them important places, but the line from Valmontone to the sea is still unbroken. A B.B.C. commentator says breezily: "Rome, of course, is a prize, but how much better for General Alexander to surround Kesselring and settle his hash before entering the city." Oh yes? Is it? We are not strategists, armchair or otherwise, but we have practical knowledge of the urgent need of liberating Rome.[35]

Her term "urgent need" probably referred to the general belief that the Germans would loot the city if they decided against making a defense of it. The German occupation troops under General Maelzer had been vigorous participants in the black market, and there was no reason to believe that they would resist the temptation to take with them everything that they could carry. Maelzer himself accumulated large stores of tobacco which his agents disposed of to the Italian black market dealers without disclosing their principal. A few days later, the commander of Rome sent SS units to raid the dealers and confiscate their stocks, which were then returned to his stockpile.[36]

In another diary entry, Jane Scrivener commented:

Although many Germans left yesterday, at present the hotels near the station are crowded with them. They must be those who have come in from the Castelli on their way north. All last night heavy vehicles, tanks and lorries rumbled northward through the streets, Via Cassia, Via Salaria, and Via Flaminia being still open for them. Yesterday, near here in Piazza Fiume, Germans systematically emptied a hardware shop, packing all the goods very carefully in a covered truck, so as to travel without shifting and to take the smallest space possible.[37]

However, black market goods, especially food, were beyond the reach of most ordinary families. The lack of food had a dramatically slimming effect not only on the poor but on most of the middle class. It became a matter of tact to avoid commenting on a friend's loss of weight.

Fortunately for the civilian population, the approach of the Allies began to act as a deterrent to the actions of even such Germans as Maelzer. Father Carroll-Abbing notes:

> The Germans were more realistic . . . a popular uprising at that moment would have been a disaster. There was even a free distribution of flour in the poorer quarters of Rome. General Maelzer could not refrain even now from having the photographers there, but this time he did not have the soldiers retrieve the food after the photographs had been taken. The madman, who had ruled Rome like a Nero, was nearing the end of his reign of terror.[38]

There were others in Rome who had an interest in the approach of the Allied troops. Peter Tompkins enjoyed listening to the broadcasts of progress by the Fifth Army radio station but complained: "I wish to God, though, they would quit broadcasting the names of Italian spies for the Germans. We have hundreds and hundreds of them listed, with names and addresses and telephone numbers, and have our men ready and waiting, not to catch them, but to shadow them and that way get at the real spies, not just the small fry. Now, every time a name is mentioned over the Fifth Army radio the SS drive up to the guy's house, pick him up (whether he wants it or not) and send him off to northern Italy. So I wish to God they'd shut up broadcasting the names."[39]

Sam Derry, the British officer who directed the escape route for Allied soldiers from a post inside the Vatican, not only listened to the broadcasts, but actually originated one. A radio operator in the Vatican told him that the British forces were contacting him in an effort to find out whether the Germans intended to try and hold onto the city. Derry took over the microphone:

> "Who are you?" crackled a voice.
> "Major Derry, First Field Regiment."
> "Where the hell are you?" asked the liaison officer.
> "In the Vatican," I answered.

"Yes — have you any idea what is going on in Rome?"

At that moment I had a very good idea indeed. From the high window where I stood, there was a clear view of German vehicles and lines of infantrymen, in single file with their weapons at the trail, crawling comfortably northward along the Via Aurelia, which flanked the Vatican City's high wall. "The Jerries appear to be withdrawing from the city very nicely," I said.[40]

One more voice is worth listening to. Regarding the atmosphere of the city, Lieutenant General Kurt Maelzer, in a statement he gave to his Allied captors after the war, said: "As for the mood of the Roman population, it was depressed by the events in prospect. When the population was notified by the German side that Rome would not be defended and that no blasting would be done, it received the news with satisfaction. There were two schools among the population: one, though the minority, inclined to enter into active opposition against the retreating Germans, the other willing to remain loyal. The Roman agencies, thinking disturbances probable and touching upon this question towards the Germans, were advised by them that 'Rome's fate is solely and entirely in the hands of the Romans themselves.' The Roman population understood these words and acted accordingly. Thus, the Allied encouragement, issued over the radio on the evening of 3 June 1944 and again on the morning of 4 June, to participate in the final battle against the Germans remained unheard."[41]

There is no question that Maelzer misread the mood of the Romans. What he believed to be a majority who "remained loyal" consisted, in reality, of those who read a sincere threat into the statement that Rome's fate was in their hands. The plain truth is that they did not know whether Rome would be defended. And neither did the Allies.[42]

An American bomber pilot who had been shot down and taken prisoner by the Germans and who escaped during this period told Allied intelligence officers: "I heard many Germans declare that they intended to make Rome a second Stalingrad."[43]

General Clark sent a telegram to all units voicing his uncertainty. Today he declares: "We were reading the German's mail pretty good [i.e., getting first-class intelligence reports] and we didn't think he would defend."[44] But a message that he sent to the commanding officer of the 339th Infantry Regiment certainly indicates that he was less than confident: "We are now approaching Rome. Do not know if the Krauts are going to defend. It is urgently desired that private and public property in Rome not [be] damaged. Firing into Rome depends upon Krauts. If opposed, Battalion Commanders and higher Commanders have power to eliminate same by fire and movement."[45]

There were others who had serious doubts that Rome would escape the devastation that occurs when the possession of a city is decided through a series of street-by-street fights. The Pope, no doubt aware that Adolf Hitler would be acting in a highly untypical manner if he concerned himself over the sanctity of the Eternal City at a time when his own capital, Berlin, was undergoing almost nightly bombing attacks, held a series of emergency meetings with German generals and diplomats. Afterwards, on June 2, he told his College of Cardinals that it was his hope that "moderate treatment will prevail," and then voiced this warning, obviously meant for both warring sides: "We do not hesitate to repeat once more with equal impartiality and dutiful firmness that whoever would dare lift a hand against Rome would be guilty of matricide before the present world and in front of the eternal judgment of God."[46]

Neither he nor any other resident of the Vatican was sure that his words would be heeded. Father Carroll-Abbing noted as late as June 3: "There was still no definite idea as to what the Germans would do: withdraw peacefully from Rome or blow up the bridges and hold the northern bank of the Tiber. From the Janiculum and the Monte Mario hills, their guns could dominate the rest of the city."[47] This uncertainty also seemed to be shared by the Germans themselves. A summary in *Time* magazine during this period read: "The Germans could not seem to make up their minds whether they would defend Rome or not. A Berlin radio

announcement that Rome would positively be defended was con-
tradicted by Adolf Hitler's own newspaper."[48]

The question of whether or not Rome was ever truly entitled to
"open city" status became crucially important. The term connotes
that an area will not be the scene of military activity. Yet the
Germans had used it continually as a supply center and a conduit
for troop dispersion. The Allies wanted it for the same reason.
Clark's primary concern was that the bridges across the Tiber
remain undestroyed so that his men would have a clear route
through the city and into the north, where he could pursue, as he
said on many occasions, "our principal business, which is killing
the enemy."

The Germans, to this day, maintain that the effect of their
original declaration of intent, echoed by Marshal Badoglio and
Pope Pius XII, was enough to create the status of "open city." The
Allies said no. President Roosevelt had told the world, "If the
German forces were not entrenched in Rome, no question would
arise concerning the city's preservation."[49] In effect, he was
saying, "When the Germans stop using Rome as an arsenal, we
will respect its neutrality; until then it is a legitimate military
target." The view was not an unpopular one among the Allied
nations, even in those countries with a large Catholic population.
A Gallup poll taken in America during this period indicated that
seventy-four per cent of the citizenry approved bombing of "historic and religious shrines" for military necessity.[50]

On May 15, despite a story by a Swiss correspondent, reported
in the New York *Times*,[51] which said that German military
movement through the city had tripled since the Anzio landing,
the American State Department did, in fact, make an effort to
achieve neutrality for Rome. But General Sir Henry Maitland
Wilson, the theater commander, refused to consider it. His position was that such an agreement would now benefit only the
Germans. The Germans had no power left with which to defend
the city and, once taken by the Allies, it would be essential for the
maximum prosecution of the campaign in the north. He extended

reassurances to the Vatican that even if a fight did ensue within the city's environs, the neutrality of the Vatican would be respected, and since Kesselring had already made similar representations, it could have been concluded that the Pope need have no fear for sanctity of his enclave.

However, no one seriously believed that any property, however hallowed or historic, would be spared in an inner-city struggle.

On June 3, Kesselring obtained permission from his high command to contact the Allied leaders through the Vatican to work out a plan whereby security for the Church properties would be guaranteed. This was ignored by Alexander; on the same day he broadcast a message calling upon the Romans to join the battle to drive the Germans from the city. Had they responded, unquestionably the Vatican would have been included in the combat zone.[52]

It seems safe to say that the Allies acted correctly in refusing to join in an "open city" declaration with the Germans. Kesselring had already extracted the last bit of military benefit from his occupation of the city, and, at this late date, if Alexander had permitted himself to be boxed into a high-sounding position, he would have severely penalized his future efforts.

As a matter of fact, the status was later officially adjudicated by the Italians themselves. On August 3, 1957, the highest court in Italy, the Supreme Court of Cassation, handed down an opinion which defined the activities of the Partisans in Rome as legitimate "acts of war." The court based its decision on the fact that Rome had never been an open city because of the German military concentrations within its territory — a fact which precluded Allied recognition of open-city status.[53]

<< 4 >>

In its final phase, the drive on Rome flared into a sudden pursuit across the ten or twelve miles of open space between the city and the Alban Hills. To avoid a complete rout, the Germans deployed a number of rearguard forces to fight delaying actions while their battered armies retreated northward through the city.

The Allies, fearing that the bridges across the Tiber would be dynamited as part of the German withdrawal plan, sent a number of task forces streaking on ahead of the main bodies of advance. The Tiber runs south through the city and then continues southwest toward the sea. The Aniene River flows west from the mountains and joins with the Tiber just north of Rome. This angle where the rivers meet contained the goals of the task forces. The river crossings here were vital if the Fifth Army was to maintain contact with the enemy. To keep the two railroad and seventeen highway bridges intact, the task forces were ordered to cross to the far side and establish secure positions.

By June 3, II Corps had completed its wheel to the west and was now advancing toward Rome on Highway 6. The Germans' solid opposition to VI Corps had been cracked by the 36th Division's coup at Velletri, and resistance along this entire section of the front was now slowly weakening.

Although the Germans were falling back on every front, the retreat never assumed the proportions of a rout. Kesselring may have been guilty of bad judgment in several key situations, but he had not lost his capacity to produce extraordinarily skillful defensive maneuvers under pressure. The enemy showed no tendency to give up. As late as June 1, General von Mackensen clearly demonstrated that he felt that the Tenth Army, coming up from the Cassino sector, might help him make a successful stand, and to prepare for it he ordered every member of his Fourteenth Army to "defend himself where he is placed as long as he has ammunition and is capable of fighting."[54]

Of course, not all the German soldiers were that resolute. In one town in the VI Corps line of advance, 130 soldiers mutinied and were shot by their officers, who, in turn, were killed by the rest of the unit, which then promptly gave itself up to the first elements of Truscott's force reaching them.[55]

One captured German told VI Corps interrogators, "sixty per

cent of my battalion were casualties, mostly due to your accurate small-arms fire. Many of my friends have been killed by hand grenades thrown by your soldiers in the dugouts where we have been trying to hide."[56]

The inconclusive winter had given way to electric achievement. The recollections of these days are studded with dramatic vignettes not likely to be forgotten by the men who lived through them. One 36th Division man remembers the people of the village turning on the petty Fascist officers who had governed them in the days of Mussolini's sway. "I saw them marched over to a cemetery where they were made to dig their own graves. Then they lined them up against a concrete wall and killed them all. I was told one man faced his own brother and pulled the trigger."[57]

W. A. Garrard, a platoon sergeant, recalls an especially poignant incident: "My lieutenant told me to take my squad and search a large house and some buildings about one hundred yards left of the road. Snipers were everywhere. Halfway to the house I heard a door slam. I looked up to see a man running from the house and down the road.

"I yelled 'Halt!' But he looked back at me and ran faster. I opened up on him with my machine gun but he continued running. As he passed a concrete post, the dust flew and I could see that I was shooting about six inches behind him. I led him a little more with a short burst before he went behind a mound by the side of the road.

"Approaching the house, I saw a German sitting down against a wall near it. After watching a little while I could see that he was dead. He had been shot four or five times through the chest, perhaps by one of our raiding tanks. He was gripping a brand-new American pistol in his right hand, which was blood-soaked. He probably had got it from an American colonel who had been captured at the roadblock that morning. As I was pulling the pistol from his hand, one of my boys yelled at me from the porch, 'Hey, Sarge, you got that son-of-a-bitch you were shooting at!'

"He was laying sprawled in the road about five hundred feet

away. The bullet had caught him under the right jaw and went out the top of his head. I felt a little empty looking at him, not knowing whether he was Italian or German. He was wearing civilian clothes, about thirty-five years old, and looked to be German.

"Soon, two old Italian men came walking by. I pointed at the body and said, 'Italian?' They hardly looked at him and both said, 'No! Tedeschi,' meaning German.

"Right then antiaircraft guns began blasting, so we scrambled into the house and down into the basement. Some Italian civilians were in there and they very coldly left as we came in. Later, we found that the German company had been in this village since 1939. The one that I had shot had married a girl here and they had a young daughter. I shall never forget her screams of horror and sobbing when she found him dead at the aid station."[58]

Other scenes no less intense were to be found on every road to Rome during these days. Eric Sevareid recalls:

The air was charged with excitement, with savage triumph and obscene defeat. German vehicles were smouldering at every bend of the road, and dead Germans lay sprawled beside them, their faces thickening with the dust sprayed over them by the ceaseless wheels that passed within inches of the mortifying flesh. Shells were screaming over in both directions, but in the general frenzy not even the civilians paid them much notice. By wrecked gasoline stations, in the front yards of decapitated homes, flushed Americans were shoving newly taken prisoners into line, jerking out the contents of their pockets and jabbing those who hesitated with the butt ends of their rifles. A child was vigorously kicking a dead German officer, until a young woman shoved the child aside and dragged off the man's boots.[59]

It was just short of chaos. Everyone wanted to be in on the capture of Rome. The atmosphere approached so feverish a pitch that even Mark Clark began to be concerned that there was a danger of misplaced emphasis. He remembers: "There was a thought in the back of my mind that 'Hell, we shouldn't even be *thinking* about Rome — all we should be thinking about is killing

Germans!' I remember putting out something just before the final attack which concerned the destruction of the German forces, but, of course, he had to put up a battle before you could kill him and right now he was falling back pretty fast.

"But I must admit that I and all my commanders were always thinking that 'if we can just capture Rome because it's such a big milestone.' *Everything* had been so unglamorous, and here was the first Axis-dominated capital to get it before Ike went across. I didn't know of *anybody* who didn't feel that way. Whether or not now they say 'the hell with Rome' I don't know, but then there was always the feeling that Rome was certainly a great prize and the sooner that we stepped out and got it, then we were in a new and final phase of the war."[60]

Clark was not overstating the situation. It did, indeed, seem as if everyone wanted to participate in the triumph. A delegation of Yugoslav officers asked Clark if they could take part in the victory parade. Churchill sent a message asking that the Poles be included. Colonel van de Velde, working in a II Corps intelligence tent, looked up from his maps that morning and saw Crown Prince Humbert waiting to talk with him about joining the procession. The French, who had just linked with II Corps, were certainly entitled to be present, and of course the British could hardly be denied representation.

Colonel James W. Holsinger, one of II Corps's key staff officers who later became a major general, remembers the traffic problems presented by the understandable British desire to participate. "The British had come up Highway 6," he said, "the French had come up through the mountains, and everyone wanted to be first in Rome. The British element moving toward the city demanded the right of way on the highway. As a matter of fact, they had not been scheduled to cross the Tiber River but to move to the right and go up east of the Tiber. One of their brigadiers threatened our military detachment trying to direct the traffic. So, farther up the road, the corps provost marshal effected a traffic jam in a very vulnerable position, and this made it possible for the American troops to stay on the Rome side and to delay the British."[61]

General Keyes heard about the row. "The British corps commander," he recalls, "wanted permission to use our main roads and the bridges in our sector to get his division through. In my opinion, this would have disrupted II Corps [operations] to give him the road for an indefinite period of time. He came over to my headquarters in the middle of the night, and Willems [the chief of staff] woke me up to ask me about it. I told him no. I thought we might make some kind of a deal to give him part-time, but our experience with the British before was that when they got a foot or a wheel on a road, then you never got it back without difficulty. But we finally got word from Fifth Army to let them use these roads. I think it was intimated that Alexander and then [Anthony] Eden got Churchill mixed up in it so they finally got through and got up on the right of the whole operation."[62]

Robert Porter found that his logistical problems were not solved by the order that finally came down from Fifth Army arraying the troops. "The boundaries separating the various corps," he said, "all stopped just short of the city of Rome. This was of great concern to me. We had set up task forces to capture each of the bridges over the Tiber River because we wanted them intact. So I called up the operations officer for Fifth Army and asked him to please draw the corps boundaries through Rome so that we wouldn't start fighting each other in the city. In answer, I was told that General Clark had decided that the boundaries should remain as they were — that there was a horse race on to Rome. General Keyes immediately got Bob Frederick in and asked him to organize two task forces to go into Rome. The First Special Service Force had done a fine job for us and we wanted them to be in on the kill."[63]

Early in the morning of June 3, the First Special Service Force received orders from II Corps attaching an armored column to it for its coming spearhead into the heart of the city. This was Task Force Howze, and its commander was the redoubtable Ham

Howze, who during the breakout from the Anzio beachhead had dispatched the tank force that had rumbled into the battle. The orders, in effect, assigned the sixteen hundred men of Frederick's outfit to an area extending the entire width of the II Corps.

This was just one of the task forces under Frederick's command. Another involved one of his captains, who, in one of the most colorful episodes of the campaign, preceded everyone else into the city. The captain, Taylor Radcliffe, a taciturn man, had established some kind of a record a few weeks earlier by being captured and escaping three times in one night from the Germans.

The mission was assigned in mid-morning on June 3. Radcliffe was told by his regimental commander to report to General Keyes, who would brief him on the job to be done. Upon arriving at corps headquarters, Radcliffe found himself in the company of men picked from every unit in II Corps for their bravery and ability as soldiers. Keyes told him that this was to be an elite patrol on a secret mission and that he had been selected to command it because "the officers of the First Special Service Force, through their proven ability to get the job done the way I wanted it done, had earned the right to have one of their number lead the way into Rome."

"We were sixty men in eighteen jeeps," recalls Radcliffe, "and our mission was to get into Rome in any way possible and send back information on the enemy situation. We were also told to post II Corps signs along the prominent streets and squares, and, to document the posting, we also had a movie and two still cameramen and a newspaperman attached.

"We left corps headquarters early that afternoon and headed for Frascati, where we were to go through an infantry unit and join up with the Ellis Task Force, which was one of the spearheads in the drive in this sector. Since they had tanks, we were to accompany them as far as possible before we broke ahead of them.

When we arrived at Frascati, we were told that the infantry

outfit we were supposed to go through had already left and that the Ellis Task Force had gone through them about an hour before.

"So we lit out, and fifteen minutes later we came to a long convoy of troops that had been stalled by a concentration of snipers. Since we had been given priority passes by General Keyes, we passed this convoy and went on ahead. As I passed the lead tank of the convoy, I noticed a bewildered look on the face of the tank commander, but I thought nothing of it at the time.

"About five minutes later we were fired on by another nest of snipers. This held us up until we could deploy and kill them.

"We went on and soon we were fired on again, this time by cannons and a number of machine guns. The lead tank of the convoy behind us, hearing the fire fight, came up and helped us knock out the enemy. I took a platoon of infantry from the convoy and advanced farther up the road, where I found a roadblock covered [by] infantry and machine guns. We forced them to withdraw, killing and wounding some and capturing the others.

"During this delay, I went back to the convoy that had pulled up behind us. The captain in that lead tank said, 'What in hell are you doing here? Are you crazy or are you lost?' I told him that we were trying to catch up with the Ellis Task Force. He said, 'Hell, man — that's me!' We had been leading the task force for the last seven miles without knowing it."

After the road was cleared, Radcliffe and his men started out again on their way into the city. They were held up several times by concentrations or pockets of German soldiers, but each time managed to blast their way through. By nightfall they had reached a point just south of the city from which, after a brief fight with enemy tanks, they were able to advance into the suburbs which contained most of the movie studios of Rome. This is where they stayed that night.

Next morning they found that another task force accompanied by a swarm of correspondents was approaching, so they got under way as quickly as they could pile into their jeeps. The correspondents, attempting to keep pace, suddenly lost their ambition when a new concentration of snipers opened fire. The speed of Radcliffe's force paid an extra dividend when they reached one major overpass, mined for demolition, which the Germans left unexploded at the sight of Radcliffe and his men tearing up the boulevard toward them.

At 6 A.M., June 4, the force passed through the gate guarding the Via Tuscolana, and found themselves in Rome. The cameramen with the party began snapping pictures of everything in sight, an activity that came to an abrupt halt as enemy machine-gun fire began pouring into the group. Radcliffe pulled his men back, and it was not until noon that they were able to return into the city and spend the rest of the day successfully completing the mission assigned them by General Keyes. Radcliffe and his men thus became one of the task forces who later claimed first entry into Rome.[64]

Back with the main body of troops during the day, General Keyes, flying overhead in a Cub plane, dropped orders to Ham Howze to hurry his command up the road. Howze immediately put on a burst of speed that catapulted his task force through several potentially deadly tank roadblocks and, by dusk, was close enough to the city to see St. Peter's dome.[65] During the night, Frederick — now a brigadier general — arrived with the three regiments of the Devil's Brigade and absorbed the tankers into his command.

« 5 »

Sunday, June 4, was a day so crammed with confusion, drama, and historic high-water marks that even now there is no one source which can accurately state, "This is the way it happened and this is the order of events."

It is still impossible, for example, to say with certainty who was the first in Rome. There were so many task forces and spearheads reaching toward the city, all shifting from one highway to another as resistance developed, that sometimes they actually crossed over into another's line of advance. Official credit has been given to an 88th Division reconnaissance platoon, but its commander, Major General John E. Sloan, admits that "the platoon wasn't strong enough to maintain its position inside the city limits. It's quite probable that the First Special Service Force beat us in strength. However, we followed them very closely, and in our race there with the Special Service Force, we actually collided and had a little fire fight due to misunderstanding between the two forces."[66]

It has been generally conceded that the Canadians and Americans of Frederick's force made the earliest penetration into the heart of the city. They had been assigned the capture of almost half of the city's bridges and by eleven o'clock on the night of June 4 had succeeded. General Frederick, while overseeing the mission, was wounded twice that day, bringing his total of Purple Hearts for the campaign up to nine and thereby easily establishing himself as the most shot-at-and-hit general in American military history.[67]

All through the day, the roads east of Rome were choked with tightly packed columns advancing toward the city while mobs of cheering Italians jammed the banks and walks of the suburbs. The only opposition was offered by the mobile rear guards left behind by Kesselring, hoping to win enough time to get the remnants of his armies through the city. At only one point did a real battle develop. In an area rimmed by Highway 6 and Via Pronestina, a northbound road, the Germans had placed a comparatively heavy concentration of infantry and self-propelled guns which succeeded in stopping the First Special Service Force and the 351st Infantry Regiment for almost nine hours. But since these elements were already so far ahead of the rest of the Allied army, the holdup did not result in their losing their place at the head of the line.

Colonel Kingsley S. Andersson, an engineer officer who received a Silver Star for his bravery that day, remembers an incident during that delay: "General Keyes was sitting up there on a rock all by himself. There was a good deal of sniper fire going on all around him. So I went up to him and I said, 'General, you know better than to sit out here where the snipers are shooting,' and he answered, 'Go away Andersson, this is the first quiet spot I've seen in weeks. If I go back anywhere, they'll get me on the telephone.' "[68]

Late that afternoon, General Mark Clark flew up in his light plane to where the advance was stalled. Impatiently, he asked General Keyes and General Frederick for the reason. Frederick answered that he did not want to use artillery to blast the German block loose because of the number of civilians in the area. Clark refused to consider this much of a reason. "I wouldn't hold up too long," he told Frederick. "We've got to get in there." Just then one of the photographers accompanying Clark suggested that the three generals pose in front of a pole upon which was nailed a directional sign reading, *Roma*. After the photograph was taken, Clark said, "Golly, Bob — I'd like to have that sign in my command post."

Frederick went up the pole himself after the sign, but, at that moment, a hidden German sniper, evidently unable to resist a target consisting of a trio of generals, cut loose with his Schmeisser. The three men dove into a nearby ditch and, before they crawled back to a safer position, Frederick surrendered to an irresistible urge. "That," he told Clark, "is what's holding up the First Special Service Force!"

After Clark had left, Frederick asked Keyes why Clark was so impatient. Keyes answered, "Well, France is going to be invaded from England the day after tomorrow and we've got to get this in the paper before then."[69]

Finally, the block was broken by Task Force Howze and a regiment from the First Special Service Force. Colonel Howze recalled: "This attack was smooth, a knockout. It rolled right in, the tanks working beautifully with the infantry. We made five thousand yards in two hours against a lot of opposition. When the Germans folded, my infiltrators went in to the bridges without serious opposition. My liaison officer went in ahead of them and sat on a bridge but had to kill three Germans to stay there. Later, another one of my staff got shot three times through the legs and Frederick was shot twice, although not seriously. Also, fortunately, they shot a jobless engineering colonel that had been in my hair for the whole day, thus saving me the trouble."[70]

In the general melee, quite a few of the units of the Fifth Army found themselves shooting at other Allied soldiers. The rivalry over boundaries became intense. General Keyes remembers: "The advance of the 36th Division had been exceptionally good, so much so that it released quite a bit of pressure on the VI Corps. But then it began to look as if the 36th and either the 85th or the 88th were going to cut the line of advance of VI Corps into Rome. Their chief of staff began yelling to ours like a pig caught under a fence that if we didn't stop, we'd cross *their* boundary and *their* highway, and if we did, he intimated, they were going to shoot it out with us."[71] There was no reason for VI Corps to have a complex over priorities at this point. Admittedly, they had faced the bulk of the German opposition in the toughest terrain around Rome, but they were still able to crash through by six that evening and secure the bridges and strong points that had been assigned to them.

Even General Clark's mother back in the States felt the tension that these days had produced. While recovering from an illness, she wrote her son, "Please take Rome soon. I can't stand the wait much longer. I'm all frazzled out." Clark answered the day before the city fell: "You'll stand it all right, darling. You've been in three wars . . . and you can take it."[72]

And because they could not influence the day's events, the population of the city became even more excited than the combatants. The diary of Jane Scrivener is one of the few coherent sources available to reconstruct the impact of the moment:

Sunday June 4th

This has been a day of such stirring experiences that they will perhaps "break through language and escape" before they can be written down. They are joint experiences, put together when we pooled our impressions and information; so much happened in so many directions. We had been suddenly deprived of the telephone (cut off); of newspapers (none out); of the radio (electric current cut off); of trams and buses (for the same reason); but the grapevine information service began functioning with incredible efficiency.

The Germans went on, wild-eyed, unshaven, unkempt, on foot, in stolen cars, in horse-drawn vehicles, even in carts belonging to the street cleaning department. There was no attempt at military formation. Some of them dragged small ambulances with wounded in them. They went, some with revolvers in their hands, some with rifles cocked. On Corso Umberto when one of them stumbled his rifle went off and caused a panic among the crowd; for a moment there was some indiscriminate shooting. Whereas last September they came with machine guns trained on the Romans, it was a different matter now. They were frightened. They had a clear idea of the strength of the underground movement, the power of the armed patriots and their determination to take action when and if necessary. Most of the "Republicans" had fled the day before, but in the German rout were to be seen handsome motorcars with Fascist dignitaries looking anything but dignified in their anxiety to get away.

In the Campo Verano cemetery, already damaged by Allied bombs, and over which the Germans had held up horrified hands and shed torrents of crocodile tears, they blew up six large plots where they had stored ammunition, causing some casualties among civilians who happened to be there at the time. The Tiburtina, the Prenestina, and the San Lorenzo railway yards were destroyed, together with surrounding buildings. The telephone plant was blown up at the Ministero delle Comunicazioni, and in Piazza Regina Margherita they set fire to a lorry loaded with ammunition which exploded and wrecked neighbouring houses. At the railway station in Via Marsala numbers of small buildings were set on fire and railway carriages destroyed.

Only lack of time and the skill and courage of patriots prevented the destruction of many public buildings, bridges and waterworks.[73]

A small group which included Major Sam Derry stood silently on the top floor of the building which housed the British legation in the Vatican. He remembers: "Our eyes were glued on the farthest corner of the wide road along which we had seen so many men and machines stream northward in the last few days. Suddenly a line of vehicles swept into view, following the same familiar course — but with such a difference; these were pursuers, not pursued. It was the veritable point of the Allied spearhead, an American tank-busting unit of about thirty vehicles, including a jeep bearing the single star of a brigadier, and I, who had never come across the American forces in battle before, thought it was quite the most beautiful sight I had ever seen.

"Diplomat and butler, soldier and priest, felt a surge of common emotion; cheering, clapping, slapping each other on the back, shaking hands, laughing wildly, and all talking at once, we seemed to throw off in an instant the strain that had settled on us all. The reservation of the diplomat, the caution of the soldier, the calm of the priest, were alike swallowed up in a giddy whirlpool of delight and relief."[74]

Derry spent the rest of the day trying to convince the escapees in Rome to remain in their billets until the last of the Germans had cleared out. When he returned to the Vatican he found that the British legation offices had turned into bedlam. Everyone seemed to be calling on them for instructions, advice, or help. Finally, despairing of ever taming the flood of problems produced by the imminent liberation — and being made promptly aware by the Vatican Secretariat of State that he was expected to make the strict neutrality of the Vatican his first order of business — Sir D'Arcy Osborne, chief of the British legation, appointed Major Derry to act as liaison officer between the legation and the Rome Area Command, whoever it might be and as soon as it was announced. In effect, Sam Derry became temporary military attaché to the Holy See.

Peter Tompkins found himself no less occupied. He remembers: "On the morning of the 4th I sent an agent up to [General] Maelzer's office to find out what was going on. He found Maelzer stinking drunk, cackling in lousy French and in a state of funk.

Obviously, this had been the best job he'd ever had, and he really had a good time at it. Otherwise he was a nobody, and now he was going, he was leaving Rome, and it was an emotional thing and he was drunk and not about to do anything one way or another."

When the agent reported back, Tompkins prepared orders on OSS letterheads and stamped liberally with an OSS stamp that he had had made up, commanding the Italian Army to take over and guard all of the public utilities in Rome. He signed these orders "In the name of General Alexander." The Italian officers to whom he had issued these orders were so grateful for the chance to demonstrate their loyalty to the oncoming Allies that they immediately flooded the city with the thousands of policemen who were still under their command.[75]

Thus, for a substantial portion of June 4, Peter Tompkins supplanted General Maelzer as "King of Rome." This didn't keep him from being arrested several times that day by bands of Partisans or by the police whom he had set at work. Tompkins, an extraordinarily brave man, has never received proper credit for the cool competence he displayed in keeping the few frail threads of governmental continuity from snapping that day. Incidentally, his report of how he became first aware that the Americans were in the city is typically irreverent:

I could hear shouting from the far end of the lane. Figuring the Germans must be up to something with the local population, we decided to keep out of the way. An old man came jogging up the lane and I asked what it was all about, but he didn't seem to know. Then a young girl came tearing across the piazza.

"They're at San Paolo!" she kept shouting.

"How do you know?" we asked her.

"Because one of them gave a man a can of meat and beans!"

To the others this sounded like a rumor, or a trick to get the Partisans to come out into the open, but I knew damned well it was the truth. If they had said tanks and guns and American uniforms, I might have doubted it, but not *meat and beans*. Only a GI could be dishing out those goddamn "C" rations to the populace![76]

By late afternoon, the streets were almost empty of Germans. A rumor spread that there would be a curfew at six o'clock and that everyone was to stay inside. No one paid any attention to it. But as the night wore on, the population grew strangely quiet, almost as if they were a theater audience in that last split second before the curtain rises. Then, from the direction of Porta Pia, there came a wild burst of cheering. The Americans were entering Rome in force. The sounds of cheering rose and the whole city seemed to come to life. Talk and laughter filled all the streets and everywhere there was clapping and shouting as the troops marched in. Many of the men and women in the crowd found it difficult to see through their tears of joy. The crowds swarmed over the tanks, throwing flowers and kissing the men. The older women sobbed and everyone pressed forward with wine and fruit and whatever else they could find as gifts for the soldiers.

The welcome was like nothing the young men of the Fifth Army had ever experienced. The Italians poured out their gratitude in what amounted to hysteria, milling about the tanks and jeeps in such numbers that, at times, forward passage became impossible.

And, of course, after months of fighting in the mud and ruins, the soldiers were almost as thrilled by seeing the broad avenues of Rome. Grimy, unkempt, with the mud of the mountains still on many of their uniforms, the young men discovered that the role of conquering hero was very much to their liking. That night all of Rome saluted them as liberators and, evidently, genuinely meant it. It would take a few more weeks before the expressions of love and gratitude would give way to cool skepticism.

But while it lasted, it was a wonderful experience. Many a young GI got "lost" that night in the company of an adoring signorina. There wasn't a whorehouse in Rome that did not have a line outside it, and even those infantrymen not searching for sexual release found pleasure in just being guests of an appreciative Italian family and sleeping that night between clean sheets and on a soft mattress for the first time in months.

« 6 »

This was the 275th day that had passed since the Allied troops had landed at Salerno. The campaign had cost the Fifth Army 124,917 casualties. The dead numbered 20,389, of whom 11,292 were American, 5017 British, 3904 French, and 176 Italian. The losses were proportionately severe in the British Eighth Army.[77]

But Rome had fallen. Sacked by the Gauls in 390 B.C., almost burned to the ground in Nero's fire, sacked again in turn by Alaric's Visigoths, the Vandals and the German barbarians, and then seized by Napoleon the Great and Napoleon the Little and, finally, by Mussolini, it now had been taken again. But this time the commanding general of the invaders spoke as no one had in all the centuries before him. Sir Harold Alexander told the inhabitants of the city: "Rome is yours. The future of Rome is in your hands."

CHAPTER X

JUNE 5 AND BEYOND

---

*Wayne wasn't averse to publicity, but he wasn't
alone in that. I might say that many of our Allied
friends were publicity-minded. I think that's rather
universal.*

— AMBASSADOR ROBERT MURPHY[1]

THERE were very few sour notes sounded as the troops marched into Rome. Some of the men wondered just how big a percentage of the cheering crowds packing the sidewalks had been Fascists or German sympathizers and just who had stood in the same spot roaring the same approval when Mussolini's troops returned from one of their periodic acts of aggression.

Many infantrymen realized that the non-fighters would soon take over the prize. Later, Bill Mauldin, the almost official voice of the enlisted men, was to write bitterly of the brass hats who, after preempting the luxuries of Rome, would close out participation in them to the GI's of the mud and mountains.[2] Quite a few of the marching men were cynically aware that their hard-won victory would soon become a haven for that considerable percentage of rear-echelon administrators who find life in the wake of a fighting army to be a much sweeter deal than they had ever enjoyed as civilians.

A Fifth Army staff officer that day exulted to a reserve officer, "Just think! This means I'm going to get my permanent promotion to colonel!" and it seemed to the reservist[3] as if the regular army man was rubbing his hands over the twenty thousand Allied soldiers who had died along the way.

A precious pair of correspondents devoted their first story from Rome not to the soldiers or the Partisans or the brave secret agents and priests who had made the victory possible, but to the joyful reunion they had just effected with their favorite prewar bartender, and it nauseated almost everyone in Rome who read it.[4]

Few of the soldiers would have been pleased by the reaction back home on June 5. The American emotion was relief rather than elation. Everyone seemed glad that the city had been taken before the historic and religious monuments had been destroyed, but the reporters who rushed to the Italian colonies in the various cities across the country were disappointed to find an absence of hysteria. Contrary to the stereotyped beliefs of the editors, the Italian-Americans were less concerned with the drama of liberation than they were with the welfare of their sons and friends. There seemed to be very few hyphenated Americans fighting under Clark.[5]

The San Francisco *Chronicle* summed it up after determining that in California there had been no organized demonstrations by Italians or special editions put out by Italian-language newspapers: ". . . the overall reaction was calm acceptance of awaited good news," read the report.[6]

A parody became the closest thing to an Italian-American gesture that the reporters could find. And this happened in Rome — on Mussolini's balcony. Sergeant John A. Vita climbed up onto the famous podium overlooking the Piazza Venezia, and delivered a mock harangue, using all of Mussolini's gestures and postures. Vita spoke in Italian to the mystified crowd who gathered below. As he shouted "Victory, victory, victory to the Allies," he brandished his clenched fist, and the crowd broke into cheers and laughter. "Death and destruction to Mussolini and all his Nazi masters!" Vita continued, and the crowd roared. Some shot revolvers into the air.

When the news of the incident came back over the wires to the States, reporters rushed to Vita's home in Port Chester, New York, sure that they had at last uncovered a genuine "Italian-American" angle. But his mother didn't cooperate. Instead of making a dramatic statement about the land of her forefathers, she simply shrugged and said, "It was just like him. Johnny said he would do it for me and I knew he would."[7]

Of course, these were only minor discolorations in a large picture. The general atmosphere of the city continued to be one of carnival. That day, Rome was a city of parades. The civilians cheered every jeep moving along the street as if it contained Mark

Clark, and they formed innumerable processions of their own. Some of the marchers carried Communist flags, but the majority carried the Stars and Stripes, the Union Jack, and the French Tricolor, and no one seemed to know how so many bits of bunting had been assembled so quickly from so many long-hidden sources.

Most of the parades seemed to have no particular political significance; they simply consisted of large numbers of Italians who had spontaneously agreed to march together and who bumped into each other at intersections and snarled up traffic for hours while they happily disentangled themselves.[8]

Corporal Wade Jones, writing in the *Stars and Stripes* (which, amazingly enough, had found a plant and published an issue that first day in Rome,) said:

At the Prison of Via Tasso, where the Germans kept many of their political prisoners, Frances Thompson (Anglicized) of Yugoslavia, meets Boris Bertot, of Yugoslavia. The Germans have persecuted and nearly starved Thompson to death in the last seven months. They have had Bertot in their Prison of Via Tasso. The two men never met until they bumped into each other at the prison and then they had so much to say they could hardly say it.

Something, somewhere in this paper, must be said about the women of Rome. It is easier to write about the women of this city than any other aspect.

The women of Rome are well dressed and judging by what can be determined from a seat in a vehicle moving through most of the principal streets, they are extremely glad to see us.

They look like the best of American women, they wave at you as you pass, and yell "Viva" something or other and seem enormously happy about the whole thing.[9]

One impromptu parade turned into a snake dance. Since there were only a few musical instruments on hand, most of the members of the line pumped their arms up and down in simulated trombone solos or puffed and blew through imaginary clarinets and trumpets. In the middle of this scene, a correspondent caught sight of an American soldier shepherding through the line a German sniper he had just captured in the Colosseum.

But the loudest applause of the morning seemed reserved for three thousand *carabinieri* (civilian police force) who arrived from Naples in Allied Military Government trucks. During the occupation, the *carabinieri* had so frequently delayed carrying out German orders that Kesselring had finally dissolved the organization. Now the Allies brought them in to help keep order. As they drove through the streets, men in civilian clothes jumped from the crowd and on to the running boards of the trucks. These were policemen who had gone underground in Rome after being fired by the Germans and were now rejoining their friends.

As might be expected, a full-blown black market in American cigarettes, clothes and food immediately came into being. The soldiers were passing these items out with lavish hands and few Italian families could afford to pass up the prices being offered for them by the profiteers. Within a few weeks the market expanded to include equipment, vehicles and medical items supplied by Allied officers with an eye for a quick dollar. One colonel sent home ten thousand dollars in that first month.[10]

The Italian nobility also evinced great joy at the arrival of the Americans. But it must be noted that many of these either had been Fascists or had effected convenient arrangements with the Germans. They greeted the soldiers with every appearance of pleasure, but there were few Fifth Army officers who were not aware of a thin edge of reserve. "They were glad to see us," said one, "but it was obvious that they felt we were perhaps a bit on the crude side."

Unfortunately, the day was marred by acts of violence. A. W. Ovenden, a soldier with the First Special Service Force, noted in his diary: "It's June 5th and the British and French are pushing through Rome in huge numbers. The city is completely taken over, people were very happy. Now the boys are drunk, raping women and disgusting the Italians who are becoming repelled. The British stand out as the neatest looking soldiers."[11]

Eric Sevareid is a witness that violence was not confined to the Allies:

There was a burst of tommy-gun fire in the police headquarters on the square. Several of us worked our way through the gates of the building just in time to see several tough-looking young men, wearing the banner of their underground political group, dashing down a corridor, firing blindly ahead of them. There was a frightening look in their eyes, an expression of sheer bloodlust and hatred. The rat hunt was on. This was not like war; this was a personal matter, and they were out to kill for the sake of killing. There were more shots, the bullets coming our way and when the hunters scrambled frantically back toward us, we shoved our way out of the building in undignified haste.

More vigilantes were in operation at every corner. They were smashing in the plate glass of shops that presumably were owned by Fascists or German sympathizers. A terrified man ran out of one, his hands in the air. He was slugged and kicked and went stumbling through the street with blood running down his face. If this was Europe's vengeance upon its tyrants, I knew I did not like the sight of it. I tried to tell myself that these present victims had done frightful things to countless others, that savage oppression must result in savage release. But it remained a sickening thing to see.[12]

Major Sam Derry was bustling about the Vatican that morning on errands connected with his new job when word came to him that he was to be available for the coming visit to the legation by a very important person. Later, when called to meet the VIP, he found himself facing General Sir Harold Alexander.

Within a few minutes, Derry found that Sir Harold was very well aware of his activities during the German control of Rome. As the conversation developed, it became obvious that the days of the Rome Escape Line organization were over. But the curiously empty feeling that this engendered in Derry quickly passed when he was asked to spend the next few months preparing a list of those who had helped the Allied prisoners escape. It was Alexander's intention to see that they were all compensated for their sacrifices.[13]

Peter Tompkins found himself in a state of frustration. Despite his efforts, it seemed impossible to explain the complicated political situation to the Allied officers designated as military governors for the area. He saw literally hundreds of opportunists endear themselves to the Allies, and he knew that they were nothing more than turncoats who had profited under Mussolini and under the Germans and were now establishing themselves securely in the new occupying force.

He didn't like some of his first experiences with the American and British generals who were now taking over. "The mentality of some of these senior officers," he told us, "was incredible. The *first* thing they wanted us to do was to provide women for them. I had this apartment which I used in my work, and by God, if I didn't come home that night and there is this fancy young American general who wanted to know what *I* was doing there.

"Then his aide appeared with some girls and he was something you will not believe. This one was a prize — you know, riding boots and breeches and so forth.

"I was so outraged that some guy would come along and requisition my apartment that I just stomped out of there right down to Clark's office to prove to them that no goddamned brigadier general was going to get my place. And he didn't, either. But that was the atmosphere of the immediate post-liberation.

"As far as I was concerned, once the city was captured, I wanted no part of these characters; I just wanted to get on with the work, which was sizable. We had the agents left by the Germans in Rome, you see, so work didn't stop for us. It only stopped for about two hours while we had a couple of brandies, and then we went right back to work again at the liberation."[14]

« 2 »

The end of the era of German domination marked only the beginning of a furious fight for control of the Italian government by dozens of factions, but since we are primarily concerned only with the politics in Rome during the days of its liberation, it is enough to note that King Victor Emmanuel III kept his promise to Robert Murphy, Mason MacFarlane and the other Allied diplomats and abdicated on June 5.

It had been his wish to make the declaration in Rome; but the diplomats, sniffing the possibility of more of the kind of royal wiliness that had enabled the little king to hang on to his throne so far, made him execute the document at his summer residence at Ravello. The reason officially assigned for this refusal was that the underground was practically standing in line to assassinate him.

With the signing of the decree, Prince Humbert, the erstwhile visitor to Robert van de Velde's tent, became the new "Lieutenant General of the Realm." Victor Emmanuel refused to relinquish his titles of "King of Italy and Head of the House of Savoy," but since these were now empty posts, the Allies were satisfied. The old Marshal Pietro Badoglio stepped down as Prime Minister and his place was taken by another gray-haired veteran, Ivanoe Bonomi, the only man that all of the political factions could agree upon at that point.[15] Little attention was paid to the new ruler, Prince Humbert. He was unaware of the formation of the new cabinet until after it was publicly announced. In taking the oath of office, the new ministers swore loyalty to the nation instead of the crown.

Although Mason MacFarlane, as British representative, accepted the new cabinet, Winston Churchill later tried to overturn it in an effort to restore the monarchy. This was vigorously resisted by the Americans, and until the Italian political situation finally achieved some kind of stability in the postwar world, civilian authority over the country rested with the groups banded together in the CLN.

All of the world figures made some sort of pronouncement that day and evening. Adolf Hitler, in a broadcast, implied that the capture of Rome really was not a very important achievement and predicted that actually the Allies would find it an embarrassment, since they had now assumed the responsibility of feeding approximately two million more people. In effect, Hitler told the German people that they were better off for having lost Rome.[16]

Winston Churchill sent a lengthy telegram to Premier Stalin, stressing that the capture of Rome was a delayed benefit of the Anzio operation and that now all efforts would be concentrated on killing as many Germans as possible. Stalin replied on the same day, offering his congratulations and adding that "this has been greeted in the Soviet Union with great satisfaction."[17]

That evening President Roosevelt stressed in a speech broadcast all over America that Rome was only the first of the Axis capitals to be captured and that now it was "one up and two to go." Although his tone was jubilant, he closed with the warning that while victory was certain, Germany had not yet been "driven to the point where she will be unable to recommence world conquest a generation hence."[18]

In Rome, at 5 P.M., at least one hundred thousand people jammed the square in front of St. Peter's Cathedral as Pope Pius XII walked or (in the words of one of the correspondents) "seemed to flow out on the balcony, his white robes shimmering in the dusk."[19] While the mass of people below knelt, the Pope delivered a short, but eloquently thankful prayer. "We must give thanks to God for the favors we have received," he said, his arms outstretched. "Rome has been spared. Today she sees salvation with new hope and confidence. This day will go down in the annals of Rome."

Some correspondents felt that the appearance was simply a masterpiece of showmanship. Others found themselves in the grip of deeply religious emotions. But none was left unmoved. Representatives of every faith agreed that they had just shared in a profoundly beautiful moment.

« 3 »

The pageantry and laughter and violence of June 5 eddied about, but never quite touched, most of the soldiers. The race to Rome might be over for the administrative officers and enlisted men, many of whom now became primarily concerned with locating the attractive billet and the understanding girl friend, but the bulk of the Fifth Army continued to move northward to hunt down Germans. The men marching in the ranks or clanking through Rome in their tanks and jeeps were beginning to understand that for them the capture of the Eternal City was simply a landmark, a prize package of memories that they would open and wonder over only after the war had ended.[20]

All day the long columns continued to wind through the city, fusing in the north with other Allied units that had been denied even a tourist's glimpse of the victory on their way up from Cassino and the rest of the battlefields in the south. Every road in central Italy wide enough to pass a wagon became choked with men and their equipment, some fleeing and some pursuing.

When Mark Clark was asked, years later, to describe his emotions as he entered Rome that day as the first general to have taken the city from the south since Belisarius in the sixth century, he answered: "Well, I give you my word I never thought about somebody capturing Rome from the south or the north or wherever. I mustn't say that I wasn't proud, because this was a big city, bigger than the whole of England. It was a milestone, and I, as the commander, was proud. I was always proud of commanding an army — my army, the Fifth Army — which rightfully should have gone to Patton at the time the decision was made, but I happened to be the boy on the ground. I'll never stop being grateful that I was given this opportunity, and I didn't picture myself as superior to anybody else when we went in.

"When I went into Rome, it was with a sense of satisfaction. But I was also concerned with our ability to proceed on and do the job, because right away they started to make these withdrawals from our army to send into southern France. A more effective pursuit [of the withdrawing Germans] might have been launched if I had had more troops. The troops that I had were pretty tired by then. It just seems to me that here was a time when the army had had a lift by virtue of taking an important intermediate objective and that it was wrong to dilute it by taking away the troops we needed for the next job."[21]

General Clark's actual entry into Rome resulted in another of those awkward incidents which dogged him through Italy.

The day began inauspiciously. In the early hours of June 5, Colonel Robert Porter was contacted at his headquarters in a small schoolhouse outside Rome by a staff officer and told to organize a guard of honor to accompany General Clark in his entry into the city later that morning. The staff officer, a man known for his fussiness, ordered Porter to have the tanks and other vehicles of the 91st Reconnaissance washed and polished and the men in clean uniforms so that they would form a properly impressive escort.

Porter, going about his chore, was surprised to look up an hour later to find General Clark landing in a light plane in a nearby wheatfield. Porter began to apologize for his delay, saying that it would take several more hours to get all the vehicles properly washed.

"Oh, the hell with that," answered Clark. "Come on, let's take them in the way they are. I don't care whether or not the men have shaves. The important thing is to get into Rome before the Germans do something about it." As he talked, he began getting into the nearest jeep. "We'll go in this," he said. "We'll have a couple of these L-5's [light observation planes] overfly our column to see that we're safe."[22]

With this, he headed for Rome accompanied by three other officers. His goal was the Campidoglio, on the Capitoline Hill, where he had scheduled a meeting with his corps commanders. But on the way he got lost. Finally, in St. Peter's Square, they hailed a priest who gave them the directions in English. When he had finished, he added, "I like to help American boys. I originally came from Detroit."

The general answered with pleasure, "That's sure nice. My name's Clark."

The priest smiled and walked two steps away and then returned, a look of wonderment on his face. *"General* Clark?" he asked. The party in the jeep broke into laughter. So did the crowd that had collected around them. Finally, the priest joined in, laughing harder than anyone else at his offer of help to the latest conqueror of Rome. Two young boys on bicycles volunteered to lead the way for the general.[23]

And this was Clark's entry into Rome. So far so good. If it had stopped there, it would have become a legend and Clark would have been widely acclaimed for his lack of pretension.

But, instead, the meeting with the corps commanders turned out to be a contrived affair, with Clark pointing in every direction that the photographers requested, while Truscott, Keyes, Crittenberger, and Juin flushed in embarrassment at the charade. Then Mark Clark made a speech. He was too brief. All that he said was, "This is a great day for the Fifth Army and for the French, British, and American troops of the Fifth who have made this victory possible." Omitting to salute the Eighth Army and all the other units who had spilled so much blood on the way to this triumph was inexcusably thoughtless, and almost every correspondent there later reported a feeling of embarrassment.

Only Geoffrey Keyes was charitable. He later explained: "The thing was staged, there's no question about it. But Clark had this public relations fellow who built this up quite a bit. But I can understand General Clark. He wanted to make sure that Fifth Army got the glory. I don't think it was intentional that he left the British and French out. But it did kind of hurt them, and, of course, that's what Eric Sevareid objected to so strenuously, in his book — that he left the others out."[24]

« 4 »

Now it was June 6, the first of the days in which the scars of the German occupation would begin to fade.

The Allied Advisory Council, a governmental group representing the nations in alignment against Germany, arrived early that morning and began its job of restoring some semblance of order to the lacerated country. Robert Murphy was a member of that body. One of his first missions was to meet with Pope Pius XII.

The Pontiff told Murphy of his gratitude that Vatican City and Rome had been spared from destruction but went on to say that he was puzzled by the effect which he evidently produced upon the Allied soldiers. Other people, said the Pope, generally showed enthusiasm at a papal audience, but these soldiers (and he had been meeting with as many as possible in order to personally express his gratitude) always remained silent and reserved.[25]

Ambassador Murphy explained to the Pontiff that the reaction did not indicate reserve, but rather a feeling of awe and respect. The Pontiff seemed pleased with this reply. But evidently he was either not completely satisfied or else he had found it a good conversational icebreaker. Next day, he met with General Clark and asked him exactly the same question. Clark, describing the scene in *Calculated Risk*, wrote:

> I hastened to clear up his misunderstanding, although I am not sure I did a very good job of explaining the difference in religious attitude between Americans and the people in the Mediterranean countries. I assume, however, that I made it clear that the American soldiers were less demonstrative and that their background prompted them to maintain a reverent silence in the presence of the head of the Roman Catholic Church. At least he seemed to understand and to be pleased.[26]

Harry Sions arrived in Rome to help in setting up the offices for *Yank* magazine. As combat correspondent of that publication, he was obviously one of the more important voices of the enlisted men of the Fifth Army and, as a result, was later invited to a papal audience.

"I was allowed to have about twenty minutes with Pope Pius," he recalls, "and my impressions were that I was meeting with a man who had been beautifully briefed. He knew I was not a Catholic, knew that I came from Philadelphia, and spoke in excellent, although heavily accented English. His skin was very pale, almost greenish.

"At the end of our talk, he asked me if he could bless my parents, and, of course, I agreed. Then he asked me if there was anyone else, so I asked him if he would bless the men of *Yank* magazine who were scattered all over the world. Then I asked him if he would bless the American soldiers in Italy who were here to liberate the Italian people. And you know what he did — he blessed the Americans and then he blessed the Polish soldiers, then the South African soldiers, and then he blessed every god-damned unit in all of the Allied forces. Of course, he didn't bless the German soldiers, but he was taking no chances of having anybody say that he was singling out the Americans.

"I have a feeling that he was a clever man. There was impressive strength there."

When asked whether or not he had been influenced by the elaborate display attending the audience, Sions answered, "Well, don't forget that I was just a GI who had been taken through this cycle of rooms. You are taken from one room to another so it's a skillfully built-up drama. You have all the medieval atmosphere of Swiss Guards and the papal attendants, all dressed in their very, very attractive and dramatic garb — and then you're all by yourself finally in the papal waiting chamber. It's a little room, and you're standing by yourself and before you know it you hear a swish of garments and you turn around and there he is.

"He's very tall. He could have been right out of the Inquisition. He had that palish green face, the burning eyes, and the whole wonderful robe of white and gold. Before I knew it I was kissing the ring. Before I did it I had said to myself, 'By golly, I'm not going to,' and then I did because it would have been bad form not to, somehow or another. Then I rose and we talked.

"There's no question that he was an enormously well-educated man. I think he was strong because he always knew exactly what he was doing. As I evaluate him now, I realize that he displayed a great deal of strength during those days. He had marked out a very carefully calculated plan and, as a result, he succeeded in saving the Vatican from being crushed by the Germans. He wasn't concerned with anything but the preservation of the Vatican. So, from that point of view, he was strong. But I don't believe that he was spiritually strong, because he didn't speak out against the murder of millions of people. So when I talk about his strength, I mean it was political rather than spiritual. He set out a course for himself and he followed it. I don't know how else you'd measure strength."[27]

General Keyes was also given one of the first audiences with Pope Pius during these days. He asked several of his staff officers to accompany him. One of them recalls: "I remember we were taken into an audience room in which there was a little platform at the front with a throne on it. We were seated on gold chairs around the sides facing the opposite wall, which contained a mural of the Abbey of Monte Cassino. I've often wondered whether that was done deliberately.

"When the Pope came in, he said, 'You are all of you my children, even those who don't want to be, are my children,' and then he delivered a little talk in which he expressed his relief over the safety of the city and people of Rome.

"The Pope didn't impress me as a saintly man, although of course, I am not a Catholic. He gave me the feeling of being a strong man of the world, a good man. Instead of feeling that he was spiritual, I felt that he was a man who honestly wanted to do good.

"Keyes surprised me. He's a staunch Catholic, but his attitude was almost as if he were meeting the Pope on equal terms. It seemed as if he felt: *This is the leader of our church, but I am a general in the U.S. Army, and we are both trying to do our best.*

"He even made a few light jokes at which everyone, including the Pope, smiled. All of the rest of us were surprised. It was almost as if you had met Churchill or Roosevelt, and even if you were an important man, you just wouldn't feel free to make jokes unless you were terribly, terribly sure of yourself. And, I guess having taken Rome with his II Corps, Keyes felt that way. He just wasn't awed as I thought he might be in a meeting with the head of his church. But, after thinking it over, I can't recall Geoffrey Keyes ever having been awed by anyone, irrespective of his rank. He was content with just being courteous to everyone he met."[28]

Another of the officers present at that meeting, Robert van de Velde, adds: "Of course, we all showed a tremendous amount of respect to Pope Pius. But, remember, by then we were pretty hardened soldier types, so underneath that obvious respect was a sense of relaxation. In effect, we felt, *We've just liberated Rome and by golly the Pope had better be thankful.* Maybe that accounted for the general atmosphere of the audience."

The next night, Pope Pius broke all precedents by allowing a mob of correspondents and soldiers to meet with him, a courtesy which he had never extended to the Germans. The correspondents turned the audience into a raucous press conference,[29] while the photographers shouted requests for various poses. Eric Sevareid couldn't resist the opportunity to whisper to Clark's publicity officer, who was standing nearby, "Do you want me to dateline this story *'With the Fifth Army in the Vatican'?*" The officer just shuddered.[30]

One other figure of interest to us met with Pius XII that day. Major Sam Derry was accorded an audience through the intervention of the priests who had helped him during his long secret stay, and like the other visitors, he was greatly impressed by both the physical presence and the intangible aura. As Derry rose from his kneeling position, the Pontiff looked him full in the face and asked, "And how long have you been in Rome?"[31]

« 5 »

The fighting continued in Italy for almost eleven months before Kesselring finally surrendered the German armies on April 29, 1945. The possibility is strong that this period could have been materially shortened. Both Alexander and Clark pleaded with their superiors against what they considered to be a dissipation of a golden opportunity to destroy the German forces in Italy, but the American political and military leaders insisted that the previously agreed-upon invasion of southern France take place. As a result, the Fifth Army and the Eighth Army were heavily drained to mount and sustain the new operation.[32]

The debate over the merits of the Italian campaign continues until this day. Every step of the way has been violently criticized, from the landings at Salerno to the withdrawal of troops for use in the invasion of southern France. The whole concept of the fight for Italy, in fact, has been questioned. Many reputable writers, historians, and military leaders consider the entire affair a waste of manpower and materiel, pointing out that these resources could have been used to infinitely better advantage in other arenas.[33] The question will never be settled, because, as General Eisenhower once said, "Speculation about the past, of course, leads nowhere except to more speculation."

Admittedly, the campaign was smeared with blunders. Anzio was poorly executed, the Sicilian campaign was a botch, and the best that can be said of Salerno was that it was an arena in which neither side distinguished itself.

But the one massive blunder belonged to the Germans. At Kesselring's urging, they were drawn into a fight for southern Italy and thereby squandered priceless reserves. Almost every German general of the period, after blaming Hitler for every defeat, notes how desperately other fronts needed the divisions that were decimated in Italy.[34] This was Kesselring's big mistake, and it overshadowed every error the Allied generals might have made. At his urging, the German army entered a game which it simply did not have enough chips to win. He staked too much on the terrain and his own ability.

Actually, General Eisenhower blueprinted the victory in Italy with two decisions.[35] He agreed to the invasion of the mainland after Sicily. Once there, he insisted that his troops maintain contact with the enemy, giving them no chance to draw back and reflect.

General Eisenhower emerges as the decisive factor. If it is conceded that the campaign served a vital purpose, then the conclusion is that part of Churchill's great record of achievement rests on Eisenhower's willingness to stand in the middle, reconciling the differences between the American and British planners. There is no question that he made the key decision; it was Eisenhower who enlarged the Italian campaign into a major conflict, and it was Eisenhower who choked it off after he had gone to England as commander of OVERLORD. He drew away the sinews of Alexander's and Clark's forces after the fall of Rome because he saw that once his armies had gone across the Channel into France, the fighting in Italy had further value only as a diversionary thrust. Until then, Italy had been the main arena, the only place where the fight against the Germans could be made on the ground. But after June 6, the place where the war would be won was obviously to be within Germany's territorial limits.[36]

Admittedly, the Allies committed many blunders during the campaign. But, it should be remembered that logic dictated that Kesselring would not fight for southern Italy and that a speedy occupation of all the territory up to Rome would follow the landings on the mainland. After all, the only conceivable usefulness of Italy to Hitler lay in its manufacturing and industrial complex — in the north. Because this logic was disregarded by the Germans, the Allies landed in Italy without a realistic plan. The campaign became a series of improvisations which, in retrospect, were reasoned judgments made under difficult circumstances.[37]

It is important to note that the highest levels of Allied intelligence sources initially argued that the Germans would find it impossible to hold a position in southern Italy because of the difficulties of maintaining transportation and communication lines through the mountains, especially in the light of Allied superiority in the air. In spite of steady Allied bombardment of bridges, supply points and railroad and truck routes, Kesselring kept his armies mobile and at almost full strength up until the last days before Rome's capture.

Further, the bad decisions for which Clark and Alexander are generally blamed were invariably political ones made on levels above them.[38] No one has ever seriously criticized their abilities as generals. Even the complaints against Clark by the survivors of the "Rapido Massacre" are rarely considered today to be much more than emotional reaction.

The words of General George C. Marshall should not be forgotten when considering the merits of the Italian campaign. He said that in wartime, there is "a political necessity for action. The public demands it. They must have action. The party opponents utilize the lack of it to attack those in power."[39]

Kesselring himself admitted three years after the war, before he had formally arranged his thoughts for his memoirs, "If you had never pitted your divisions in the Mediterranean, you would not have won the victory in the West."[40]

« 6 »

By the end of 1944, some striking changes occurred in the Allied High Command. The theater commander, Sir Henry Maitland Wilson, was transferred to Washington as the chief British military representative with the Combined Chiefs of Staff. His place was taken by Field Marshal Sir Harold Alexander. Mark Clark succeeded to the command of the Allied armies in Italy, and Lucian Truscott took over the Fifth Army.

Geoffrey Keyes left Italy after the surrender to assume command of the U.S. Occupation Zone in Austria. He subsequently became commander of all the occupation troops in the U.S. Zone of Germany and, finally, relieved Mark Clark as High Commissioner of Austria. After his retirement he moved to Arizona, where he is frequently visited by his former staff officers, all of whom seem to retain the admiration for him that was so much in evidence during the campaign in Italy.

His career cut short by a physical disability, Lucian K. Truscott, Jr., reached the rank of four-star general before he retired in 1947. He died in 1965.

General Clark has continued to devote his life to public service. After World War II, he capped his military career by being named to succeed General Douglas MacArthur as commanding officer of the United Nations forces during the Korean War. Upon his retirement in 1953, he assumed the presidency of the Citadel in South Carolina, and served on many governmental commissions. As late as December 1966, he was asked to head a board studying proposed revisions of the draft law.

He has been joined on that board by his old friend Ambassador Robert Murphy, who offered us a final look at Clark's maturity by recalling: "Later on, when Wayne came out to Tokyo as the U.S. Commander in Korea, and in Japan, I had occasion to visit with him. It was amazing how much he had improved over the days of World War II. In the past, he had been impatient of political considerations, but by the time he got to Tokyo he had become an accomplished diplomat. He handled himself beautifully in a situation that, being within the United Nations contract, was quite difficult — much more so than it had been in Africa and Italy."[41]

There is no question that Mark Clark has matured. In Italy, he was actually an embodiment of the young Americans who were sent there — politically unsophisticated, brash, and avid for publicity, although he showed no aptitude for its proper handling or attraction.

When asked if some other general, perhaps Eisenhower, could have done a better job than Clark in Italy, even those who dislike him replied in the negative. As a matter of fact, some said that he uniquely benefited the Italian campaign because through his friendship with Ike and the respect in which he was held by General Marshall, he was probably able to get a fraction more supplies and reserves than any other general who might have held the post.

One of his subordinates was once questioned by a correspondent about the plan for a coming battle. The aide replied, "We have fifty-seven plans, and you can bet that General Clark is going to use every one of them." To an objective viewer, this only evidences Clark's overwhelming ambition to win. He may have been impatient, arrogant, and even a bit ruthless, but as Robert Porter observed, "Clark was the ideal man for the job. He's a soldier, a leader, and a driver, and that's what you needed there. You can't win in the mountains without crawling up those mountains, and you can't get forward without closing with the enemy, particularly when he's sitting up there on the heights and is going to stay there until you dislodge him. I feel Clark was the man, and he did the job. Anybody given his job to do would have been criticized. You could have put Eisenhower there and they would have been just as sharp with him as they were with Clark."[42]

This evaluation indicates what is probably the correct estimate of Mark Clark in the Italian campaign. It was a frustrating campaign, incapable of a dramatic victory, and as commanding officer, Clark came to be the symbol of its difficulty. He had none of Dwight Eisenhower's instinctive sophistication and therefore performed exactly as he had been trained to do at West Point. The country owes him respect and gratitude, because he was a commander who did everything that could have been done under the circumstances.

Robert Porter has fulfilled the expectations of his II Corps associates in Italy. As a four-star general, he now commands our southern defenses, dividing his time between his headquarters in the Canal Zone and the Pentagon.

His friend Nic Malitch continued to be colorful to the end of his days. When the French divisions were taken out of the Fifth Army to prepare for the coming invasion of southern France, General Keyes asked Marshal Juin if Malitch could receive his formal discharge from the French Foreign Legion. At first, it seemed as if this could not be done. There was a suspicion on the part of the French authorities that Malitch had been involved in certain questionable activities and there was talk that they wanted him back so that he might be court-martialed.

However, Keyes finally secured the Russian's release. Three months later, after Porter had returned to the United States, Keyes fulfilled a promise to Porter by taking Malitch with him to Seventh Army headquarters in Germany. Here, Nic did not fare so well. His gambling and his penchant for brutality caused much dissension in intelligence circles, and after it became known that Malitch had attended a drinking party where a girl had been thrown out of a hotel window to her death, he was separated from service with the United States Army.

Porter, back in America, heard of this episode, and at the same time he was told that Malitch, in addition to outliving his usefulness to the Seventh Army, had been placed on the "Wanted" list by the Russian Army as a result of several espionage coups. Through friends, an arrangement was made to bring Nic to America.

Malitch apparently reformed after leaving Europe. He married an American girl and settled down to a variety of jobs, none of which, however, held as much interest for him as his wartime activities.

In 1952, General Porter received a letter from Mrs. Malitch announcing Nic's death after a three-month struggle with cancer.[43]

« 7 »

At midmorning on June 6, the writers and photographers in the building set aside for the press were interrupted by a man shouting, "It's just come over the wire! Eisenhower has invaded Europe!" The correspondents looked at each other in common understanding. That afternoon they began to pack and, within a few days, were on their way to where the new big event was unfolding. The story of Rome had been returned to the historians.

That evening, at a cocktail party, an Italian princess approached a Fifth Army staff officer. "I want to congratulate you," she said with evident sincerity. "Do you realize that you are the first of the barbarians to have taken Rome from the south?"[44]

ACKNOWLEDGMENTS

A special note of thanks is due from the authors to Mrs. Lois Aldridge, World War II Records Division, National Archives, Alexandria, Virginia; Hobart F. Berolzheimer, head of the Literature Department, Free Library of Philadelphia, Pa.; H. L. Kownatsky, Photo-Duplication Department, Free Library of Philadelphia, Pa.; and Miss Katherine Howell, Wilmington Public Library, Wilmington, N.C.

CHAPTER NOTES

FOREWORD

1. William Dickinson, now managing editor of the Philadelphia *Bulletin*, was the United Press bureau chief in the Southwest Pacific during much of World World II. In that capacity he was in close contact with General MacArthur. This statement represents his considered judgment of General MacArthur's attitude.
2. Lt. Col. Chester G. Starr's book *From Salerno to the Alps* is the complete chronicle of Fifth Army activities from 1943 to 1945. It details its elements, engagements, movements and chains of command and is recognized as its most accurate history.

CHAPTER I

1. Eric Sevareid, *Not So Wild a Dream*, p. 408.
2. Excerpt from letter, Max E. Shaffer to the authors, July 10, 1966.
3. For a detailed description of the army as it was composed during this period, see the January 1959 edition of *The Army Almanac*, published by the Stackpole Company. Pp. 57–111 will be especially helpful.
4. From the unpublished report Battle for Rome and Retreat Northward. This was edited by Generalleutnant Heinrich Greiner (the commanding general of the 362, I.D.) and was documented by the division's combat reports from May 23 to May 27, 1945, German diaries, and the report of a conference held by the division commander with his staff "taken down in writing" after the conclusion of the battle for Rome. Particular attention should be paid to Section "B," titled "Defensive Fighting Near Velletri, 27 to 31 May, 1944."
5. Walker. Reel 9, USMA.
6. Walker, Reel 9, USMA.
7. Van de Velde, Reel 6, USMA.
8. Keyes, Reel 4, USMA.
9. Greiner, *op. cit.*, pp. 12, 13.
10. Translation of a document dated May 25, 1944, captured by Allied soldiers. The first name of the German general does not appear.
11. J. Patrick Carroll-Abbing, *But for the Grace of God*, p. 92.
12. Porter, #2, Reel 8, USMA.
13. Ernest F. Fisher's excellent description of the battle, "A Classic Stratagem on Monte Artemesio," *Military Review*, Feb. 1963, p. 79, states; "The 36th Division . . . had acquired among American troops, the reputation of being a 'hard luck' division."
14. Van de Velde, Reel 6, USMA.
15. Clark, Reel 1, USMA.
16. Unpub. notes in authors' possession. The source did not wish to be identified.
17. Van de Velde, Reel 6, USMA.
18. Lynch, Reel 10, USMA.
19. Letter, M/Sgt. Kennedy to authors, May 1966.
20. Walker, Reel 9, USMA.
21. Regimental Commander's Comments — Operations in Italy, May 1944, Headquarters, One Hundred Forty-Second Infantry U.S. Army, July 1, 1944, p. 5 (unpublished).

22. Lynch, Reel 10, USMA.
23. Sevareid, *op. cit.*, p. 404.
24. From completed questionnaire in authors' possession.
25. Kenneth L. Dixon, "The Night of the Knife," *Argosy*, Sept. 1964.
26. Kennedy letter, *op. cit.*
27. Shaffer letter, *op. cit.*
28. From completed questionnaire in possession of authors.
29. From completed questionnaire in possession of authors.
30. From completed questionnaire in possession of authors.
31. From completed questionnaire in possession of authors.
32. Quoted by Fisher, *op. cit.*
33. Porter, #2, Reel 8, USMA.
34. Letter to authors, dated Apr. 7, 1966.
35. Shaffer letter, *op. cit.*
36. John P. Delaney, *The Blue Devils in Italy*, p. 91.

CHAPTER II

1. Murphy, Reel 8, USMA.
2. *Ibid.*
3. Henry L. Stimson and McGeorge Bundy, *On Active Service in Peace and War*, p. 525.
4. *Ibid.*, p. 526.
5. Trumbull Higgins, *Winston Churchill and the Second Front*, p. 154.
6. The whole of Chapter 9, Book 3, of John T. Flynn's *The Roosevelt Myth* amplifies this point.
7. Lord Moran, *Churchill: Taken from the Diaries Of Lord Moran*, p. 37; Murphy. Lang, Reel 8, USMA; Marquis Childs, *Eisenhower: Captive Hero*, p. 67.
8. James Leasor, *War At The Top* (based on the experience of General Sir Leslie Hollis), p. 173.
9. Moran, *op. cit.*, p. 110.
10. Forrest C. Pogue, *George C. Marshall: Ordeal and Hope*, p. 402.
11. *Ibid.*, p. 163.
12. *Ibid.*, p. 405.
13. Higgins, *op. cit.*, p. 155. The accuracy of General Marshall's concept is further underlined by a statement appearing in the *ROTC Manual #145-20*, issued by the Department of the Army, titled *American Military History 1607-1958*, which reads, "Perhaps equally important [the North African victory], American troops and commanders had gained experience in both combat and logistical operations, and the stage was set for the campaigns that were to follow" (p. 430).
14. Peter Tompkins, *The Murder of Admiral Darlan*, p. 125.
15. Conversation, Mrs. Clark and authors, Sept. 22, 1966.
16. The material dealing with General Clark's early years is to be found in Clark, Reel 1, USMA. See, also *Encyclopaedia Britannica Book of the Year — 1945*.
17. Pogue, *op. cit.*, p. 83.
18. *Ibid.*, p. 84.
19. Clark, Reel 1, USMA.
20. Quoted in Childs, *op. cit.*, p. 50.
21. Clark, Reel 1, USMA.
22. Maurine Clark, *Captain's Bride, General's Lady*, p. 97.
23. Conversation with authors, Aug. 1966.
24. Liese, Reel 3, USMA.
25. Winston S. Churchill, *The Hinge of Fate*, p. 526.

26. Harry C. Butcher, *My Three Years with Eisenhower*, p. 75.
27. Clark, Reel 1, USMA.
28. Lang, Reel 8, USMA.
29. Clark, Reel 1, USMA.
30. Arthur Bryant, *Triumph In The West* (based on the diaries of Field Marshal Lord Alanbrooke), p. 98.
31. Quoted by Sir John Kennedy, *The Business of War*, p. 315.
32. Moran, *op. cit.*, p. 118.
33. Pogue, *op. cit.*, p. 406.
34. Butcher, *op. cit.*, p. 134.
35. Maurine Clark, *op. cit.*, p. 168.
36. Godfrey B. Courtney, "General Clark's Secret Mission," *100 Best True Stories of World War II*, p. 559.
37. Butcher, *op. cit.*, p. 150.
38. Courtney, *op. cit.*, p. 562.
39. An expert discussion of the problems inherent in the North African political situation during this period can be found in Robert Murphy's *Diplomat Among Warriors*. Ambassador Murphy was the senior American diplomatic representative on the scene at the time and his presentation of the factors involved contains dimensions that are almost unrecognized in the memoirs of the generals and the journalists who also participated in the events. As a supplement, attention should be also paid to Clark, Reel 1, USMA, wherein General Clark delivers a rather salty summary of his and General Eisenhower's estimates of the various French political and military figures with whom they were in contact.
40. Quoted in Pogue, *op. cit.*, p. 418.
41. Murphy, Reel 8, USMA.
42. Quoted in Butcher, *op. cit.*, p. 271.
43. Murphy, Reel 8, USMA.
44. Clark, Reel 1, USMA.
45. A brief military summary of the campaign which contains a description of every key tactical move can be found in the *ROTC Manual, op. cit.*, pp. 425–430. Its statement ". . . this was the turning point of the war in Europe" can be considered authoritative.
46. Moran, *op. cit.*, p. 87.
47. Leasor, *op. cit.*, p. 227. For an excellent listing of the reasons underlying Sicily's choice as the next step, see Martin Blumenson, "Sicily and Italy," *Military Review*, Feb. 1966, pp. 62, 63.
48. Albert C. Wedemeyer, *Wedemeyer Reports!:* "But the British test of friendship was not always loyalty to one's own conceptions of the right thing to do for both parties. To the British — negotiating, arguing, and fighting in the international arena — the true friend might be the man who could be manipulated or enticed to see things as the British themselves saw them. There was no give and take between British and American planners. It was all 'take' on their part, with the pattern established by centuries of negotiations and now symbolized by the voluble Mr. Churchill and the sensitive Sir Alan Brooke" (p. 188). It should be remembered, however, that General Wedemeyer has always been considered as holding conservative views, an attribute which let him function as a balance wheel as a member of General Marshall's key planning group.
49. Higgins, *op. cit.*, p. 92.
50. Wedemeyer, *op. cit.*, p. 185.
51. Thomas A. Bailey, *Presidential Greatness*, pp. 158, 159.
52. Unpublished notes in possession of authors. The source did not wish to be identified.

53. Bryant, *op. cit.* The thread of Brooke's ambivalent attitude toward General Marshall is woven throughout the book. On p. 44, writing of his impatience with American planners (headed by Marshall), he notes, ". . . I am tired of seeing our strategy warped by their short-sightedness and by their incompetency!"; on p. 110: "It is quite clear to me from Marshall's wire that he does not begin to understand the Italian campaign"; on p. 162: "It is quite clear in listening to Marshall's arguments that he has not even now grasped the true aspects of the Burma campaign." Evidently General Marshall produced the same effect on other British leaders; Sir John Dill, writing from Washington to Lord Alanbrooke, noted: "It is odd how that charming person Marshall can fly off the handle and be so infernally rude. Also he gets fixed ideas about things and people which it is almost impossible to alter" (Lord Alanbrooke, *Personal Files*).
54. Lord Cherwell to General Marshall, quoted in Leasor, *op. cit.*, p. 173.
55. Wing Commander J. C. Slessor in his 1937 Gold Medal Essay, quoted in Higgins, *op. cit.*, p. 188.
56. Murphy, Lang, Reel 8, USMA.
57. Charles de Gaulle, *The Complete War Memoirs of Charles de Gaulle*, p. 308.
58. Leasor, *op. cit.*, a letter from "Stalin's Correspondence," quoted on p. 230.
59. *Ibid.*, p. 173n.
60. Clark, Reel 1, USMA.
61. Clark, Reel 1, USMA.
62. Van de Velde, Reel 6, USMA; van de Velde, Interview #2 (notes in possession of authors). From completed questionnaires in possession of authors.
63. Porter, #1, Reel 7, USMA.

CHAPTER III

1. Winston S. Churchill, *Closing the Ring*, p. 662.
2. Hanson W. Baldwin, *Battles Lost and Won*, pp. 228–235. Omar N. Bradley, *A Soldier's Story*, p. 159, contains a detailed discussion of some of the personal characteristics of General Patton which met with something less than widespread admiration, e.g., "In that unhappy part of his career [the Mediterranean war] George's theatrics brought him much contempt, and his impetuousness outraged his commanders."
3. Unpub. notes in possession of authors. The source did not wish to be identified. Baldwin, *op. cit.*, p. 202.
4. Testimony on this point is so abundant that pinpointing it here would be meaningless. Reference can be made to the memoirs of almost every American general with whom Montgomery had contact.
5. "Tedder's Memoirs Laud Eisenhower," New York *Times*, Oct. 9, 1966.
6. The authority for this report is an American general who held a combat command during the Sicilian campaign, but did not wish to be quoted. Unpub. notes in possession of authors.
7. Field Marshal Earl Alexander of Tunis, *The Alexander Memoirs 1940–1945* (ed. John North), p. 45.
8. Bradley, *op. cit.*, p. 161.
9. Lang, Reel 8, USMA.
10. Here, too, criticism of an American general is a continuing theme in Lord Alanbrooke's diaries. This phenomenon was not confined to the CIGS. It is a rare British memoir in which an American leader's military ability is mentioned with such approval as Alanbrooke's description of General MacArthur: "the biggest general I have yet seen during the war. He is head and shoulders bigger than Marshall" and "the greatest general and the best strategist that the war

produced" and "masterly genius." These estimates are noted in Douglas Mac-Arthur, *Reminiscences*, p. 290.

11. One of the authors was stationed in England when this incident occurred. The news of it was greeted with such relish by British soldiers and civilians alike that it seems fair to say that the wholehearted admiration with which the English public regarded Eisenhower had its roots in this moment.

12. For an excellent outline of the aims and constituting personnel of this and other conferences of the leaders of the Allied nations, see Trevor Nevitt Dupuy, *Strategic Direction of World War II* (The Military History of World War II, Vol. XVIII), pp. 29–43.

13. Attention is invited to three authoritative discussions of the military and political background and problems inherent in Italy's collapse at this point: Ralph S. Mavrogordato, "Hitler's Decision on the Defense of Italy," *Command Decisions* (ed. Kent R. Greenfield), pp. 303–322; Robert Murphy, *Diplomat Among Warriors*, pp. 186–205; Norman Kogan, *Italy and the Allies*, pp. 13–90.

14. Robert E. Sherwood, *Roosevelt and Hopkins*, pp. 695–697; Albert Wedemeyer, *Wedemeyer Reports!*, p. 186; J. F. C. Fuller, *The Second World War*, p. 265; Hanson W. Baldwin, *Great Mistakes of the War*, pp. 24, 25.

   The following is from a letter to the authors from Robert Murphy (Nov. 20, 1967): "My recollection of Casablanca regarding 'unconditional surrender' is a little different. I was with Mr. Roosevelt when he sprang it on Mr. Churchill who went along, it seemed to me, for tactical reasons. Perhaps it was an 'honest statement of feeling' on his part but I don't think so. I personally liked the policy because the then high pitch of emotion in the United States would not have tolerated a negotiation about terms with the Nazi leadership. With whom could we have negotiated a conditional surrender? Mr. Roosevelt had that very much in mind but Mr. Churchill's position vis-a-vis the British public was different. They were more tired than we!"

15. The quotations in this and the preceding two paragraphs of the text are from a New York *Times* report, Dec. 15, 1966.

16. Wedemeyer, *op. cit.*, p. 230. This suspicion of Churchill and his aims was also shared by Hitler and his advisers (Mavrogordato, *op. cit.*, p. 309). Fleet Admiral William D. Leahy, *I Was There*, suggests (pp. 220–221) that there may have been other reasons for Russia's willingness to back the American position. See also Sir John Kennedy, *The Business of War*, pp. 298, 299; James Leasor, *War at the Top* (based on the experience of General Sir Leslie Hollis), pp. 238, 239; Kenneth S. Davis, *Experience of War*, pp. 452, 453.

17. This was one of the basic decisions of the Italian campaign. By making it, Eisenhower set in motion the forces in a conflict that in earlier eras, would have been considered a major war by itself. See Davis, *op. cit.*, pp. 430, 431; Lang, Reel 8, USMA; Dwight D. Eisenhower, *Crusade in Europe*, pp. 183, 184, 488. Baldwin, *op. cit.*, pp. 198–235, contains a masterful review of the Sicilian campaign which focuses upon all the influences leading to the Eisenhower decision. See also J. F. C. Fuller, *op. cit.*, p. 260; Winston S. Churchill, *The Hinge of Fate*, pp. 816–826, wherein the Prime Minister presents the carefully marshaled arguments which persuaded Eisenhower to make a decision that few of the American planning group looked favorably upon; Harry C. Butcher, *My Three Years with Eisenhower*, p. 374; Alan W. Dulles, *The Secret Surrender*, p. 53.

18. Leasor, *op. cit.*, p. 239; Fuller, *op. cit.*, p. 260; Kennedy, *op. cit.*, p. 300.

19. Attention is again invited to the discussions by Kogan, Murphy (specifically p. 191), and Mavrogordato, cited in note 13, above.

20. Albert Kesselring, *Kesselring: A Soldier's Record*, p. 207.

21. Peter Tompkins, *Italy Betrayed* (N.Y.: Simon & Schuster, 1966) contains an

exhaustive discussion of the motives of the King and his prime minister. A less harsh view will be found in Kogan, *op. cit.*, pp. 31–79.

22. In his memoirs, Kesselring noted: "This period before Italy's defection was for my commanders and me one of exceptional nervous strain. To me as a soldier this duplicity forced upon me by our Allies and by Hitler was intolerable. I could not reconcile the apparently reasonable chance of our allies' playing us false with my implicit trust in my Italian associates, and my belief in the King's and Badoglio's word. This worry, on top of my far from pleasant exchanges with the Führer's headquarters, together with the burden of military work, the spread of the air war to the whole of Italy, and the gloomy prospects ahead gradually frayed my nerves. Yet on the day of surrender — which brought with it a bombing raid on my general headquarters, the Allied invasion in the Bay of Salerno and the flight of the royal family and the Government from Rome — I was glad to say I had done everything in my power both to prevent the Italians from taking this step and to safeguard the German cause from avoidable injury" (*op. cit.*, p. 212).

23. Murphy, *op. cit.*, Chapter 13; Murphy, Reel 8, USMA; Eisenhower, *op. cit.*, p. 184.

24. Murphy, *op. cit.*, p. 203.

25. Franco Maugeri, *From the Ashes of Disgrace*, pp. 184, 185; Kogan, *op. cit.*, p. 40.

26. The code name used by the German High Command to describe their plan for taking over Italy in the event of an Allied invasion.

27. Louis P. Lochner (ed. and trans.), *The Goebbels Diaries*, p. 437.

28. "Smiling Albert," *Newsweek*, Feb. 21, 1944, p. 25; "Nazis' New Broom?" *Time*, Apr. 2, 1945, p. 31.

29. Porter, #2, Reel 8, USMA.

30. VI Corps Intelligence Report, May 26–27, 1944 (unpublished).

31. Frido von Senger und Etterlin, *Neither Fear nor Hope*, p. 127.

32. As an example, the widespread belief that the Italians would support his forces in the event of an Allied invasion: Karl Doenitz, *Memoirs — Ten Years and Twenty Days*, p. 363. This sentiment concerning Kesselring's occasionally unrealistic combat estimates characterizes many of the interviews with captured German commanders described in the "Unpublished Sources" section of the Bibliography.

33. Kesselring, *op. cit.*, p. 202n.

34. The most complete discussion of this possibility is found in Ian Colvin's book, *Chief of Intelligence*. See also Hugh Pond, *Salerno*, p. 8.

35. Clark, Reel 1, USMA.

36. Porter, #2, Reel 8, USMA.

37. Churchill, *The Hinge of Fate*, pp. 828, 829; Eisenhower, *op. cit.*, pp. 168, 169.

38. "The Arsenal City," *Time*, July 26, 1943; Quentin Reynolds, "While Rome Burned," *Collier's*, Aug. 28, 1943; "Raid on Eternal City Stirs Prelate and Laymen but Catholics Are Split," *Newsweek*, Aug. 2, 1943.

39. *Newsweek*, Aug. 2, 1943.

40. Quoted in *Newsweek*, Aug. 2, 1943.

41. Jane Scrivener, *Inside Rome with the Germans* (introduction by Carlton J. H. Hayes, former American ambassador to Spain), pp. ix–x.

42. William L. Shirer, *The Rise and Fall of the Third Reich*, p. 999; reported in more detail in Saul Friedländer, *Pius XII and the Third Reich*, pp. 198, 199.

43. Lochner, *op. cit.*, p. 409.

44. Ernest F. Fisher, "Rome: An Open City," *Military Review*, Aug. 1965, p. 72.

45. *Ibid.*, pp. 73, 74; Vatican radio broadcast, Oct. 19, 1943.

46. Fisher, *op. cit.*, p. 76.

47. Two fine critiques of this book are Guenter Lewy, "Was Silence The Only

Solution?" *Saturday Review*, May 21, 1966, p. 26., and "Pius XII and the Third Reich," *Look*, May 17, 1966, p. 34.
48. Friedländer, *op. cit.*, p. 8.
49. Harry F. Ward, "Vatican Fascism," *Christian Century*, June 7, 1944, p. 693.
50. "Behind the Pope's Pleas for Peace," *Christian Century*, Sept. 6, 1943, p. 1031.
51. Maugeri, *op. cit.*, p. 214.
52. Lochner, *op. cit.*, p. 166.
53. *Ibid.*, p. 161.
54. *Ibid.*, pp. 271, 409, 410; Dulles, *op. cit.*, pp. 61, 62.
55. "A Pius Role in Plot on Hitler Reported," New York *Times*, Dec. 31, 1965.
56. Interview, 1966. Notes in possession of authors.

CHAPTER IV

1. Lang, Reel 8, USMA.
2. Clark, Reel 1, USMA; Mark W. Clark, *Calculated Risk*, pp. 183–195.
3. Hugh Pond, *Salerno*, p. 204.
4. J. F. C. Fuller, *The Second World War, 1939–1945*, p. 270; Harry C. Butcher, *My Three Years with Eisenhower*, p. 420.
5. "Beyond the Bridge Head," *Time*, Oct. 4, 1943; Fuller, *op. cit.*, p. 270.
6. But further testimony to his private pessimism can be found in the discussions with his associates concerning the preparation of a set of plans for reembarkation as detailed in Pond, *op. cit.*, pp. 165, 188.
7. Maurine Clark, "Letters from a General," *Collier's*, Dec. 4, 1943.
8. Pond, *op. cit.*, p. 22. Clark, *Calc. Risk*, p. 195. The incident is also mentioned in many of the completed questionnaires in the possession of the authors.
9. The deteriorating relationship between Clark and Walker was mentioned in discussions with the authors by almost every officer who knew the two men.
10. Clark, Reel 1, USMA.
11. Quoted in Pond, *op. cit.*, pp. 194, 195.
12. Letter, General Walker to Harold Bond (author of *Return to Cassino*), Sept. 28, 1965. This correspondence file is in the possession of General Walker, who made the letter quoted available to the authors.
13. Quoted in Butcher, *op. cit.*, p. 420.
14. In possession of the authors.
15. Fuller, *op. cit.*, p. 268; B. H. Liddell Hart, *Strategy*, p. 304.
16. Albert Kesselring, *Kesselring: A Soldier's Record*, p. 225; and see also pp. 220–228 for an excellent summary of the German reactions and countermeasures to the Allied landings, as well as a discussion of the political factors obtaining in Hitler's headquarters during the period.
17. Sir Francis de Guingand, *Operation Victory*, p. 322.
18. Clark, Reel 1, USMA. Clark, *Calc. Risk*, Chapter 9; "Salerno: A Near Disaster," pp. 183–216.
19. Clark, *Calc. Risk*, p. 211.
20. De Guingand, *op. cit.*, p. 186.
21. Robert Murphy, *Diplomat Among Warriors*, p. 190.
22. Wynford Vaughn-Thomas, *Anzio*, p. 26.
23. Other contemporary descriptions which have been drawn upon for the portrait used here are Martin Blumenson, *Anzio: The Gamble That Failed*, p. 10; Frank L. Kluckhohn, "Attack — Attack Again Is Alexander's Motto," New York *Times Magazine*, August 8, 1943, p. 20; "Master Strategist of the Year: General Sir Harold Alexander," *Newsweek*, Sept. 6, 1943, p. 32; Frank Gervasi, "Alexander the Modest," *Collier's*, Feb. 12, 1944, p. 12. These journalistic reports seem to convey a more illuminating description of General Alexander's impact on his associates and the era than do the word-portraits emerging from the biographies and memoirs appearing after World War II.

24. Charles de Gaulle, *The Complete War Memoirs of Charles de Gaulle*, p. 607.
25. Omar N. Bradley, *A Soldier's Story*, p. 207.
26. Aug. 8, 1943.
27. Lord Moran, *Churchill: Taken from the Diaries of Lord Moran*, p. 126.
28. Gervasi, *op. cit.*
29. *Ibid.*
30. As quoted in Norman Kogan, *Italy and the Allies*, pp. 70, 71. Evidently the Italians were offering something considerably more than a gesture. William L. Shirer, in *The Rise and Fall of the Third Reich*, says: "Moreover, no effort seems to have been made by Eisenhower's Command to try to utilize the large Italian forces in conjunction with its own, especially the five Italian divisions in the vicinity of Rome. Had Eisenhower done so — at least such was the contention of both Kesselring and his chief of staff, General Siegfried Westphal, later — the predicament of the Germans would have become hopeless. It was simply beyond their powers, they declared, to fight off Montgomery's army advancing up the peninsula from the 'boot,' throw back General Mark Clark's invasion force wherever it landed, and deal with the large Italian armed formations in their midst and in their rear" (p. 1001).
31. Louis P. Lochner (ed. and trans.), *The Goebbels Diaries, 1942–1943*, p. 479.
32. Jane Scrivener, *Inside Rome with the Germans*, p. 32.
33. Franco Maugeri, *From the Ashes of Disgrace*, pp. 198–201.
34. Scrivener, *op. cit.*, pp. 19–21.
35. Kesselring, *op. cit.*, pp. 268, 269.
36. Alexander, *The Alexander Memoirs, 1940–1945*, p. 111.

CHAPTER V

1. Clark, Reel 1, USMA.
2. Dwight D. Eisenhower, *Crusade in Europe*, pp. 202, 203. Martin Blumenson, "Sicily and Italy: Why and What For?" *Military Review*, Feb. 1966, pp. 66, 67; Sir Harold Alexander, *The Alexander Memoirs, 1940–1945*. This was the second critical decision made by Eisenhower, and it was so recognized by Alexander, who wrote, "Here was the true moment of birth of the Italian campaign" (*op. cit.*, p. 117). This was also General Marshall's sentiment; see Harry C. Butcher, *My Three Years with Eisenhower*, pp. 423, 424.
3. Eisenhower, *op. cit.*, p. 189; Gordon R. Young, ed., *The Army Almanac*, p. 591.
4. J. F. C. Fuller, *The Second World War, 1939–1945*, p. 270.
5. Frido von Senger und Etterlin, *Neither Fear nor Hope*, p. 226.
6. The authors are indebted to General Keyes for this biographical information. See Keyes, Reel 4, USMA and *Register of Graduates, U.S. Military Academy, 1964*. The relationships and evaluations of General Keyes are to be found in Clark, Reel 1, USMA; Holsinger, Walter and Liese, Reel 3, USMA; Willems, Reel 5, USMA; van de Velde, Reel 6, USMA, Porter, #1, Reel 7; Sloan and Lynch, Reel 10, USMA. There is much additional information in the possession of the authors attesting to the regard for General Keyes seemingly held by everyone with whom he came in contact.
7. The relationship between General Keyes and Colonel Porter has been substantiated in interviews with almost every ranking member of the II Corps staff as it was constituted in Italy during the period referred to in the text. Taped comments can be found in van de Velde (who was also present at the meeting between Pope Pius XII and General Keyes), Reel 6, USMA.
8. George S. Patton, Jr., *War as I Knew It* (paperbound edition), p. 67. General Keyes has always rejected the adverse comments of General Patton's detractors. He regarded himself as Patton's protégé and, in a letter to the authors dated June 5, 1967, he said, "General Patton was a very close friend and patron of mine whom I admired very much. In spite of his few failings of temper, temperament

and language which were always exaggeratedly stressed by his critics, he was the No. 1 aggressive in the American army in Europe."

9. The authority for this statement is General Keyes himself. See Keyes, Reel 4, USMA.
10. Copy in possession of authors.
11. Robert H. Adleman and George Walton, *The Devil's Brigade*, p. 122.
12. Unpub. notes in possession of authors.
13. Liese, Reel 3, USMA.
14. Unpub. notes in possession of authors. The source did not wish to be identified.
15. Holsinger, Reel 3, USMA.
16. Willems, Reel 5, USMA.
17. Interview #2, van de Velde and others (unpub. notes in possession of authors).
18. Liese, Reel 3, USMA.
19. Unpub. notes in possession of authors. The source did not wish to be identified.
20. Porter, #1, Reel 7, USMA. However, there were quite a few interviews (notably Liese, Reel 3, USMA), which testify that Malitch did, indeed, infiltrate behind the enemy lines on many occasions. Since these interviews were conducted by the authors with former II Corps intelligence and operations officers, it must be assumed that knowledge of the trips was withheld from Colonel Porter.
21. Van de Velde, interview #2 (unpub. notes in possession of authors).
22. Walter, Reel 3, USMA.
23. Willems, Reel 5, USMA.
24. Clark, Reel 1, USMA.
25. Interview #2, van de Velde and others (unpub. notes in possession of authors).
26. Keyes, Reel 4, USMA.
27. The most complete descriptions of the reaction of the principals to these conferences are to be found in Robert E. Sherwood, *Roosevelt and Hopkins*, and Winston S. Churchill, *Closing the Ring*. Other memoirs have been written by those in attendance, notably Lord Alanbrooke, Admiral Leahy, Lord Moran, and General Sir Leslie Hollis. Perhaps one of the most balanced presentations of the events is offered by a nonparticipant, Richard M. Leighton, in "OVERLORD Versus the Mediterranean at the Cairo-Teheran Conferences," in Kent R. Greenfield, ed., *Command Decisions*, pp. 255–285.
28. Sir John Kennedy, *The Business of War*, p. 308.
29. *Ibid.*, p. 310.
30. Sherwood, *op. cit.*, p. 775.
31. Kenneth S. Davis, *Experience of War*, p. 452. When asked by the authors to comment on President Roosevelt's disposition to allow greater latitude to his military commanders than did Winston Churchill, Ambassador Robert Murphy replied, "Well, you must remember that as the war went on, the President had less vitality, he was a sick man" (Murphy, Reel 8, USMA). To be coupled with this is the factor of the President's enormous respect for General Marshall. Upon the occasion of choosing a commander for OVERLORD, he decided against selecting Marshall (among other reasons) because "I could not sleep at nights knowing that you [Marshall] were out of the country." Many of the American military leaders felt the English habit of making the major decisions in London was a serious hindrance to operational efficiency, e.g., Admiral Leahy, in *I Was There:* "this completely divided control was serious enough in my opinion to account for most of the British air failures in the war. Unity of command of all available forces — land, sea and air — was essential to success. It was my intention, if the British persisted in exercising operational command of the Royal Air Force from England, to insist that our American air arm be divorced completely from the British Air Command and turned over to the Supreme Allied Commander of the area concerned" (p. 197). When General Clark was questioned by the authors on this point, he stated that he had been given so large a latitude that,

he implied, sometimes he wished a bit more guidance from above (Clark, Reel 1, USMA).

32. See Leighton, *op. cit.*, for many comments upon this point.

33. Leasor, *War at the Top*, p. 239. Many of the memoirs of the period assert that Winston Churchill was dominated by the World War I debacle at Gallipoli and, therefore, this explains his great interest in seeing the Italian campaign succeed.

34. Sherwood, *op. cit.*, pp. 780, 781.

35. John R. Deane, *The Strange Alliance* (New York: Viking Press, 1947), p. 43.

36. Hanson W. Baldwin, *Great Mistakes of the War*, p. 35; Maurice Matloff, "The ANVIL Decision: Crossroads of Strategy," *Command Decisions*, ed. Kent R. Greenfield, p. 273.

37. Churchill, *Closing the Ring*, p. 356.

38. Matloff, *op. cit.*, p. 387.

39. Sherwood, *op. cit.*, pp. 780, 781; Leighton, *op cit.*, p. 273; Arthur Bryant, *Triumph in the West*, pp. 64, 65.

40. The thread that ran through Churchill's and Sir Alan Brooke's arguments was that it would be inconceivable to keep a large army standing idly by for the six - months it would take to complete OVERLORD. See Churchill, *Closing the Ring*, p. 370; Bryant, *op. cit.*, p. 53.

41. Leighton, *op. cit.*, p. 277.

42. Clark, *Calc. Risk*, p. 256; Clark, Reel 1, USMA; Matloff, *op. cit.*, p. 389; Churchill, *Closing the Ring*, p. 424.

43. Bryant, *op. cit.*, p. 67.

44. Leahy, *op. cit.*, p. 205; Bryant, *op. cit.*, p. 62.

45. Clark, Reel 1, USMA.

46. Murphy, Reel 8, USMA.

47. Norman Lewis, *The Honored Society* (New York: Putnam, 1964), pp. 9–24.

48. Clark, Reel 1, USMA; Murphy, Reel 8, USMA.

49. Quoted in Bryant, *op. cit.*, p. 86n.

50. *Ibid.*

51. *Ibid.*, p. 87.

52. Lucian K. Truscott, Jr., *Command Missions*, p. 289.

53. Clark, *Calc. Risk*, p. 263.

54. Ernie Pyle, *Brave Men*, p. 215.

55. Alexander, *op. cit.*, p. 117.

56. Pyle, *op. cit.*, p. 98; C. L. Sulzberger, "The Doughboy's Grim Road to Rome," New York *Times Magazine*, Feb. 20, 1944, p. 5.

57. Eric Sevareid, *Not So Wild a Dream*, p. 378.

58. Unpub. notes in possession of authors. The source did not wish to be identified.

59. Unpub. notes in possession of authors. The source did not wish to be identified.

60. Unpub. notes in possession of authors. The source did not wish to be identified.

61. Completed questionnaire in possession of authors.

62. Written recollections (unpub. notes) of Colonel George Walton.

63. One of the authors was present at this lunch.

64. Authors' notes.

65. Van de Velde and others, Interview #2 (unpub. notes in possession of authors).

66. Bill Mauldin, *Up Front*, p. 28.

67. Interview with authors (unpub. notes in possession of authors).

68. Sions, Reel 8, USMA.

69. Clark, Reel 1, USMA.

CHAPTER VI

1. Keyes, Reel 1, USMA.

2. General Eisenhower's selection as commanding officer of OVERLORD was the result of a long and involved series of discussions involving almost every Allied

leader of importance. The post was a coveted one and the selection was not made lightly. The appointment was announced on Dec. 6, 1943, and detailed descriptions of the circumstances surrounding it can be found in Richard M. Leighton, "OVERLORD Versus the Mediterranean," *Command Decisions*, ed. Kent R. Greenfield, pp. 271–285; Winston S. Churchill, *Closing the Ring*, pp. 300–306, 313, 335–340, 365–369, 377–379, 385, 418, 419; Robert E. Sherwood, *Roosevelt and Hopkins*, pp. 802, 803. William D. Leahy, *I Was There*, p. 213; Arthur Bryant, *Triumph in the West*, p. 74; Dwight D. Eisenhower, *Crusade in Europe*, pp. 207–209; Harry C. Butcher, *My Three Years with Eisenhower*, pp. 446, 448, 452, 453; Kenneth S. Davis, *Experience of War*, 421, 422, 444 448, 456–460.

3. Eric Sevareid, *Not So Wild a Dream*, p. 379.
4. Described in detail in *Anzio Beachhead, 25 January–25 May 1944*, (American Forces in Action series), p. 3.
5. Telegram, Churchill to Roosevelt, Dec. 25, 1943, quoted in Churchill, *op. cit.*, p. 437.
6. Eric Linklater, *The Campaign in Italy*, p. 152; Lucian Truscott, *Command Missions*, p. 286. In a press conference (reported in *Time*, Oct. 4, 1943), Lt. Gen. Joseph T. McNarney, U.S. Deputy Chief of Staff, said: "Today in Italy we are faced with nearly 20 German divisions; beyond Italy are the Alps, a formidable natural defense line, and many more German divisions. At the present time, Germany is capable of opposing any attack on a vital portion of her European defense with at least ten times the German forces defeated in Sicily."
7. Wynford Vaughn-Thomas, *Anzio*, pp. 17, 18; Clark, Reel 1, USMA.
8. Winston Churchill later wrote of this request: "If I had asked for a three-division lift I should not have got anything. How often in life must one be content with what one can get!" (quoted in Vaughn-Thomas, *op. cit.*, p. 191).
9. Recalled for the authors by an officer who was present but does not wish to be identified. See also Mark Clark, *Calculated Risk*, pp. 254, 255.
10. James Leasor, *War at the Top* (based on the experience of General Sir Leslie Hollis), p. 267.
11. Martin Blumenson, *Anzio: The Gamble That Failed*, p. 50.
12. *Anzio Beachhead, op. cit.*, p. 3.
13. For a discussion of the worth of the intelligence reports upon which the Anzio invasion plan was based, see Truscott, *op. cit.*, pp. 305–307; Fred Sheehan, *Anzio — Epic of Bravery*, pp. 29, 30, 39; Martin Blumenson, "General Lucas at Anzio," *Command Decisions*, ed. Kent R. Greenfield, pp. 328–331.
14. Clark, *op. cit.*, p. 254; Blumenson, *Anzio*, p. 50.
15. Clark, Reel 1, USMA.
16. A good description of both the rehearsal for the operation and the constitution of the naval force can be found in Sheehan, *op. cit.*, pp. 22–24.
17. Truscott, *op. cit.*, p. 292. General Clark's version is that he received a note from Truscott *after* the naval rehearsal, saying: "I believe you know me well enough to know that I would not make such a point [concerning the mismanagement] unless I actually felt *strongly* [Truscott's italics] about it. If this [Anzio invasion] is to be a forlorn hope or a 'suicide sashay,' then all I want to know is that fact. If so, I'm positive that there is no outfit in the world that can do it better than we [the 3rd Division] even though I reserve the right (personally) to believe we might deserve a better fate" (*Calc. Risk*, p. 269).
18. Vaughn-Thomas, *op. cit.*, p. 80.
19. As quoted in Blumenson, *Anzio*, p. 55.
20. Blumenson, *Lucas*, pp. 346, 347.
21. Albert Kesselring, *Kesselring: A Soldier's Record*, pp. 230, 231. The English journalist Vaughn-Thomas presents a detailed summary of Kesselring's concepts and plans in anticipation of the Anzio invasion (*op. cit.*, pp. 52–54).
22. Clark, *Calc. Risk*, pp. 250, 251, 256.

23. Clark, Reel 1, USMA.
24. Lucas Diary, as quoted in Blumenson, *Lucas*, p. 333.
25. Samuel Eliot Morison, *Sicily-Salerno-Anzio* (History of United States Naval Operations in World War II, Vol. IX), p. 328.
26. A good description of Kesselring's alternate provisions is contained in General-leutnant Kurt Maelzer's report The Problem of Rome During the Period of the Fighting near Anzio-Nettuno until the Evacuation of Rome on 4 June 1944 (unpublished).
27. Hanson W. Baldwin, "Men of Destiny — Leaders in North Africa," New York *Times Magazine*, June 20, 1943; Frank Gervasi, "The French Fight for Rome," *Collier's*, Feb. 26, 1944; Will Lang, "Big Charley's Men," *Life*, Feb. 1944; Charles de Gaulle, *The Complete War Memoirs of Charles de Gaulle*, pp. 603, 604, 605; Paul-Marie de la Gorce, *The French Army*, p. 342.
28. Eric Sevareid, *Not So Wild a Dream*, pp. 378, 379.
29. De Gaulle, *op. cit.*, p. 606.
30. In a conversation with the authors (1966), General Clark stated that this was a probability. He added, quite emphatically, that he was extremely grateful for the posts to which he had been assigned and for the opportunities he had had to serve his country. See, also, Sevareid, Reel 2, USMA; Vaughn-Thomas, *op. cit.*, p. 46.
31. Clark, *Calc. Risk*, p. 271.
32. *Ibid.*, p. 270.
33. Keyes, Reel 4, USMA.
34. Quoted in Fred Majdalany, *Cassino: Portrait of a Battle*, p. 90 (entry dated Jan. 22, 1944).
35. Harold L. Bond, *Return to Cassino*, p. 53.
36. Majdalany, *op. cit.*, pp. 66, 67.
37. Clark, *Calc. Risk*, p. 277.
38. The recorded interviews with the commanders, staff officers and journalists involved contain abundant comment upon the circumstances surrounding this engagement. Particularly helpful to the student or historian are Clark, Reel 1; Liese, Reel 3; Keyes, Reel 4; Porter, #1, Reel 7; Lang, Reel 8; Walker, Reel 9, USMA. Since Clark, Keyes and Walker were the three commanding generals primarily involved, their versions of the action are particularly illuminating.
39. United States Congress, House of Representatives, Committee on Military Affairs, *U.S. 79th Cong. 2 Sess. House Comm. on Military Affairs, Rapido River Crossing.* Page "iv" reproduces the conclusions reached by Robert P. Patterson, Secretary of War. This document contains the most complete summary of all of the facts and views of the engagement and should be read in its entirety. The British view is contained in the War Office publication *Current Reports from Overseas, No. 47*, dated July 22, 1944.
40. This is a report marked "Secret" which was declassified after World War II.
41. Unpub. notes in possession of authors. The source, interviewed in 1966, did not wish to be identified.
42. Sid Feder, "They'll Never Forget Mark Clark," *Saturday Evening Post*, May 18, 1946.
43. Truscott, *op. cit.*, p. 295.
44. Bond, *op. cit.*, p. 54. See also Frido von Senger und Etterlin, *Neither Fear nor Hope*.
45. "Murder at the Rapido?" *Time*, Jan. 28, 1946, p. 24.
46. Lang, Reel 8, USMA.
47. Sheehan, *op. cit.*, pp. 45–47.
48. Majdalany, *op. cit.*, p. 66.
49. *Ibid.*, p. 67.
50. Keyes, Reel 4, USMA.
51. Churchill, *op. cit.*, p. 488.

52. Blumenson, *Anzio*, pp. 51, 52.
53. These diary entries of General Lucas are quoted throughout Blumenson, *Lucas*.
54. Vaughn-Thomas, *op. cit.*, p. 44.
55. By midnight of D-Day, 36,034 men and 3069 vehicles had been landed (Morison, *op. cit.*, p. 343).
56. Blumenson, *Lucas*, p. 337.
57. Kesselring, *op. cit.*, pp. 233–237.
58. D. J. Fitzgerald, *History of the Irish Guards in the Second World War* (London: Gale and Polden, 1949).
59. In a 1966 discussion with the authors, General Keyes said that General Lucas had told him: "Clark and Alexander were there almost continually with me, breathing down my neck. If they didn't like what I was doing, they had plenty of opportunity to tell me, but they didn't" (Keyes, Reel 4, USMA). See also Blumenson, *Lucas*, p. 340.
60. Kesselring, *op. cit.*, p. 233.
61. Maelzer, *op. cit.*, pp. 3–5.
62. Quoted in Peter Tompkins, *A Spy in Rome*, p. 65.
63. Quoted in Churchill, *op. cit.*, p. 482.
64. Tompkins, *op. cit.*, 65.
65. J. Patrick Carroll-Abbing, *But for the Grace of God*, p. 52.
66. Franco Maugeri, *From the Ashes of Disgrace*, p. 265.
67. *Ibid.*, p. 266.
68. *Ibid.*, p. 267.
69. Bryant, *op. cit.*, p. 107; diary entry of Lord Alanbrooke.
70. Churchill, *Closing the Ring*, Appendix, Feb. 1944.
71. Blumenson, *Anzio*, pp. 140, 141. Alexander, *op. cit.*, p. 126.
72. Conversation with authors, Sept. 1966.
73. Alexander, *op. cit.*, p. 126.
74. Truscott, *op. cit.*, pp. 311, 312.
75. Interview, Mathews and others with Marshall, July 25, 1949, OCMH files, as cited in Blumenson, *Lucas*, p. 347.
76. Alexander, *op. cit.*, p. 125. General Kesselring was also in agreement. In an interview with an Associated Press correspondent in January 1946, he said, "It would have been the Anglo-American doom to overextend themselves. The landing force was initially weak, only a division or so of infantry, and without armor. It was a half-way measure as an offensive that was your basic error" (quoted in Majdalany, *op. cit.*, p. 74).
77. Keyes, Reel 4, USMA.
78. This is not the unsupported view of the authors. On two occasions Winston Churchill made the point in a not too subtle manner to General Alexander that he was remiss in not moving more promptly to insist upon the replacement of Lucas. In a letter dated Feb. 10, 1944, to Alexander he said: "I have a feeling that you may have hesitated to assert your authority because you were dealing so largely with Americans and therefore *urged* an advance instead of *ordering* [Churchill's italics] it. You are, however, entitled to give them orders . . ." (quoted, at greater length, in Churchill, *op. cit.*, pp. 448, 449). Two days before this he wrote to Field Marshal Dill in Washington: "My comment is that senior commanders should not 'urge' but 'order' " (*ibid.*, p. 487).

CHAPTER VII

1. J. Patrick Carroll-Abbing, *But for the Grace of God*, p. 67.
2. Bill Mauldin, *Up Front*, pp. 28, 29. In a conversation with the authors, Mr. Mauldin identified the corps commander (unnamed in the book) as Lucian K. Truscott, Jr.

3. The story about Patton slapping a soldier in a hospital in Sicily was first broken by Drew Pearson. After the war, references appeared to it in the memoirs of Eisenhower, Butcher, Bradley, Alexander and many others. However, the authors have additional material in their files indicating that General Patton's abuse of the soldier was not an isolated occurrence. He was evidently guilty of this kind of conduct on several occasions.

4. Although these statements are supported by many reports in the authors' files, the most concise (and illuminating) contrast of Clark, Patton and Truscott will be found in Fred Sheehan, *Anzio: Epic of Bravery*, pp. 114–116. And, in spite of generally good relations with the press, Sir Harold Alexander also occasionally found himself with "image" trouble. Once, during the period of the beachhead containment, he found it necessary to call all of the correspondents together and formally apologize to them for what had turned out to be unfair criticism on his part. See "Alexander's Rocket," *Newsweek*, April 3, 1944, p. 87.

5. Two excellent contemporary profiles; "Gen. Truscott, Chief of Allied Army," Chicago *Tribune*, May 30, 1944, and Will Lang, "Lucian King Truscott, Jr.," *Life*, October 2, 1944, do much to explain the impact of General Truscott on his associates and troops. See also Trevor Nevitt Dupuy, *The Military History of World War II*, Vol. XVII, *Combat Leaders of World War II*, pp. 14, 15; Wynford Vaughn-Thomas, *Anzio*, pp. 30, 31, 182; Martin Blumenson, *Anzio: The Gamble That Failed*, 144–147.

6. Winston S. Churchill, *Closing the Ring*, pp. 493, 494.

7. See Samuel Eliot Morison, *Sicily-Salerno-Anzio* (History of United States Naval Operations in World War II, Vol. IX), pp. 364–371. A description of the terrain is detailed in *Anzio Beachhead, 25 January–25 May 1944* (American Forces In Action series, issued by the Historical Dept. of the Army), pp. 4, 5.

8. Robert H. Adleman and George Walton, *The Devil's Brigade*, pp. 166–199.

9. A summary of the military activities at Anzio can be found in David Chandler, ed., *A Guide to the Military Battlefields of Europe*, Vol. II, pp. 87, 88. See also Earl Alexander of Tunis, *The Alexander Memoirs, 1940–1945*, p. 177; Albert Kesselring, *Kesselring: A Soldier's Record*, pp. 229–245; Mark Clark, *Calculated Risk*, pp. 283–310; Clark, Reel 1, USMA. John Lardner wrote a particularly good summary, "Our First Continental Invasion — Seven Bloody Months of Fighting," for *Newsweek*, May 22, 1944, pp. 28, 29.

10. Authoritative accounts of the Cassino battles in World War II are to be found in Fred Majdalany, *Cassino: Portrait of a Battle*; Clark, *Calc. Risk*, pp. 311–333; Alexander *op. cit.*, pp. 179–181. Chandler, *op. cit.*, pp. 94–96; Frido von Senger und Etterlin, *Neither Fear nor Hope* (in its entirety); Eric Linklater, *Campaign in Italy*, pp. 164–184, 217–230; Clark, Reel 1; Keyes, Reel 4; Porter, #1, Reel 7; and Lang, Reel 8, USMA.

11. *Newsweek*, May 22, 1944, p. 29.

12. Clark, *Calc. Risk*, p. 311.

13. VI Corps Intelligence Report, 26–27 May 1944; Senger, *op. cit.*, p. 181.

14. Alexander, *op. cit.*, pp. 120, 121. On another occasion, Sir Harold wrote to Sir Alan Brooke: "We are fighting the best soldiers in the world — what men!" (Alexander to CIGS, Mar. 22, 1944, Lord Alanbrooke, *Personal Files: Notes on My Life*, XIII, 15).

15. Majdalany, *op. cit.*, pp. 96–105.

16. Clark, Reel 1, USMA.

17. Porter, #1, Reel 7, USMA.

18. Keyes, Reel 4, USMA.

19. Clark, *Calc. Risk*, pp. 314–323.

20. But Etterlin emphatically disagrees with these estimates of Clark's conduct (*op. cit.*, pp. 204, 205).

21. George Walton, one of the authors of this book, was the air support officer involved. This is his recollection.
22. Clark, *Calc. Risk*, pp. 322, 323.
23. Carroll-Abbing, *op. cit.*, pp. 71, 72.
24. Interview with the authors, 1966.
25. Peter Tompkins, *A Spy in Rome*, pp. 159, 160; Carroll-Abbing, *op. cit.*, p. 75.
26. E. Piscitelli, *Storia della Resistenza Romana* (Rome: Barit Laterza, 1965), p. 259.
27. Robert Katz, *Death in Rome*, pp. 8, 9; Christopher Hibbert, *Il Duce*, pp. 269, 270.
28. Carroll-Abbing, *op. cit.*, p. 75.
29. Norman Kogan, *Italy and the Allies*, pp. 171–177.
30. Sions, Reel 8, USMA.
31. Kesselring, *op. cit.*, pp. 120–122, 196.
32. Porter, #1, Reel 7, USMA.
33. Robert Capa, *Slightly Out of Focus*, pp. 103, 104.
34. Quoted in Katz, *op. cit.*, p. 43.
35. Franco Maugeri, *From the Ashes of Disgrace*, pp. 201, 202.
36. Jane Scrivener, *Inside Rome with the Germans*, p. 121.
37. II Corps Journal File, G–2, June 1944. This was a captured Regimental Order of the 1028 PGR, dated 2 April 1944.
38. Ernest F. Fisher, Jr., "Rome: An Open City," *Military Review*, Aug. 1965; Scrivener, *op. cit.*, p. 147.
39. Maugeri, *op. cit.*, pp. 296, 297; Scrivener, *op. cit.*, pp. 94, 179, 185; Fisher, *op. cit.*, p. 77. A British officer in the city said, "The Germans were turning the Eternal City into a sort of front-line base. Divisions from all over northern Italy were converging upon it" (Sam Derry, *The Rome Escape Line*, p. 128). The matter was exhaustively discussed in Kesselring's trial before a postwar Italian court, and the German use of the city as a rail center was conclusively established; see Katz, *op. cit.*, pp. 232, 233. Also, cf. notes 37 and 38 to Chapter III, above.
40. Fisher, *op. cit.*, pp. 74, 75.
41. Many of the questionnaires returned to the authors by American officers and enlisted men indicate that one of the questions asked of them with great frequency by the Romans in the first days after Rome fell was: "Can we ride our bicycles?"
42. Kesselring, *op. cit.*, pp. 271, 272. There may have been some basis for this belief; see Kogan, *op. cit.*, p. 101.
43. Kogan, *op. cit.*, p. 101; Hibbert, *op. cit.*, p. 269.
44. Maugeri, *op. cit.*, p. 291.
45. The remarkable book by Robert Katz, *Death in Rome*, is a full documentation of this period. The authors have found much corroborative material in Scrivener, *op. cit.*, pp. 144–147; Maugeri, *op. cit.*, *passim*; Fifth Army Interrogation Reports — June 1944, (unpublished); a captured 5th Mountain Division (German) Report dated Mar. 3, 1944; Michael Stern, *An American in Rome*, p. 17; Hibbert, *op. cit.*, p. 270.
46. Katz, *op. cit.*, *passim*.
47. 5th Mt. Division report, *op. cit.*
48. Katz, *op. cit.*, pp. 232–234.
49. *Ibid.*, pp. 11, 12.
50. This material appeared in a 1966 telecast over the National Educational Television network, in a program devoted to his life, which appeared as part of the series *Biography*.
51. One of the authors of this book, George Walton, was present.

52. Pope Pius XII, Encyclical, *Divini redemptoris*, as quoted in Saul Friedländer, *Pius XII and the Third Reich*, pp. 80, 81; see pp. 82–86 for more discussions of the Pope's attitudes toward Russia and the Communists.
53. Katz, *op. cit.*, 253–258.
54. *Ibid.*, pp. 12n., 13n. See also, in its entirety, *Wartime Correspondence between President Roosevelt and Pope Pius XII*, with an introduction and explanatory notes by Myron C. Taylor (New York: Macmillan, 1947).
55. Quoted in Katz, *op. cit.*, p. 13n.
56. These are quoted in full throughout Friedländer, *op. cit.*
57. See comments by Father Lieber on *Pius XII and the Third Reich*, *Look*, May 1, 1966.
58. James Efron, "Israeli Author Says Efforts of Pius XII Saved Many Jews," New York *Times*, April 24, 1966; *The Last Three Popes and the Jews* (New York: Hawthorn Books, 1967).
59. Efron, *op. cit.*
60. Lieber, *op. cit.*; Stern, *op. cit.*, pp. 21, 22; Carroll-Abbing, *But for the Grace of God*, p. 41.
61. Efron, *op. cit.*
62. Sions, Reel 8, USMA.
63. The anecdotes in this and the immediately preceding paragraphs are to be found in Derry, *op. cit.*
64. Vaughn-Thomas, *Anzio*, pp. 188, 189; Katz, *op. cit.*, p. 91.
65. James Byrnes, *Speaking Frankly*, pp. 56, 57.
66. Harry C. Butcher, *My Three Years with Eisenhower*, p. 515. See also Churchill-Roosevelt correspondence quoted in Churchill, *op. cit.* pp. 503–505.
67. Churchill, *op. cit.*, p. 705.

CHAPTER VIII

1. Heinrich von Vietinghoff, The Campaign in Italy: The Operations of the 71st German Inf. Div. During the Month of May 1944 (unpublished), pp. 39, 40.
2. Captured German documents pertaining to the period prior to the beginning of the Allied attack on May 11, 1944, prove that the deception was successful and that the Germans seriously underestimated the Allied order of battle. "This poor estimation of our capabilities resulted in the enemy being completely surprised when our attack began" (II Corps Operations Report, June 1944, p. 2).
3. For a description of the German deployment, see Vietinghoff: ". . . it must be stated that at that time all commands . . . misjudged the value of the French divisions" (op. cit., p. 3).
4. The memoirs of both commanders on this point offer unmistakable evidence that there was no real meeting of the minds. See Mark Clark, *Calculated Risk*, pp. 338–342, and Earl Alexander of Tunis, *The Alexander Memoirs, 1940–1945*, ed. John North, pp. 127, 128.
5. As a sampling of the general feeling that Rome was a major prize, see Alexander, *op. cit.*, p. 128; Clark, *Calc. Risk*, pp. 334–366 *passim.*; Albert Kesselring, *Kesselring: A Soldier's Record*, pp. 229–245; Sir John Kennedy, *The Business of War*, p. 310; Arthur Bryant, *Triumph in the West*, p. 102; Eric Linklater, *The Campaign in Italy*, p. 96; Martin Blumenson, "General Lucas at Anzio," *Command Decisions*, ed. Kent R. Greenfield, p. 324n.
6. This list is detailed in Sir Harold's dispatches in Lord Alanbrooke, *Personal Papers*. See also Alexander, *op. cit.*, p. 155.
7. Clark, Reel 1, USMA.
8. "General Clark Sees F.D.R. in Secret Before Big Drive," Chicago *Tribune*, May 13, 1944.

9. Maurine Clark, *Captain's Bride, General's Lady*, pp. 115, 116.
10. For a description of the German attitude and the German troop disposition, see German Estimation of the Situation, Effects of Allied Attacks and German Countermeasures During the May 1944 Offensive (unpublished), pp. 117–131. This document represents information from various German staff levels secured immediately after the surrender of the German forces in Italy. See also Chester G. Starr, *From Salerno to the Alps*, pp. 209–213.
11. Kesselring, *op. cit.*, p. 239.
12. Sydney T. Mathews, *The French in the Drive on Rome*, p. 122; Heinrich Greiner, ed., Battle for Rome and Retreat Northward (unpublished), May 28, 1947, pp. 3–8.
13. Vietinghoff, *op. cit.*, pp. 39, 40.
14. Conversation with authors, November 1966; Clark, *Calc. Risk*, p. 338.
15. Frido von Senger und Etterlin, *Neither Fear nor Hope*, pp. 244–247.
16. Charles de Gaulle, *The Complete War Memoirs of Charles de Gaulle*, pp. 608–612; Vietinghoff, *op. cit.*; Mathews, *op. cit.* (in its entirety); "French Units Punch Hole in Gustav Line near Key Strongpoint," *Stars and Stripes*, May 16, 1944. Note also extract from the translation of a letter addressed to his wife by Rittmeister (Captain) van der Borch, commanding 115 Rcn. Bn. (letter was found on the battlefield): "You can have no idea how hard this retreat is or how terrible . . . our French and Moroccan opponents are remarkably good. My heart bleeds when I look at my beautiful Abteilung after 5 days; 150 men lost . . . the supply train is already far in the rear . . . my command tank and all the radio and wire equipment have been demolished by a French tank . . . Perhaps we will succeed in escaping a collapse of the entire Italian front, but there seems to be small hope of this" (quoted in VI Corps Report, 26–27 May '44).
17. Clark, *Calc. Risk*, p. 348; Clark, Reel 1, USMA.
18. Porter, #1, Reel 7, USMA.
19. De Gaulle, *op. cit.*, p. 607.
20. *Ibid.*, p. 610.
21. "Allies Supply Missing Pieces for Jigsaw Puzzle of Attack," *Newsweek*, May 29, 1944, p. 21.
22. *Ibid.*, p. 22.
23. Vietinghoff, *op. cit.*, pp. 40, 41.
24. Porter, #1, Reel 7, USMA.
25. Interview with van de Velde, June 1966 (notes in possession of authors).
26. Wladyslaw Anders, *An Army in Exile*, p. 153. Alexander, *op. cit.*, p. 155.
27. Winston S. Churchill, *Closing the Ring*, p. 604.
28. *Ibid.*, pp. 605, 606.
29. This surge is described in detail in Lucian K. Truscott, Jr., *Command Missions*, pp. 370–380; George F. Howe, *The Battle History of the 1st Armored Division*, pp. 317–334. Starr, *op. cit.*, pp. 176–220. *Anzio Beachhead 25 January–25 May 1944* (American Forces in Action series), pp. 117–119.
30. *Stars and Stripes*, May 24, 1944. The daily issues of this newspaper contain illuminating sidelights, in addition to offering accurate daily combat summaries. The May and June 1944 issues of the New York *Times* and the Chicago *Tribune* are especially helpful in constructing a composite picture of events from the breakout until the day Rome fell.
31. From a letter written in 1966 to the authors in response to a request for personal recollections.
32. This anecdote appears in almost every published description of the linkup between the Anzio forces and the bulk of the Fifth Army advancing up the penin-

sula. The two military sources (out of many) used were the VI Corps Report, May 23–25, 1944 (unpublished), and *Stars and Stripes*, May 26, 1944.
33. Franco Maugeri, *From the Ashes of Disgrace*, p. 294.
34. Many Roman newspapers during this period contained exhortations signed by Kesselring and other German leaders (and also by Italian Fascist leaders) to join in the last-ditch fight against the approaching Allied armies. There is little evidence of an affirmative response.
35. Peter Tompkins, *A Spy in Rome*, p. 209.
36. Jane Scrivener, *Inside Rome with the Germans*, p. 181.
37. There are simply too many sources of adverse criticism to be listed in this space. However, many of the documents listed in the Bibliography under "Unpublished Sources," as well as such memoirs as Senger's *Neither Fear nor Hope* (e.g., pp. 246, 247) indicate that Albert Kesselring was not an object of unflawed admiration to his subordinates.
38. Kesselring, *op. cit.*, p. 238.

CHAPTER IX

1. Second interview with Dr. van de Velde, 1966. Notes in possession of authors.
2. Sydney T. Mathews, "General Clark's Decision to Drive on Rome," *Command Decisions*, ed. Kent Robert Greenfield, p. 352; Mark Clark, *Calculated Risk*, pp. 340, 341.
3. Earl Alexander of Tunis, *The Alexander Memoirs, 1940–1945*, ed. John North, p. 127. In a letter dated May 28, 1944, Winston Churchill told General Alexander: "At this distance it seems much more important to cut their line of retreat than anything else. . . . A cop [sic] is much more important than Rome, which would anyhow come as its consequence. The cop is the one thing that matters" (Winston Churchill, *Closing the Ring*, p. 607).
4. Clark, Reel 1, USMA.
5. In a conversation with the authors (September 1966), Clark said that there were a number of roads that the German Tenth Army could have used for a northward retreat. His opponent, General Frido von Senger und Etterlin, was not of the same opinion; in his memoirs, *Neither Fear nor Hope*, he says: "The remaining available mountain roads east of the Via Casilina were now of doubtful and limited value in view of the enemy's overwhelming air superiority" (p. 249).
6. General Clark's views of the controversy are presented in a somewhat softer version in his memoirs, *Calculated Risk*, pp. 340–361. But see Mathews, *op. cit.*, pp. 351–363.
7. Clark, Reel 1, USMA.
8. Murphy, Reel 8, USMA.
9. General Truscott's version appears in his memoirs, *Command Missions*, pp. 368–376.
10. Harold L. Bond, *Return to Cassino*, pp. 184, 185.
11. Truscott, *op. cit.*, p. 369.
12. Murphy, Reel 8, USMA.
13. Senger, *op. cit.*, p. 251.
14. *Ibid.*, p. 252.
15. Memo, Gruenther to Clark, May 26, 1944, cited in Mathews, *op. cit.*, p. 361.
16. Alexander, *op. cit.*, p. 127.
17. Clark, Reel 1, USMA.
18. Truscott, *op. cit.*, 368–376. This criticism of Clark will be found throughout the section cited.
19. Telephone conversation, Truscott to Brann, VI Corps War Room Journal, May 25, 1944, cited in Mathews, *op. cit.*, p. 360.

20. Martin Blumenson, *Anzio: The Gamble That Failed*, p. 192.
21. Morning Report, 339th F.A. Bn., 88th Inf. Div., May 30, 1944.
22. Keyes, Reel 4, USMA.
23. Clark, *Calc. Risk*, p. 360.
24. This was underlined in the report edited by Heinrich Greiner, Battle for Rome and Retreat Northwards, May 28, 1947 (unpublished) : "As might be anticipated, a large number of men became separated from their units during the extremely hasty withdrawal movement through Rome; by means of a network of straggler collecting points, disposed in depth, organized by the rear services upon order of the 362 Division, and which proved very satisfactory, a large number of these stragglers was collected. The stragglers were assembled in straggler-units, in platoons, or in companies, and brought up to the fighting front; wherever possible they were assigned to covering positions behind the fighting front or to positions previously selected for future occupation" (p. 30). Further evidence of the fighting ability of these men is given by Fred Sheehan in *Anzio — Epic of Bravery*: "Nowhere was their ability for reconstituting, from broken battalions and other shattered elements, rear guard units of unimpeachable fortitude more dramatically demonstrated than during these last days before Rome. Of the 377 prisoners taken at Velletri, there were representatives of fifty different companies from a variety of battalions and regiments and divisions. Yet they fought on as a cohesive unit until overwhelmed" (p. 206).
25. Conversation with authors, November 1966. Notes in possession of authors.
26. Keyes, Reel 4, USMA.
27. At 1400 hours, May 29, 1944. The forces placed under II Corps are detailed in George F. Howe, *The Battle History of the 1st Armored Division*, p. 334. Also given are the geographical boundary lines separating II Corps, VI Corps, and the British Eighth Army.
28. In subsequent conversations with the authors, Dr. van de Velde (June 1966) and General Porter (Porter, #2, Reel 8, USMA) supplied the description of Malitch's activities during this period.
29. Porter, Reel 7, USMA.
30. This was the considered opinion of many II Corps operations and intelligence officers who participated in the planning sessions and who were later interviewed by the authors. See also Porter, Reel 7, USMA.
31. Porter, Reel 8, USMA.
32. Interview #2 with Dr. van der Velde (notes in possession of authors).
33. Porter, Reel 8, USMA.
34. Franco Maugeri, *From the Ashes of Disgrace*, pp. 296, 297.
35. Jane Scrivener, *Inside Rome with the Germans*, p. 191.
36. *Ibid.*, p. 190.
37. *Ibid.*, p. 193.
38. J. Patrick Carroll-Abbing, *But for the Grace of God*, p. 94.
39. Peter Tompkins, *A Spy in Rome*, p. 331.
40. Sam Derry, *The Rome Escape Line*, p. 217.
41. Kurt Maelzer, The Problem of Rome During the Period of the Fighting near Anzio-Nettuno Until the Evacuation of Rome on 4 June 1944, (unpublished), pp. 11, 12.
42. The lead story on page 1 of the *Stars And Stripes* for Monday, June 5, 1944, carried the five-column headline "YANKS BATTLE WAY INTO ROME." The subhead, over two columns, read, "City's Fate Uncertain: Nazis May Pull Out or Fight for Capital."
43. 34th Division Intelligence Summary. Information given by Lieutenant Douglas Plowden, 86th Fighter Bomber Group, who had been shot down in January 1944 and escaped from the Germans on May 30, 1944.

44. Conversation with Mark Clark, November 1966 (notes in possession of authors).
45. Operations Report, 339th Inf. Regt., 85th Inf. Div., June 1944 (quoted in part).
46. "Pope's Fears for Rome Take New Turn as City Becomes a German Target," *Newsweek*, June 12, 1944, p. 68.
47. Carroll-Abbing, *op. cit.*, p. 96.
48. June 5, 1944, p. 29.
49. Occurring in a letter to President Eamon de Valera of Ireland, April 19, 1944.
50. *Newsweek*, June 12, 1944, *op. cit.*, p. 70.
51. April 2, 1944, p. 19.
52. Ernest F. Fisher, Jr., "Rome: An Open City," *Military Review*, August 1965, p. 75.
53. Robert Katz, *Death in Rome*, pp. 239, 240.
54. G–2 Historical Summaries, Fifth Army, June 1944–April 30, 1945.
55. "German Soldiers Mutiny," New York *Times*, June 5, 1944.
56. History of 351st Inf. Regt., June 1944, p. 2.
57. Bennis G. Pullen, Completed questionnaire (in possession of authors).
58. Letter to authors, 1966, in possession of authors.
59. Eric Sevareid, *Not So Wild a Dream*, p. 408.
60. Conversation with authors, November 1966 (notes in possession of authors).
61. Holsinger, Reel 3, USMA.
62. Keyes, Reel 4, USMA.
63. Porter, Reel 7, USMA.
64. Patrol to Rome, unpublished report of Captain Taylor Radcliffe (written about 1945).
65. Hamilton H. Howze. The Rome Operation, unpublished recollections, written June 6, 1944.
66. Sloan, Reel 10, USMA.
67. Robert H. Adleman and George Walton, *The Devil's Brigade*, pp. 217, 218.
68. Andersson, Reel 3, USMA.
69. Conversation with General Frederick, 1965 notes in possession of authors. See also Clark, *Calc. Risk*, p. 364.
70. Howze, *op. cit.*, pp. 18, 19.
71. Keyes, Reel 4, USMA.
72. "Clark's Mother Happy," New York *Times*, June 5, 1944.
73. Scrivener, *op. cit.*, pp. 194–197.
74. Derry, *op. cit.*, p. 222.
75. Tompkins, Reel 3, USMA.
76. Peter Tompkins, *A Spy In Rome*, p. 339.
77. Clark, *Calc. Risk*, p. 365.

CHAPTER X

1. Murphy, Reel 8, USMA.
2. Bill Mauldin, *Up Front*, p. 163.
3. George Walton, one of the authors of this book.
4. Jack Foise, "Relief Rather than Elation Felt at Home on Rome's Fall," *Stars and Stripes*, Mediterranean Edition, June 7, 1944.
5. *Ibid.*
6. June 6, 1944.
7. William Strand, "G.I. Harangues All Rome from Duce's Balcony," Chicago *Tribune*, June 6, 1944; *Stars and Stripes*, Mediterranean Edition, June 6, 1944, p. 1.
8. Some especially good contemporary descriptions of the day's impact upon the Italian population are Daniel Lang, "Letter From Rome," *New Yorker*, June 17,

1944, pp. 58, 59; Frank Gervasi, "Rome Lives Again," *Collier's*, Sept. 9, 1944, p. 11; History, 351st Infantry Regt., June 1944, pp. 8, 9; Wade Jones, "All is Confusion in City, but All Are Having Fun," *Stars and Stripes*, Mediterranean Edition, June 7, 1944.

9. Jones, *ibid.*

10. Descriptions of the black market which followed the Allied entry into Rome are to be found in almost every memoir covering the period. The authors have used Gervasi, *op. cit.*, and a letter dated April 19, 1966, from Dr. van de Velde (in possession of authors) as primary sources.

11. Copy in possession of authors.

12. Eric Sevareid, *Not So Wild a Dream*, pp. 412, 413.

13. Sam Derry, *The Rome Escape Line*, p. 227.

14. Tompkins, Reel 3, USMA.

15. *Stars and Stripes*, Mediterranean Edition, June 6, 1944, p. 1; Robert Murphy, *Diplomat Among Warriors*, pp. 203, 204; Norman Kogan, *Italy and the Allies*, pp. 76–79; "Sunshine and Scars," *Time*, June 19, 1944, p. 38.

16. "Northwest of Rome, Nazis Say," Chicago *Tribune*, June 5, 1944.

17. Winston S. Churchill, *Closing the Ring*, pp. 610, 611.

18. President Roosevelt's speech is placed in perspective by the editorial "The Victory of Rome," New York *Times*, June 6, 1944. See also Anne O'Hare McCormick's brilliant critique, "Abroad: The Americans Lead the Way into Rome," New York *Times*, June 5, 1944.

19. Sevareid, *op. cit.*, p. 415.

20. An excellent description of the passage of combat troops through Rome that day is contained in Harold L. Bond, *Return to Cassino*, pp. 216–231.

21. Clark, Reel 1, USMA.

22. Porter, Reel 7.

23. Mark Clark, *Calculated Risk*, pp. 365, 366. The story was broadened in its telling by some of the Fifth Army officers present that day.

24. Keyes, Reel 4, USMA. See also Sevareid, *op. cit.*, pp. 413, 414.

25. Murphy, *op. cit.*, p. 204.

26. Clark, *Calc. Risk*, pp. 374, 375.

27. Sions, Reel 8, USMA.

28. The officer was Colonel George Walton.

29. "Pope Greets Americans In Vatican," *Life*, June 26, 1944.

30. Sevareid, *op. cit.*, p. 416.

31. Derry, *op. cit.*, p. 239.

32. Murphy, *op. cit.*, p. 205.

33. General Albert Wedemeyer, one of the most influential of the American military planners, has never softened his convictions: "I, for one, still think of the Mediterranean [the Italian campaign] as a trap which prolonged the war in Europe by a year. It was a sideshow and it cost many unnecessary lives" (*Wedemeyer Reports!*, p. 168). Major General J. F. C. Fuller, a military commentator of considerable importance, showed his agreement with those who considered the Italian campaign a waste by his writings during and after World War II. For example, in a *Newsweek* article, "The 'Second-Hand' Front in Italy" (March 13, 1944), he concludes, "We should never have embarked upon this Italian adventure because it was unstrategic from the start." There are other negative opinions from sources that are worthy of a respectful hearing. But there are also important voices on the other side. Field Marshal Albert Kesselring, before he had arranged his concepts for his memoirs, told his Allied captors in 1947: "If you had never pitted your divisions in the Mediterranean, you would not have won the victory in the West" (U.S. Naval Inst. *Proceedings*, LXXX, 31). Sir Harold Alexander, in discussing the concept of entering upon the

campaign, said, "It was the Germans, not the Allies, who were contained in Italy; and, as the record shows, the drain on their strength was greater than on our own" (*The Alexander Memoirs, 1940–1945*, pp. 158, 159).

34. "The conclusion is that the battle for Italy was not only justified but even imperative and the problem one of simply doing whatever seemed best for one's own theatre, irrespective of the general strategic plan. Of course if the objective was to bring the war to an early end, regardless of what chances remained of snatching a semi-political victory, then the Mediterranean war must be considered unnecessary, but this is a view I cannot share" (Albert Kesselring, *Kesselring: A Soldier's Record*, p. 167).

"The effect of our success in Italy makes impossible withdrawal of German forces to assist their defense against OVERLORD" (Harry C. Butcher, *My Three Years with Eisenhower*, p. 551).

"I have staked a great deal on the Italian campaign in all our arguments with the Americans. I felt throughout that we had wonderful opportunities of inflicting a real telling defeat on the Germans which would be worth anything in connection with the cross-Channel operations" (Sir Alan Brooke, diary entry, May 20, 1944, quoted in Arthur Bryant, *Triumph in the West*, p. 141).

"At another conference on December 27, 1943, General Zeitzker, Chief of the [German] General Staff, repeatedly stressed the difficulty of finding reserves to halt the Russians: 'We will have to look around for new forces . . . If we could just straighten that out a little and get some fresh troops, we could get going again' " (F. Gilbert, *Hitler Directs His War*, pp. 79, 89, 93).

"Although the Quebec decisions satisfied no one entirely at the time, they were probably the best possible for the successful prosecution of the war at that stage. It would have been a mistake not to continue the Italian campaign, for there was no other way open to us, in the coming winter of 1943–1944, of engaging the Germans on land in any appreciable strength and of drawing reserves from the Russian front. We could almost certainly have occupied the whole of Italy quite quickly had we devoted more of our resources to the effort. But this could hardly have been done without either postponing the landing in France, or reducing the scale of operations in the Pacific against the Japanese" (Sir John Kennedy, *The Business of War*, p. 300).

35. General Eisenhower discusses his reasoning in *Crusade in Europe*, pp. 166–168.

36. "Of the American service leaders, Eisenhower was the leading soldier-statesman; only he could have held together the vast amalgam of U.S. and British Armies, Navies and Air Force. Eisenhower was no strategist, but then he did not have to be one. There were quite enough, if not too many, without him" (James Leasor, *War at the Top* — based on the diaries of General Sir Leslie Hollis). And see General Alexander's tacit acceptance of Eisenhower as the dominant influence in the Italian campaign, evidenced by the somewhat bitter summary in Alexander, *op. cit.*, pp. 41–43. See also General Clark's summary, Clark, *Calc. Risk*, pp. 368–371. In a New York *Times* story ("Eisenhower Role In Planning Cited," June 7, 1967), the historian Alfred J. Chandler, Jr., is quoted as describing General Eisenhower to a meeting of the Organization of American Historians as "the architect of the first truly unified Allied command, which helped achieve . . . victory."

37. There is reason to believe that Winston Churchill was never really convinced that the capture of Rome was the great propaganda tool that he spoke of so constantly. It seems to the authors that the Prime Minister and his staff were honestly convinced that the Italian campaign was vital, but, in order to simplify the issues, they used Rome as the focus, somewhat in the spirit of the comment, "If there were no God, it would be necessary to invent one."

38. Will Lang, the *Time-Life* correspondent who earned widespread general respect for the honesty, balance and insight of his combat reports, told the authors in 1966, "Mark Clark's role in all this [the Italian campaign] was one of following orders and then finding himself with a major difficult campaign in mountainous territory with really too few troops and not enough vessels (Lang, Reel 8, USMA). In substantiation, note the general criticism of Clark as a result of the Anzio debacle. Yet Kesselring, interviewed by American correspondents immediately after his capture, said that the biggest Allied mistake at Anzio was in landing a force too small to accomplish its mission. As we have seen, Clark is on record as protesting the size of the force well before the operation was launched.

39. Quoted by Trumbull Higgins in *Winston Churchill and the Second Front*, pp. 152, 153.

40. See note 33, above.

41. Murphy, Reel 8, USMA. Also, an illuminating portrait of General Clark's ability to deal with the Russians in Austria during the immediate postwar period can be found in "An American Abroad," *Time*, June 24, 1946, p. 27.

42. Porter, #2, Reel 8, USMA.

43. Porter, #1, Reel 7, USMA.

44. The officer was Colonel George Walton.

BIBLIOGRAPHY

UNPUBLISHED SOURCES

A. UNPUBLISHED MATERIAL IN POSSESSION OF THE AUTHORS

Andersson, Col. Kingsley S.: Correspondence with authors, 1966; extracts from diaries, 1944.

Clark, Gen. Mark W.: Notes on telephone conversations, Aug.–Dec. 1966; corroborating and supplementing material.

Dickinson, William: Notes of interview with authors, Aug. 1966.

Eisenhower, Gen. Dwight D.: Notes of interview with authors, Aug. 1966.

Greiner, Lt. Gen. Heinrich: Written recollections of fighting around Rome in early summer of 1944.

Howze, Hamilton H.: "The Rome Operation."

Kilroe, Col. R. H.: Notes of interview with authors, Jan. 1966.

Lynch, Maj. Gen. George E.: Correspondence with authors, 1966.

Malitch, Mrs. Lucille: Notes of interview with authors, June 1966.

Mauldin, Bill: Notes of interview with authors, Sept. 1966.

Murphy, Robert: Letter to authors, Nov. 20, 1967.

Pacatte, Andre: Notes of interview with authors, Apr. 1966.

Porter, Gen. Robert W.: Correspondence with authors, 1966.

Shaffer, Max E.: Letter to authors, July 10, 1966.

Stovall, Col. Oran C.: Letter to authors, Apr. 7, 1966.

Tittman, Harold: Notes of interview with authors, Apr. 1966.

van de Velde, Robert: Notes of interviews with authors, Oct., Nov. 1966.

Walker, Maj. Gen. Fred L.: Notes of untaped interview with authors (following taped interview listed in section C below), Jan. 29, 1966.

Walton, Col. George: Personal records, correspondence, orders, written recollections.

B. PERSONAL PAPERS AND DIARIES

In every case, this material was made available to the authors by the source himself.

Andersson, Col. Kingsley S.: Personal diaries, 1944.

Clark, Gen. Mark W.: Letters and memoranda from Winston S. Churchill.

Frederick, Maj. Gen. Robert T.: Correspondence, files.

Howze, Gen. Hamilton H.: Diary, written recollections, personal records.

Ives, Maj. Gen. Robert M.: Diary and correspondence.

Keyes, Lt. Gen. Geoffrey: Private correspondence, files, records and pictures, Inspector General's report on Rapido River crossing.

Lynch, Maj. Gen. George E.: Diaries, personal papers.

Stovall, Col. Oran: Undated letter to Dr. Robert L. Wagner evaluating accuracy of previously published accounts of 36th Division activities in Italy; letter from Maj. Gen. Fred L. Walker, May 5, 1966; written comments on accuracy of published accounts of 36th Division activities; field order directing that road be built over Mt. Artemisio, May 30, 1944; copy of memorandum "The Road That Could Not Be Built," by John Bob Parks (111th Engr. Bn.).

Walker, Maj. Gen. Fred L.: Correspondence with Harold L. Bond (author of *Return to Cassino*), Brig. Gen. Robert Stack, and members of 36th Inf. Div. Assn.

C. TAPED INTERVIEWS

The tapes itemized below have been donated by the authors to the United States Military Academy, West Point, N.Y. Citations of the tapes in the Chapter Notes are in the form "Clark, Reel 1, USMA."

Reel Number	Interviewee	Date of Interview	Place of Interview
1	Gen. Mark W. Clark	9/22/66	Charleston, S. C.
2	Eric Sevareid	8/66	Washington, D.C.
3	Col. Kingsley S. Andersson	4/22/66	Chase City, Va.
	Peter Tompkins	4/21/66	McClean, Va.
	Maj. Gen. James W. Holsinger	4/23/66	Durham, N.C.
	Maj. Gen. Mercer C. Walter	4/19/66	Alexandria, Va.
	Theodore W. Liese	5/30/66	Prescott, Ariz.
4	Lt. Gen. Geoffrey Keyes	5/66	Tucson, Ariz.
5	Maj. Gen. John Willems	5/28/66	San Diego, Cal.
6	Col. K. S. Andersson (dup.)	4/22/66	Chase City, Va.
	Robert van de Velde	4/15/66	Princeton, N.J.
	Brig. Gen. Robert Stack	4/18/66	King George, Va.
	Gen. Robert W. Porter	11/3/65	Canal Zone
7	Gen. Robert W. Porter	9/66	Washington, D.C.
8	Will Lang	9/66	New York, N.Y.
	Robert Murphy	9/66	New York, N.Y.
	Harry Sions	9/66	New York, N.Y.
	Maj. Gen. Fred L. Walker	1/29/66	Alexandria, Va.
	Maj. Gen. John E. Sloan	3/30/66	Weaverville, N.C.
9	Maj. Gen. George E. Lynch	3/28/66	Columbus, Ga.
10	Maj. Gen. Robert T. Frederick	10/66	Palo Alto, Cal.

D. UNIT REPORTS AND HISTORIES
IN THE NATIONAL ARCHIVES, WORLD WAR II DIVISION, ALEXANDRIA, VA.

Fifth Army Interrogation Reports, June 1944.

Fifth Army G–2 Historical Summaries, June 1944–April 30, 1945.

II Corps Operations Report, May 1944.

II Corps G–2 Journal and File, June 1944.

II Corps Operations Report, June 1944.

II Corps Operations in Italy Report, June–Dec. 1944.
Hq. II Corps Periodic Report, May 13–31, 1944.
II Corps Operations in Italy.
A Brief History II Corps (Editoriale Domus).
IV Corps G–3 Journal File, Jan. 16–June 1944.
Hq. VI Corps After Action Reports, Jan. 31–May 1944.
VI Corps G–2 Journal, May 16–19, 1944.
VI Corps G–2 Journal, May 20–22, 1944.
VI Corps, May 23–25, 1944.
VI Corps, May 26–27, 1944.
VI Corps G–2 Journal, May 28–29, 1944.
VI Corps G–2 Journal, May 30–31, 1944.
VI Corps Historical Record, June 1944.
3rd Inf. Div. G–2 Periodic Reports, May 1944.
3rd Inf. Div. G–2 Periodic Reports, June, 1944.
Hq. 3rd Inf. Div. Operations Report.
34th Inf. Div. G–2 Monthly Report, May 1944.
34th Inf. Div. G–2 Monthly Report, June 1944.
34th Inf. Div. G–2 Summaries, June 1944.
36th Inf. Div. G–2 Summaries, May 26–31, 1944.
45th Inf. Div. G–2 General Summary, May 1–31, 1944.
45th Inf. Div. G–2 Periodic Reports, May 11–15, 1944.
45th Inf. Div. G–2 General Summary, June 1–30, 1944.
6th Armored Inf. Regt. History, May 1944.
135th Inf. Regt. 34th Inf. Div. History, May 11–Sept. 1944.
141st Inf. Regt., May 1944.
141st Inf. Regt., June 1944.
142nd Inf. Regt. 36th Div. Operations Report.
142nd Inf. Regt. 36th Div., May 1944.
142nd Inf. Regt. 36th Div., June 1944.
143rd Inf. Regt. 36th Div. Operations Report.
143rd Inf. Regt., May 1944.
143rd Inf. Regt., June 1944.
168th Inf. Regt. 34th Inf. Div. History, May 1944.
180th Inf. Regt. 45th Div. Operations Report, May 1–31, 1944.
337th Inf. Regt. 85th Inf. Div. Operations Report, June 1944.
339th Inf. Regt. Operations Report, June 1944.
349th Inf. Regt. History, June 1944.
350th Inf. Regt. History, June 1944.
351st Inf. Regt. History, May 1944.
351st Inf. Regt. History, June 1944.
84th Cml. Mortar Bn. History, June 1944.
339th F. A. Bn. 88th Inf. Div. Morning Report.
CSDIC Interrogation Reports, June 1, 1944–June 30, 1944.

E. GERMAN MANUSCRIPT SOURCES

Some of the following manuscripts were prepared by former high-ranking officers of the German Army. These documents came into being as a result of the Foreign Military Studies Program which began shortly after the close of World War II. The Allied interrogations of certain prominent German prisoners of war were so informative that the program was expanded to the point where it became broad-based primary research. Written questions replaced oral interrogation, and later, certain highly placed German officers were asked to prepare a series of monographs. In almost every case, the authors of these monographs were key participants in the events which they described and thus were able to supply information which was not otherwise available.

Unfortunately, many of the early manuscripts were inadequately translated and sometimes received misleading titles. In quite a few cases the names of the interpreters have been lost. However, over the years, this material has been supplemented. The documents cited in this book are only a selection. The hundreds of other available manuscripts have been consulted only for confirmation or corroboration.

The following materials, plus supplementary and other subject treatments, are all to be found in the Office of the Chief of Military History, Department of the Army, Washington, D.C.

Anon., Allied Offensive (Battle for Rome) — The German View.
Estimate of the Situation: Effects of Allied Attacks and German Countermeasures during May 1944 Offensive (captured staff document).
Greiner, Heinrich, ed., Battle for Rome and Retreat Northward (dated May 28, 1944, 362nd I.D.).
Kesselring, Albert, Operations from the Start of the Major Allied Attack up to the Evacuation of Rome, Inclusive.
———, Special Report of the Events in Italy Between 25 July and 8 September 1943 (trans. A. Rosenwald; ed. Dr. Frederiksen).
Klinkowstroem, Graf von, Italy's Breakaway and the Fighting Around Rome, According to the Viewpoint of OB South (dated Sept. 16, 1947, Neustadt, Germany).
Maelzer, Kurt, The Problem of Rome During the Period of the Fighting near Anzio-Nettuno until the Evacuation of Rome on 4 June 1944.
Vietinghoff, Heinrich von, The Campaign in Italy — The Operations of the 71st German Infantry Division During the Month of May 1944 (dated Sept. 28, 1948).

PUBLISHED SOURCES

A. BOOKS

Adleman, Robert H., and George Walton, *The Devil's Brigade* (Philadelphia: Chilton, 1966).
Alexander of Tunis, Harold Alexander, Earl, *The Alexander Memoirs, 1940–1945*, ed. John North (New York: McGraw-Hill, 1962).
Anders, W., *An Army in Exile* (London: Macmillan, 1949).
Anzio Beachhead, Jan. 25–May 25, 1944 (American Forces in Action series; Washington: Historical Division, Department of the Army, 1947).
Bailey, Thomas A., *Presidential Greatness* (New York: Appleton-Century, 1966).
Baldwin, Hanson W., *Great Mistakes of the War* (New York: Harper, 1949).
———, *Battles Lost and Won* (New York: Harper, 1966).
Belot, Raymond de, *The Struggle for the Mediterranean, 1939–1945*, trans. James A. Field, Jr. (Princeton, N.J.: Princeton University Press, 1951).
Blumenson, Martin, *Anzio: The Gamble That Failed* (Philadelphia: Lippincott, 1963).
Bond, Harold L., *Return to Cassino* (Garden City, N.Y.: Doubleday, 1964).
Bradley, Omar N., *A Soldier's Story* (New York: Holt, 1951).
Bryant, Arthur, *Triumph in the West*, A history of the war years based on the diaries of Field Marshal Lord Alanbrooke, Chief of the Imperial General Staff (Garden City, N.Y.: Doubleday, 1959).
Bullock, Alan, *Hitler: A Study in Tyranny* (revised ed.) (New York: Bantam, 1961; New York: Harper, 1953).

Butcher, Harry C., *My Three Years with Eisenhower* (New York: Simon & Schuster, 1946).

Byrnes, James F., *Speaking Frankly* (New York: Harper, 1947).

Capa, Robert, *Slightly Out of Focus* (New York: Holt, 1947).

Carroll-Abbing, J. Patrick, *But for the Grace of God* (New York: Delacorte, 1965).

Carter, Bruce, *The Other Side of the Fence* (New York: Carlton, 1963).

Chandler, David, ed., *A Guide to the Battlefields of Europe* (Vol. II) (Philadelphia: Chilton, 1965).

Chandos, Viscount, and Oliver Lyttleton, *The Memoirs of Lord Chandos* (New York: New American Library, 1963).

Childs, Marquis, *Eisenhower: Captive Hero* (New York: Harcourt, Brace, 1958).

Churchill, Winston S., *Closing the Ring* (The Second World War, Vol. 5; Boston: Houghton Mifflin, 1951).

———, *The Hinge of Fate* (The Second World War, Vol. 4; Boston: Houghton Mifflin, 1950).

———, *Triumph and Tragedy* (The Second World War, Vol. 6; Boston: Houghton Mifflin, 1953).

Clark, Mark W., *Calculated Risk* (New York: Harper, 1950).

Clark, Maurine, *Captain's Bride, General's Lady* (New York: McGraw-Hill, 1956).

Colvin, Ian, *Chief of Intelligence* (London, Victor Gollancz, 1951).

Commager, Henry Steele, ed., *The Pocket History of the Second World War* (New York: Pocket Books, 1945).

Courtney, Godfrey B., "General Clark's Secret Mission," *100 Best True Stories of World War II* (Union City, N.J.: Wm. H. Wise, 1945).

Davis, Kenneth S., *Experience of War — The United States in World War II* (Garden City, N.Y.: Doubleday, 1965).

de Gaulle, Charles, *The Complete War Memoirs of Charles de Gaulle* (New York: Simon & Schuster, 1964).

De Guingand, Sir Francis, *Operation Victory* (New York: Scribner's, 1947).

De La Gorce, Paul-Marie, *The French Army* (New York: George Braziller, 1963).

Delaney, John P., *The Blue Devils in Italy* (Washington: Infantry Journal Press, 1947).

Derry, Sam, *The Rome Escape Line* (New York: Norton, 1960).

Doenitz, Karl, *Memoirs — Ten Years and Twenty Days* (New York: World, 1959).

Dupuy, Trevor Nevitt, *Combat Leaders of World War II* (The Military History of World War II, Vol. XVII; New York: Franklin Watts, 1962).

———, *European Land Battles* (The Military History of World War II, Vol. II; New York: Franklin Watts, 1962).

———, *Land Battles: North Africa, Sicily and Italy* (The Military History of World War II, Vol. III; New York: Franklin Watts, 1962).

———, *Strategic Direction of World War II* (The Military History of World War II, Vol. XVIII; New York: Franklin Watts, 1962).

Durant, Will, *The Age of Faith* (*The Story of Civilization*; New York: Simon & Schuster, 1950).

Eastlake, William, *Castle Keep* (New York: Simon & Schuster, 1965).

Eisenhower, Dwight D., *Crusade in Europe* (Garden City, N.Y.: Doubleday, 1948).

Encyclopaedia Britannica Book of the Year — 1945 (Chicago: Encyclopaedia Britannica, Inc., 1945).

Evans, Burtt, "Why Old Soldiers Never Die"; "The Colonel and the Rock," in *The Best from Yank, the Army Weekly*, Selected by the Editors of Yank (New York: Dutton, 1945).

Farago, Ladislas, *Patton: Ordeal and Triumph* (New York: Obolensky, 1964).

Feis, Herbert, *Churchill, Roosevelt, Stalin* (Princeton, N.J.: Princeton University Press, 1957).

Fergusson, Bernard, *The Watery Maze* (New York: Holt, 1961).
Flynn, John T., *The Roosevelt Myth* (New York: Devin-Adair, 1956).
Friedländer, Saul, *Pius XII and the Third Reich* (New York: Knopf, 1966).
Fuller, J. F. C., *The Second World War 1939–45* (New York: Duell, Sloan and Pearce, 1948).
Greenfield, Kent Roberts, ed., *Command Decisions* (Washington, D.C.: Office of the Chief of Military History, Dept. of the Army, 1960).
Hibbert, Christopher, *Il Duce* (Boston: Little, Brown, 1962).
Higgins, Trumbull, *Winston Churchill and the Second Front* (New York: Oxford University Press, 1957).
Historical Division — War Dept. U.S.A., *Small Unit Actions* (American Forces in Action series; Washington: G. P. O., 1946).
Holles, Everett, *Unconditional Surrender* (New York: Howell, Soskin, 1945).
Howe, George F., *The Battle History of the 1st Armored Division* (Washington: Combat Forces Press, 1954).
Infantry Journal 1939–1944, *The World at War*, A Brief History of the Origins, Military Operations and Related Events of World War II.
Ismay, Lord, *The Memoirs of General Lord Ismay* (New York: Viking, 1960).
Jacobsen, H. A., and J. Rohwer, *Decisive Battles of World War II — The German View* (New York: Putnam, 1965).
Katz, Robert, *Death in Rome* (New York: Macmillan, 1967).
Keitel, Wilhelm, *The Memoirs of Field Marshal Keitel*, trans. David Irving, ed. Walter Gorlitz (New York: Stein & Day, 1966).
Kennedy, Sir John, *The Business of War* (New York: William Morrow, 1951).
Kesselring, Albert, *Kesselring, a Soldier's Story* (New York: William Morrow, 1954).
Kogan, Norman, *Italy and the Allies* (Cambridge, Mass.: Harvard University Press, 1956).
Launay, Jacques de, *Secret Diplomacy of World War II* (New York: Simmons-Boardman, 1963).
Leahy, William D., *I Was There* (New York: McGraw-Hill, 1950).
Leasor, James, *War at the Top*, based on the experience of General Sir Leslie Hollis (London: Michael Joseph, 1959).
Lidell Hart, B. H., *Strategy* (New York: Praeger, 1954).
Linklater, Eric, *The Campaign in Italy* (London: H. M. S. O., 1951).
Lochner, Louis P., ed. and trans., *The Goebbels Diaries, 1942–43* (Garden City, N.Y.: Doubleday, 1948).
MacArthur, Douglas, *Reminiscences* (New York: McGraw-Hill, 1964).
Majdalaney, Fred, *Cassino — Portrait of a Battle* (London: Longmans, 1957).
Maugeri, Franco, *From the Ashes of Disgrace* (New York: Reynal & Hitchcock, 1948).
Mauldin, Bill, *Up Front* (New York: Holt, 1945).
Meyer, Robert, Jr., ed., *The Stars & Stripes Story of World War II* (New York: McKay, 1960).
Montgomery, Viscount, of Alamein, *Memoirs: Montgomery of Alamein* (Cleveland: World, 1958).
Moran, Lord, *Churchill: Taken from his Diaries — The Struggle for Survival, 1940–1965* (Boston: Houghton Mifflin, 1966).
Morison, Samuel Eliot, *Sicily-Salerno-Anzio, January 1943–June 1944* (History of U.S. Naval Operations in World War II, Vol. IX; Boston: Little, Brown, 1954).
Murphy, Robert, *Diplomat Among Warriors* (Garden City, N.Y.: Doubleday, 1964).
Patton, George S., *War as I Knew It* (New York: Pyramid, 1966).
Payne, Robert, *The Marshall Story* (Englewood Cliffs, N.J.: Prentice-Hall, 1951).
Peek, Clifford H., Jr., ed., *Five Years, Five Countries, Five Campaigns* (Munich, Germany: 141st Inf. Reg. Assn., 1945).
Phillips, Cabell, *The Truman Presidency* (New York: Macmillan, 1966).

Pogue, Forrest C., *George C. Marshall: Ordeal and Hope* (New York: Viking, 1966).
Pond, Hugh, *Salerno* (Boston: Little, Brown, 1961).
Pyle, Ernie, *Brave Men* (New York: Holt, 1943).
ROTCM 145-20 Dept. *of the Army ROTC Manual: American Military History 1607–1958* (Washington: Headquarters, Dept. of the Army, July 1959).
Scrivener, Jane, *Inside Rome with the Germans* (New York: Macmillan, 1945).
Senger und Etterlin, Frido von, *Neither Fear nor Hope* (New York: Dutton, 1964).
Sevareid, Eric, *Not So Wild a Dream* (New York: Knopf, 1946).
Sheehan, Fred, *Anzio — Epic of Bravery* (Norman, Okla.: University of Oklahoma Press, 1964).
Sherwood, Robert E., *Roosevelt and Hopkins*, Vol. II (New York: Harper, 1948).
Shirer, William L., *End of a Berlin Diary* (New York: Knopf, 1947).
———, *The Rise and Fall of the Third Reich* (New York: Simon & Schuster, 1960).
Skorzeny, Otto, *Skorzeny's Secret Missions* (New York: Dutton, 1950).
Snyder, Louis L., *The War — A Concise History 1939–45* (New York: Julian Messner, Inc., 1960; New York: Dell, 1964).
Starr, Chester G., ed. *From Salerno to the Alps* (Washington, D.C.: Infantry Journal Press, 1948).
Stern, Michael, *An American in Rome* (New York: Bernard Geis Associates, 1964).
Stimson, Henry L., and McGeorge Bundy, *On Active Service in Peace and War* (New York: Harper, 1947).
Story of the 36th Infantry Division, The (Washington: U.S. Army Information Service, 1945).
Sunderman, James F., ed., *World War II in the Air — Europe* (New York: Franklin Watts, 1963).
Taggart, Donald G., ed., *History of the Third Infantry Division in World War II* (Washington: Infantry Journal Press, 1947).
Tompkins, Peter, *A Spy in Rome* (New York: Simon & Schuster, 1962).
———, *The Murder of Admiral Darlan* (New York: Simon & Schuster, 1965).
Truscott, Lucian King, *Command Missions* (New York: Dutton, 1954).
United States Congress, *79th Cong., 2 Sess., House Comm. on Military Affairs: Rapido River Crossing.*
Vaughan-Thomas, W., *Anzio* (New York: Holt, 1961).
Wedemeyer, Albert C., *Wedemeyer Reports!* (New York: Holt, 1958).
We Were There (88th Infantry Division, Info. & Ed. Section, n.d.).
West Point Alumni Foundation, *1964 Register of Graduates and Former Cadets 180–21964 of the U.S. Military Academy.*
White, Theodore H., *The Making of the President: 1964* (New York: Atheneum, 1965).
Young, Gordon, ed., *The Army Almanac* (Harrisburg, Pa.: Stackpole, 1959).

B. PERIODICALS

"Alexander's Rocket," *Newsweek*, April 3, 1944.
"Allied Air-Land-Sea Teams Converge on Eternal City," *Newsweek*, Oct. 25, 1943.
"Allies Supply Missing Pieces for Jigsaw Puzzle of Attack," *Newsweek*, May 29, 1944.
"Americans Take Over Rome," *Life*, June 26, 1944.
Angell, Sir Norman, "The Real Question: Are the Allies Incurable?" *New York Times Magazine*, Feb. 1943.
"Arsenal City, The," *Time*, July 26, 1943.
"Austria — An American Abroad," *Time*, June 24, 1946.
Baldwin, Hanson W., "Men of Destiny — Leaders in North Africa," *New York Times Magazine*, June 20, 1943.

"Behind the Pope's Peace Plea," *Christian Century*, Sept. 15, 1943.
"Beyond the Bridge Head," *Time*, Oct. 4, 1943.
Biddle, Livingston, "Soldier Sketches," *Collier's*, 1943.
Bishop, J. A., "Rome's Black Monday," *Collier's*, Oct. 23, 1944.
Blumenson, Martin, "Sicily and Italy," *Military Review*, Feb. 1966.
"Bombing of Rome, The," *Life*, Aug. 9, 1943.
"Bombs Rain on Rome," *Christian Century* (editorial), July 28, 1943.
Bracker, Milton, "General Mark Clark Gets the Tough Jobs," New York *Times Magazine*, June 19, 1953.
"Divided Command One Factor Behind Lag in Mediterranean," *Newsweek*, Oct. 11, 1943.
Dixon, Kenneth L., "The Night of the Knife," *Argosy*, Sept. 1964.
Dulles, Allen W., "The Secret Surrender," *Harper's*, July, Aug. 1966.
"Enemy Retreating Everywhere but the Allied Going Is Tough," *Newsweek*, Oct. 11, 1943.
"Fall of Esperia, The," *Life*, Aug. 14, 1944.
"Fall of Rome, The," *Life*, June 19, 1944.
Feder, Sid, "They'll Never Forget Mark Clark," *Saturday Evening Post*, May 18, 1946.
"Ferocity of Nazi Defense Shows Importance of Rome Beachheads," *Newsweek*, Feb. 14, 1944.
"Field Marshal No. 8," *Time*, Dec. 4, 1944.
"First Attack: Italy," *Life*, May 29, 1944.
Fisher, Ernest F., "A Classic Stratagem on Monte Cassino," *Military Review*, Feb. 1963.
Fisher, Ernest F., Jr., "Rome — An Open City," *Military Review*, USA C & GS Sch., Aug. 1965.
Fried, Joseph P., "Bayonet Breakthrough," *Men*, 1948.
Fuller, J. F. C., "The 'Second Hand' Front in Italy," *Newsweek*, Mar. 13, 1944.
———, "The Why and Wherefore of the Italian Offensive," *Newsweek*, June 7, 1944.
Genet, "Letter from Rome," *New Yorker*, Nov. 21, 1945.
Gervasi, Frank, "Alexander the Modest," *Collier's*, Feb. 12, 1944.
———, "The French Fight for Rome," *Collier's*, Feb. 26, 1944.
———, "Rome Lives Again," *Collier's*, Sept. 9, 1944.
"Gestapo in Rome," *Life*, July 3, 1944.
Gwynn, Sir Charles, "Russia and Italy," *Fortnightly*, Nov. 6, 1943.
Hamburger, Philip, "Letter from Rome," *New Yorker*, July 7, 1945.
"Holy Hostage," *Newsweek*, Sept. 27, 1943.
"Humor in Uniform," *Reader's Digest*, Sept. 1966.
"Italy: Bridgehead to Europe," *Scholastic Mag.*, Sept. 20, 1943.
Joesten, Joachim, "Hitler's Last General," *Nation*, Mar. 31, 1945.
"Kesselring: Soft Soap," *Newsweek*, May 21, 1944.
Kluckhohn, Frank L., "Attack — Attack Again Is Alexander's Motto," New York *Times Mag.*, Aug. 8, 1943.
Lang, Daniel, "Letter from Rome," *New Yorker*, June 17, 1944; June 24, 1944; July 15, 1944.
Lang, Will, " 'Big Charley's' Men," *Life*, 1944.
Lardner, John, "Report on Italy," *Newsweek*, May 22, 1944.
Leiber, Father, "Comments on *Pius XII and the Third Reich*," *Look*, May 1, 1966.
"Letters from a General," *Collier's*, Dec. 4, 1943.
Lewy, Guenter, "Was Silence the Only Solution?" *Sat. Review*, May 21, 1966 (Review of *Pius XII and the Third Reich*).
Malloy, J. L., "Vatican City Bombed," *Catholic World*, Sept. 1943.
———, "Holy Father on Bombing of Rome," *Catholic World*, Dec. 1943.

Malone, Paul B., "The Battle for Rome," *Newsweek*, Feb. 14, 1944.
"Man Who Paved the Way, The," *Time*, June 12, 1944.
Masefield, Peter, "Italy as an Air Base," *Newsweek*, Oct. 4, 1943.
"Master Strategist of the Year — General Sir Harold Alexander," *Newsweek*, Sept. 6, 1943.
Mathews, Herbert L., "A New Chapter in Eternal Rome," New York *Times Mag.*, June 18, 1944.
Mathews, Sydney T., "The French in the Drive on Rome," Fraternité d'Armes Franco-Américaine, *Revue Historique De L'Armée*, Special Issue, 1954.
Mitchell, Donald W., "From Calabria to Cassino: Analysis of Allied Military Mistakes in Italy," *Current History*, May 1944.
"Murder at the Rapido," *Time*, Jan. 28, 1946.
"Myth of the Forty-Day Soft War on Italy," *Saturday Evening Post*, Oct. 23, 1943.
"Nazis' New Broom," *Time*, Dec. 2, 1945.
"Nightmare's End," *Time*, June 5, 1944.
"Open City," *Newsweek*, Aug. 22, 1943.
"Our Three Champions in the Resistance to Soviet War of Nerves," *U.S. News & World Report*, Aug. 30, 1946.
Paulding, C. G., "We Still Can Choose," *Commonweal*, Feb. 18 to Feb. 25, 1944.
"Pope Greets Americans in Vatican," *Life*, June 26, 1944.
"Pope's Fears for Rome Take New Turn as City Becomes a German Target," *Newsweek*, June 12, 1944.
"Raids on Eternal City Stir Prelate and Laymen but Catholics Are Split," *Newsweek*, Aug. 2, 1943.
Reynolds, Quentin, "While Rome Burned," *Collier's*, Feb. 28, 1943.
Reynolds, Robert L., and Robert S. Lopez, "Odoacer: German or Hun?" *Am. Hist. Rev.*, Oct. 1946.
"Roads to Rome," *Nation*, Nov. 6, 1943.
"Roman Social Season," *Time*, Sept. 11, 1944.
Shenkel, William T., "The Allied 'Sunday Punch' in Italy," *Newsweek*, May 21, 1944.
"Skyroad to Rome," *Newsweek*, Aug. 2, 1943.
"Smiling Albert," *Newsweek*, Feb. 21, 1944.
Sturzo, Luigi, "The Vatican and Fascism," *Commonweal*, Dec. 17, 1943.
Sulzberger, C. L., "The Doughboy's Grim Road to Rome," New York *Times Mag.*, Feb. 20, 1944.
"Sunshine and Scars," *Time*, June 19, 1944.
"Truscott, Lucian King, Jr." *Life*, Oct. 2, 1944.
"Victory Vignettes," *Scholastic Mag.*, Oct. 11, 1943.
Ward, Harry F., "Vatican Fascism," *Christian Century*, June 7, 1944.
Wilson, P. W., "The Appian Road to Rome," New York *Times Mag.*, Oct. 17, 1943.
"World Greets the Fall of Rome with Relief that City Is Safe," *Newsweek*, June 12, 1944.

C. NEWSPAPERS

"Biography of Maj. Gen. E. E. Hume (Medic)," Philadelphia *Inquirer*, Jan. 30, 1966.
Chicago *Tribune*, June 1944.
Cuneo, Dr. Ernest, "Take It or Leave It," North American Newspaper Alliance, July 9, 1966.
Davies, Lawrence E., "A Pius Role in Plot on Hitler Reported," New York *Times*, Dec. 31, 1965.
"Hitler Rejected Jets in 1942 Willi Messerschmitt Says," New York *Times*, Oct. 13, 1966.

"Israeli Author Says Efforts of Pius XII Saved Many Jews," New York *Times*, April 24, 1966.

Marshall, S. L. A., "What Men Did There" (Review of *Battles Lost and Won*), New York *Times*, Oct. 9, 1966.

New York *Times*, June 1944.

Stars And Stripes, May 26–June 6, 1944; Mediterranean Edition, June 7, 1944.

Sulzberger, C. L., "Foreign Affairs — Footnote to a Sordid Tale" (review and report on Peter Tompkins, *Italy Betrayed*), New York *Times*, Aug. 19, 1966.

"Tedder's Memoirs Laud Eisenhower," New York *Times*, Oct. 9, 1966.

INDEX

ADAM, SIR RONALD, 128
Africa. See North Africa
Air Forces, British, 81, 149, 174, 208, 215–16, 218, 279
Air Forces, U.S., 81, 95–96, 136, 149, 152–53, 174, 180–82, 197, 205, 208, 215–16, 218, 279; Fifteenth Strategic, 109–10; G-3 Air, 180
Alamo, 151
Alanbrooke, Lord, 45, 57, 73, 117, 124–27, 164
Alaric, 260
Alban Hills (Colli Laziali), 15, 18, 23, 142, 144, 146, 157, 159, 165–66, 205–6, 225–26, 233, 234, 236, 244
Alexander, Gen. Sir Harold, 68, 72, 137, 220, 238, 239, 249; isolation and pressures, 3; character, abilities, appearance, 4, 57, 99–101; wishes Eighth Army to share Rome capture, 33; relationship with Clark, 52; calls Eisenhower "dumbbell," 57, 59; relationship with Montgomery, 99–100; commands in France, at Dunkirk, 100, 231; as Army Group commander, 101; not sanguine about Italian campaign, 102; refuses Italy status as ally, 102, 105, 185; admires Italian partisans, 106; blames fighting conditions for stalemate, 128; retained as Fifteenth Army Group commander, 141; plans for Anzio landings, 141, 143–44; instructions for Anzio, 146; Kesselring's comments about landings, 146–47; orders offensive to divert from Anzio, 151, 154; satisfied with Anzio operation, 160; demands Lucas's dismissal, 164–65, 167–68, 179; opinion of Anzio, 166; admires German defense of Cassino, 176–77; difficulty with Freyberg, 178; strategy for spring offensive, 201–3, 205–7, 209; ability to harness diverse national units, 202–3; intends maximum assistance to OVERLORD, 204; relationship with Clark clouded, 207; pride in French, 209; considers Liri Valley best route to Rome, 213; jubilant message to Churchill, 214–16; masterful execution of spring offensive, 221–22; conflict with Clark, 225–33, 235; refuses to proclaim Rome neutrality, 244; gives Rome to inhabitants, 260; intends compensation to those who aided Allied escapees, 267; forces removed to France, 277–79; decisions and ability as general, 280; becomes theater commander, 280

Alexandria, Va., 5
Algeria, 65
Algiers, 48, 51, 67, 150
Allen, Gen. Terry, 36, 47, 63–64
Allied Advisory Council, 273–74
Allied Control Commission, 198
Allied High Command, 101, 280
Allied Military Government, 266
Allied relations: divergent aims emerge in North Africa, 56; strained at Casablanca, 58; over "unconditional surrender," 74–75; divided over suggested Balkan thrust, 75; agree Italian invasion useless, 76; change minds when Mussolini removed, 76; nationalistic reasons for Italian invasion, 77; Alexander's success commanding Allies, 100–101; Russians back Americans, support OVERLORD, 123–24; Russians stop surrender negotiations with Kesselring, deal directly with Badoglio, 198; friendship fading, 198; with troops, 202–3, cooperation in armed forces good, 216; see also Anglo-American relations; French leaders
Allison, Lee F., 6
Altavilla, 96
America. See United States
American Historical Society, 86
Ancon, 91
Anders, Gen. Wladyslaw, 213, 220
Andersson, Col. Kingsley S., 253–54

Anglo-American relations: smooth in North Africa, 51; poor in Italy, 51; Clark's attitude, 52; British reluctance to channel invasion, 35, 56–59; tense at Casablanca, 56–58; British resent American plans, 59; Americans dislike Montgomery, 71; criticism of Eisenhower, 73; Churchill's suggested Balkan attack opposed, 75; discord prevents Allied coup in Italy, 79; between commanders in Italy, 99; respect for Alexander, 100–101; difficulties with Montgomery, 101; relationship between Eisenhower and Alanbrooke, 117; conflict over Mediterranean versus OVERLORD and ANVIL at Teheran, 121–25; differences fostered by Teheran decision, 125; differences in British and American military systems, 126; British generals criticize American political and military capacities, 126–27; Clark criticizes British, 128; Clark irritates British correspondents, 135; agreement on proposed Anzio landings, 141–48; dispute over ANVIL, 148; American difficulty with Freyberg, 177–80; relationship between Clark and Alexander clouded, 207; cooperation within armed forces good, 216, 233; conflict over honor of capturing Rome, 223–33; Clark offends British at victory speech, 273; Eisenhower reconciles differences between British and American planners, 279; see also Allied relations
Ariene River, 245
ANVIL. See France, invasion of south
Anzio (SHINGLE), 79, 83, 145, 179, 188, 207, 235, 243, 270; landings proposed and planned for, 142–47; hoped-for achievements, 145; doubts about, 148–49, 158; offensive to divert enemy from, 150–51, 154; beaches secured, casualties, 152, 182; attack not pressed, Germans rally, 156–68; siege, 168–71, 233; hopelessness of German position, 197–99; appraisal, 278
Anzio—Epic of Bravery, by Fred Sheehan, 154   .
Appian Way. See Highway 7
Arabs, 63
Ardeatine Caves massacre, 190–92, 194
Arizona, 281

Army, British, 33, 126, 128, 150, 156, 160, 199, 202, 209, 213, 266, 273; Eighth Army, 18, 33, 55, 71, 98–99, 110, 135, 137, 141, 144–45, 178, 201–2, 205–7, 209–10, 212–16, 225–27, 233–34, 236, 240, 248–49, 260, 273, 278; I Corps, 100; X Corps, 145, 151, 155, 160, 175; XII Corps, 213; XIII Corps, 214; New Zealand Corps, 177–78, 180–81, 205; 1st Div., 100, 145, 166; 78th Div., 177; 1st Airborne, 98; 4th Indian, 177; 2nd New Zealand, 177; Intelligence, 145–46; see also Air Forces, British; Army Groups, Allied; Chiefs of Staff, Combined; strategy, Allied
Army, French, 33, 67, 145, 150–51, 158, 202, 266, 273; Free French Expeditionary Corps, 150, 207–11, 213–14, 216, 233–34, 236, 248, 260, 282; Goumiers, 208, 211; 19th Corps, 65
Army, German, 26–28, 34, 58, 66, 71, 77, 79, 81, 98, 104, 112, 115, 144, 150–52, 159, 185–86, 188, 191, 197, 199, 202, 213, 238, 277–78; Tenth Army, 106, 110, 161, 176, 208, 211, 221, 225, 229–30, 238, 245; Fourteenth Army, 110, 160, 205, 221, 225, 230, 234, 238, 245; 14th Panzer Corps, 176, 208; 76th Panzer Corps, 22, 98; 44th Div., 215; 71st Div., 209, 215; 94th Div., 215; 715th Div., 215; 362nd Div., 215; 10th Panzer Div., 66, 67; Hermann Goering Panzer Div., 215–16, 226, 234; 15th Panzer Gren. Div., 215; 26th Panzer Gren. Div., 215; 29th Panzer Gren. Div., 161; 90th Panzer Gren. Div., 161, 215; 1st Parachute Div., 19, 22, 215; Army Group C., 208; SS, 104, 239, 240; see also German Supreme Command; strategy, German
Army, Italian, 66, 79, 89, 102, 185–86, 203, 258, 260
Army, U.S., 14, 35–36, 110–11, 126, 136, 150, 184–85, 199, 274–75, 283; Third Army, 36; Fifth Army, 4, 6, 18, 20, 33–34, 51, 60–61, 94, 97–99, 110, 120, 126–27, 131, 135–38, 144–45, 147–48, 150, 154, 158–60, 172, 178, 185, 201–3, 205, 207, 209, 214–16, 219, 225–26, 228, 229–32, 236–37, 240, 245, 249, 255, 259–60, 263, 266, 271, 273, 274, 278, 282, 284; Seventh Army, 61, 71,

72, 147–48, 283; II Corps, 19, 21, 29, 30, 33, 36, 41, 55, 61, 72, 111–21, 131, 145, 151, 155–57, 177–78, 180, 193, 209–13, 218, 221, 230, 233–34, 236–37, 245, 248–50, 277, 282; IV Corps, 30, 233–35; VI Corps, 11, 18, 33, 80, 95, 131, 146, 149, 157, 164–67, 171, 173–74, 176, 182, 205, 216–19, 225, 227–28, 230, 232–34, 236, 245, 255; 1st Div., 65, 67, 118; 3rd Div., 30, 38–39, 126, 146, 155, 166, 173, 234, 236; 34th Div., 17, 145, 151, 155–56, 175, 178; 36th Div., 11, 14–15, 19–21, 29, 95–97, 112, 145, 151–56, 160, 175, 176, 185, 205, 211, 218, 228, 237, 245–46, 255; 45th Div., 17, 155; 85th Div., 30, 211–12, 236, 255; 88th Div., 30, 211, 233, 236, 253, 255; 1st Armored Div., 155, 217, 236; 135th, Inf. Reg., 177; 141st Inf. Reg., 15–16, 22–23, 28; 142nd Inf. Reg., 14, 22–28; 143rd Inf. Reg., 22, 25; 339th Inf. Reg., 242; 504th Parachute Reg., 166; Intelligence (G-2; G-3), 62–63, 65, 68, 115, 119, 159, 185; Ranger battalions, 166; 1st Special Service Force ("Devil's Brigade"), 30, 113, 156, 174, 234, 235, 249–54, 266; *see also* Air Forces, U.S., Army Groups, Allied; Chiefs of Staff, Combined; Navy, U.S.; strategy, Allied.

Army Groups, Allied: Fifteenth, 141, 154, 178, 180, 202, 227; Twenty-first, 101

Army War College, 15, 38

Aurunci Mountains, 207

Austria, 15, 114, 280

"Axis Sally," 168

Badoglio, Marshal Pietro, 76–78, 83, 89, 102, 106, 188, 191, 198, 243, 269

Bailey, Prof. Thomas A., 57

Balkans, 75, 77, 123, 160

Basuto troops, 202

Beardwood, Lt. Jack, 52

Beaty, Norman J., 97

Bechuana troops, 202

Belgian troops, 203

Belisarius, 142, 271

Benedict, St., 174

Berchtesgaden, 197

Berlin, 190, 194, 229, 242

Bertot, Boris, 265

"Big Three" alliance, 33–34, 121, 123, 198

Biscayne, 149

BOLERO, 35

Bologna, 238

Bond, Harold, 153, 228

Bonomi, Ivanoe, 269

Borghese villa and gardens, 142, 228

Bradley, Gen. Omar, 36, 47, 72–73, 100, 111, 113–15, 157

Brann, Gen. Donald W., 232

Brazilian troops, 33, 203

Breckenridge, Tex., 97

Brindisi, 98

Britain; British (England; English), 33, 35, 42, 51, 57–59, 84, 86, 113, 115, 118, 120, 123–24, 141, 143, 145, 150, 173, 183, 193; *see also* Anglo-American relations; Army, British; Air Forces, British

British Broadcasting Co., 99, 219, 239

British Combined Operations Command, 49

Brooke, Field Marshal Sir Alan. *See* Alanbrooke, Lord

Buckley, Lt. Francis X., 218

Butcher, Capt. Harry, 43, 47, 49, 93

Byrnes, James, 198

Caesar Line, 206

Cairo, 43, 82, 121–22

Calabria, 80, 82, 87, 97

Calculated Risk, by Gen. Mark Clark, 148, 179, 274

Caledon, Earl of, 100

Canadian troops, 174, 202, 205, 216–17, 253

Canal Zone, 282

Canaris, Adm., 81, 160

Capa, Robert, 186

Carabinieri, 266

Caribbean troops, 202

Carroll-Abbing, the Rt. Rev. Msgr. J. Patrick, 19, 163, 169, 181, 240, 242

Carthaginians, 209

Casablanca, 51, 60; Conference, 56–58

Casilina, Via. *See* Highway 6

Cassino, 79–81, 114, 155, 158–59, 174–77, 188, 205–6, 208–9, 212–13, 215, 216, 223, 230, 245, 271; Abbey and bombing, 174–75, 177–82, 276

Cassino—Portrait of a Battle, by Fred Majdalany, 155

Castelli, the, 239

Catholics, 82, 84, 193, 195, 243

Chamberlain, Neville, 84

Channel invasion (OVERLORD), 31, 34–35, 37, 44, 56–59, 73–76, 109, 110, 121–24, 141–43, 147–48, 173, 204, 229, 254, 279, 283

Chiefs of Staff, Combined, 75, 109, 143, 165, 280

Christian Century, 84

Churchill, Winston, 50, 54, 61, 69, 248–49, 279; "Big Three" Alliance, 33–34; concessions to Stalin, 34; promotes North African campaign, 34–35, 44; reluctance to Channel invasion, 34, 58–59; relationship with Eisenhower and Clark, 43–45; appraisal of, 46–47; upset over "Darlan deal," 53–54; at Casablanca, 56, 58; accused of self-interest in Mediterranean, 58–59; cautions against code names, 69, 71; agrees to Channel invasion, 73–74; at Quebec, 74; insists on "unconditional surrender," 74–75; desires abdication of Victor Emmanuel, 78; optimistic about Rome capture, 102; at Teheran, 109, 121–25; Cairo meeting with Roosevelt, 121–22; backs Mediterranean theater against OVERLORD, 121–24; urges capture of Rome, 122, 124; argues against abandoning Italy and ANVIL, 124–25; distrusts Stalin, 124–25; loyalty of military, 126; on Italian campaign, 128, 141; proposes Anzio landings, 141–46, 148; reaction to Anzio, 156–57, 164–65; consulted about Lucas's dismissal, 164; admires Truscott, 173; wants Monte Cassino abbey bombed, 181; distrusted by Italians, 183; Pope disapproves of, 193; directive against Communists, 198; requests publicity for Eighth Army, 214; considers Rome prize, 228; attempts to restore Italian monarchy, 269; telegram to Stalin, 270

Cisterna, 215, 217–18, 230

Cisterna-Campolene railroad, 217

Citadel, 281

Civitavecchia, 205, 238

Clark, Ann, 49

Clark, Col. Charles G., 37

Clark, Mrs. Charles G., 204, 255

Clark, Gen. Mark Wayne, 7, 68, 107, 112, 120, 125, 264, 268, 277; denied Chief of Staff office, 3, 151; blamed for Italian campaign, 3, 4; isolation and pressures, 3; leads Fifth Army, 4; character, personality, appearance, 5, 37–38, 47, 52, 60, 73, 128; charges against, 5, 130–38; discusses plans for Rome breakthrough, 11–13; relationship with Walker, 15, 20–21, 95–97; authorizes Walker's plans, 18; wants Fifth Army to capture Rome, 18, 33; eager to eliminate Velletri, 22; selected to train army for North Africa, 37; family, education, marriage, 37–38; rise in army, 38–41; relationship with Eisenhower, 37, 40–42, 61; heads II Corps, 41; in England, 41–42; relationship with Churchill, 43–45; backs plans for North African campaign, 44–45; appointed second-in-command for North Africa, 47; secret mission to North Africa to arrange French alliance, 34, 48–51; loses pants, 34, 50; admires Allied cooperation, 51; relationship with British, 52; relations with French, 52–55; opinion of British self-interest, 58; commands Fifth Army, 60; youngest lieutenant general in U.S. history, 60; friendship with Patton, 60–61; difficulties with Eisenhower and Bradley, 73; estimate of Kesselring, 81; commands at Salerno, 87, 91–94, 96–99; dog incident mars image, 94–95; rumored belittled by Walker, 95–97; irritated by British, 98–99; friendship with Montgomery, 99; costly advance, 110; appointed commander for ANVIL, 124, 147; receives little military and political guidance, 126; criticized by British and American generals, 126–28; criticizes British, 128; criticism and praise, 130–36; reaction to criticism, 137–38; continues as Fifth Army commander, 141; opinion about Anzio landings, 145–46; concern about ANVIL, 147; heads Seventh Army, 147; meets Roosevelt in Sicily, 147; relinquishes command of Seventh, 148; discusses ANVIL with Eisenhower, 148; commands offensive to divert Germans, 151; Texans' accusations and Congressional investigation of

Rapido River, 151–56; relationship with Lucas, 157–58; ambiguous order to Lucas, 159; reactions to Anzio, 160, 167; dismisses Lucas, 165, 167–68, 179; inability to communicate with men, 172; relies on artillery at Cassino, 175–76; difficulty with Freyberg, 178–79; position on bombing of Monte Cassino abbey, 179–81; successful execution of Alexander's strategy, 201; problems with national groups, 203; returns to U.S. to explain spring offensive, meets wife, 203–4; relationship with Alexander clouded, 207; admires French offensive, 209; admiration of de Gaulle, 209–10; present for Anzio breakthrough and link-up of II and VI Corps, 216, 219; efficiency in spring offensive, 220; conflict with Alexander over Rome capture, 225–33, 235; relationship with Truscott, 231–33, 235; plan to capture Rome, 234; agrees to Keyes's plan for Rome breakthrough, 235–37; reliance upon Keyes, 237; uncertain whether Germans will defend Rome, 241–42; intends to use Rome militarily, 243; desire to capture Rome, 247–48; decides on race for Rome, 249; impatience to enter city, 254; enjoys publicity, 261; reactions to capture of Rome, 271; entry into Rome, offends Allies, 272–73; audience with Pope, 274; forces removed to France, 277–79; decisions and ability as general, 280; succeeds to Allied command in Italy, 280; postwar career, maturity, 280–81; evaluation of, in Italian campaign, 281–82

Clark, Maurine (Mrs. Mark), 38, 41–42, 94, 203–4
Clark, William, 37, 41–42
CLN (Comitato di Liberazione Nazionale, 183, 188, 269
Colli Laziali. *See* Alban Hills
Command and General Staff School, 38
Commonweal, 82
Communism; Communists, 58–59, 79, 84, 123, 126, 183, 189–95
Cook, Zeke, 210
Corps commander, estimate of, 110–11
Courtney, Capt. Godfrey B., 49–50
Crimea, 67

Crittenberger, Gen. Willis, 233, 273
Cypriot French troops, 202

D-Day. *See* Channel invasion
Darby, Bill, 65–66
Darlan, Adm. Jean, 50, 53–54, 150
Dawley, Gen. Ernest J., 95, 157
De Gaulle, Gen. Charles, 50, 58, 100, 150–51, 209–10
De Guingand, Sir Francis, 98–99
Delaney, John P., 30, 33
Democratic Party, 72
Deputy, The, by Rolf Hochhuth, 4, 84
Derry, Maj. Sam, 196–97, 240–41, 256–57, 267, 277
Devers, Gen. Jacob, 167
Dickinson, William, 42
Dieppe, 31, 35, 173
Dill, Field Marshal, 164
Dixon, Kenneth, 25
Dollman, Gen. Eugene, 162
Doolittle, Hooker A., 63, 65
Dora Line. *See* Hitler-Dora Line
Dunkirk, 92, 231

Eden, Anthony, 249
Eisenhower, Gen. Dwight D., 7, 31, 53, 126, 134, 150, 157, 164, 204, 248, 281; army rise, 36, 41; relationship with Clark, 37, 40–42, 50, 51; commands American Forces in Europe, 41–42; in England, 42–43; relationship with Churchill, 43–44; plans North African campaign, 44–45; commands North African campaign, 47, 51, 54–55; called "dumbbell," 57; summarizes British attitude toward Channel invasion, 59; appointed commander of Sicily invasion, 59–60, 68; pins star on Clark, 60; creates Seventh Army, 61; relationship with Patton, 72; personality, 72, 144, 282; criticized, 73; diplomatic ability, 73, 141, 144; agrees to limited Italian sortie, 75–76; meets with Badoglio to arrange surrender, 76; concern for Salerno, 93; maintains Allied attack, 109; lack of jurisdiction produces stalemate, 109–10; estimate of, advice to Keyes, 112–13; relations with Alanbrooke, 117; appointed commander of Channel invasion force, 141; discusses Anzio landings, 143–44; discusses ANVIL with Clark, 148;

respect for Truscott, 173; decisive factor in Italian campaign, 278–79; invades Europe, 283
El Alamein, 71
El Guetter, 66
Ellis Task Force, 250–51
England. See Britain; British
Europe, 40–41, 55, 75–76, 91, 101, 119, 123

FALL ACHSE ("Axis Project"), 79
Fascists, 82, 102–3, 126, 130, 183, 192, 194, 234, 246, 256, 263, 267
Feder, Sid, 153
Flanders, 100
Florence, 238
Foggia, 75, 98, 109–10
Fondi, 235
Formia, 211, 235
Fort Myer, Va., 204
Fort Sheridan, 60
France; French, 35, 36, 44, 48, 56, 63, 73, 76, 100, 120, 130, 150–51, 160, 204, 229, 254, 283; invasion of south (AN-VIL), 123–24, 148, 204, 271, 278, 282; see also Army, French; French, in North Africa
Frascati, 250
Fredenall, Gen. Lloyd R., 47
Frederick, Gen. Robert, 7, 156, 174, 217, 249–50, 252–55
French, in North Africa, 37, 48–55, 56, 58, 62–65, 89, 137, 150
French Committee, 198
French Foreign Legion, 61, 63, 282
Freyberg, Gen. Sir Bernard, 177–80, 205
Friedländer, Saul, 4, 84
From the Ashes of Disgrace, by Franco Maugeri, 85
Frosinone, 142, 239

Gaeta, 229
Gafsa, 67
Gallipoli, 92, 123
Garigliano River, 145, 155, 160
Garrard, W. A., 28, 218, 246
Gauls, 260
George VI, King, 50
German Supreme Command, 159, 199
Germany; Germans (Nazis; Third Reich), 4, 53, 56, 58, 63, 77, 83, 119, 122–23, 130, 132, 179, 193–97, 208, 212–13, 243, 250, 268, 270, 273, 277, 280, 283; treatment of occupied ter-

ritory, 48, 78, 84, 150, 187–88, 220; military capabilities, 57; Churchill's and Roosevelt's dislike of, 74–75; Italy declares war on, 79; Pope's involvement with, 84–87; see also Army, German; strategy, German
Gestapo, 187, 220
Gibraltar, 60
Giraud, Gen. Henri, 50, 52–54
Goebbels, Dr. Joseph, 79, 83, 85–86, 102, 181, 222
Greece, 75
Greek troops, 203
Gruenther, Gen. Albert, 230–31
Gustav Line, 145, 154, 174–76, 205–6, 208–9, 211, 214–15, 221

Hague Convention, 106
Hannibal, 209
Heidrich, Gen., 19
Hewitt, Adm. Henry, 91
Highway 6 (Via Casilina), 30, 142–43, 225, 236, 245, 248, 253
Highway 7 (Appian Way), 26, 142–43, 207, 211, 217, 225
Himmler, Heinrich, 81, 162, 190
Hitler, Adolf, 74, 76–77, 80–81, 83–86 passim, 98, 100, 109, 110, 156, 162, 190–92 passim, 194–95, 197–98, 221, 242, 243, 269, 278–79
Hitler-Dora Line, 206, 211, 213–14, 221
Hochhuth, Rolf, 84
Hodges, Gen. Courtney, 36
Holiday, 133
Holland, 195
Hollis, Gen. Sir Leslie, 123, 144
Holsinger, Gen. James W., 115, 248
Hopkins, Harry, 35, 44
Howze, Col. Hamilton H., 217, 236, 249–50, 252, 254
Hull, Cordell, 74
Humbert, Crown Prince, 248, 269
HUSKY. See Sicily

Indian Ocean, 143
Indian troops, 177, 202, 216
Italian campaign, 4, 134; historical perspective, 3; isolation, 3; terrain, climate, fighting conditions, 33, 55, 76, 110, 127, 128–30, 208; troops, 33; political influences regarding, 33–35; lack of Anglo-American cooperation, 51; slow progress, 73; Allies agree on uselessness of, 76; Allies hope for

easy victory after Italian surrender, 76–77; Germans plan to defend Italy, 77; diverse national reasons for, 77; Italy surrenders, 78; Italy declares war on Germany, 79; demoralization of Italian army, 79; Germany plans to resist Allied invasion, German troops in Italy, 79; Salerno, 91–97; British landings, 97–99; political handicaps, 102; Italian hostility to Germans, living conditions, 102–6; Allies continue campaign, 109; stalemate, 109–10; II Corps under Keyes, 111, 115–16; supported by Churchill, 121–22, 124; Stalin backs ANVIL against Italian offense, 124; becomes secondary effort, 125; American political naïveté in, 126; slow progress toward Rome, 127–30, 141, 145, 147; Clark's feeling about command, 137–38; Anzio landings proposed, preparations, 141–49; offensive to divert enemy from Anzio, 160; Rapido River, 151–56; Anzio, 156–71, 173–74, 197–98; Cassino, 158–59, 174–79; Allies miss chance to capture Rome, 161–63; characterized by struggle for high ground, 175; Allied bombing of Monte Cassino abbey, 179–82; bombardment of Rome outskirts, 182; planning and execution of Allied spring offensive, 201–25; endorsed by U.S. government, 204; race for Rome, 225–38, 244–55; liberation of Rome, 255–60; casualties, 260; army moves north, 270–71; continues in north, German surrender, 277–78; debate over merits, German blunders, 278–80; *see also* Sicily; strategy, Allied; strategy, German

Italy; Italians, 71, 73, 74, 77, 80, 118, 147, 150, 183–91, 196, 212, 219, 246, 268. See Army, Italian; Italian campaign; Rome

Itri, 211

Jaccarino, Pensione, 234

Janiculum hills, 242

Jews, 85, 190, 195–96, 203

Jones, Sgt. Latham, 26

Jones, Corp. Wade, 265

Judean Hills, 196

Juin, Marshal Alphonse-Pierre, 54, 150, 202, 207–10, 220, 273, 282

Kappler, Obersturmbannfuehrer, 190

Kasserine Pass, 55

Keitel, Field Marshal, 198

Kennedy, Gen. Sir John, 121–22

Kennedy, P. F. C. Richard J., 22, 25

Kesselring, Field Marshal Albert, 109, 144, 145, 162, 219, 230, 233, 239; love of Italy, 5, 80; establishes position at Rome, 14; convinces Hitler to defend southern Italy, 76–77; believes Italy will be ally, 78–79; background, 80; relationship with Pius XII, 80; criticism, 80–81; appearance, 80; abilities, 81; does not fear Italians, orders respect for Vatican, 83–84; treatment of Rome, 83; strategy against Montgomery, 98; calls for Italians to fight with Germans, 103; annoyed by partisans, 105; promoted, delaying tactics, 110; comment about proposed landings, 146–47; plans to combat amphibious landings, 149; surprised at Anzio, 159; countermeasures, 159–61; assigns Cassino commanders, 176; criticizes Italians, 185; attitude changes toward Italians, 186, 188–89; proclaims Rome an open city, 188; orders reprisals against Romans, 190–92; attempts to convince Hitler Anzio position hopeless, 197–98; proposes surrender meeting, 198; virtuosity dims, 201; has terrain advantage, 203; commits all to offset attack, 204; misapprehension about Allied plans, 205–7; armies take pounding, 208; releases reserves to block II Corps, 210; refuses permission for withdrawal at Cisterna, 217; outgeneraled by Alexander, 221; criticized by German generals, 221, 278; defends himself from charges, 221–22; countermoves to Clark's plan, 234–35; guarantees Church property in Rome, 244; defensive maneuvers under pressure, 245, 253; dissolves *carabinieri*, 266; surrenders, 277; blunders and abilities, 278–80; opinion of campaign's importance, 280

Keyes, Gen. Geoffrey, 7, 280–83; relationship to 36th Division, 29, 112; commands II Corps, 111–15; approach to warfare, 111, 113; willingness to be unorthodox, 111, 117; background and religion, 112; Eisenhower's estimate of, suggests light approach to, 112–13; protégè of Patton, 114; character and appearance, admiration of men, 114, 280–81; moral level of headquarters, 116; relationship with Malitch, 118, 121, 282–83; never criticizes publicly, 131; respect for Clark, 132; explanation of Rapido River, 154–56; on Anzio stalemate, 166–67; at Cassino, 178–81; in spring offensive, 202, 211–12; plan for assault to north rejected, 209; links up with Truscott, 221; II Corps replaced, 233; plan for Rome breakthrough accepted, 235–37; Clark's reliance upon, 237; problems before Rome entry, 249, 253–55; authorizes task forces to enter Rome, 249–52; explanation of Clark's offense to other armies, 273; audience with Pope, 276–77; commands U.S. Occupation Zones in Austria and Germany, 280; retirement, 280–81

Khartoum, 59
King, Adm. Ernest, 31, 44
Kluckholn, Frank L., 101
Korea, 38, 126, 281
Krueger, Gen. Walter, 41

La Cosa Creek, 96
Lang, Will, 6, 7, 44, 90, 154
Lapide, Pinhas, 195
Lateran Treaty, 82, 197
Leahy, Adm. William, 125
Lear, Gen. Ben, 41
Leese, Gen. Sir Oliver, 141, 201–2, 213, 220, 228, 230
Lepini Mountains, 217
Libya, 185
Liese, Ted, 117
Life, 6, 24, 44, 132
Liri River, 202
Liri Valley, 145, 150, 207, 208, 213, 225, 228
London, 33, 43, 82, 85
Louisiana maneuvers, 36, 41
Lowry, Adm. Frank J., 149
LST's, 143–44
Lucas, Gen. John P., 95, 146, 148–49, 151–52, 157–68, 179, 225
Luce, Claire Boothe, 193
Luftwaffe, 80
Luongo, Mount, 185–86
Lynch, Col. George E., 7, 22–24

MacArthur, Gen. Douglas, 3, 73, 126, 281
MacFarlane, Mason, 269
McNair, Gen. Leslie, 38–39, 41, 94

Mackensen, Gen. Eberhard von, 159, 160–61, 174, 205, 216–17, 225, 238, 245
Madison Barracks, N.Y., 37
Maelzer, Gen. Kurt, 161, 190, 239–41, 257–58
Mafia, 126
Majo, Mount, 208
Malitch, Capt. Nicholas Vladimir, 61–68, 117–21, 152, 212, 235, 237, 282–83
Malitch, Mrs. Nicholas, 283
Marino, 27
Mario, Monte, 242
Marshall, Gen. George, 31, 35–37, 39, 44, 45, 47, 50, 56–58 *passim*, 122–23, 147–48, 157, 166, 204, 280, 281
Maugeri, Adm. Franco, 85, 103, 163, 187, 219, 238
Mauldin, Bill, 7, 133–35, 171, 263
Mauritian troops, 202
May, Rep. Andrew J., 154
Mediterranean Sea, 34, 55, 58–59, 76, 109
Mediterranean theater, 72, 75, 101, 121, 123, 141, 143, 280
Milan, 195
Minor, Lt. Col. James L., 27
Mollhaussen, Eitel F., 190
Molotov, Vyacheslav, 75
Monterey, Calif., 38–39
Montgomery, Gen. Sir Bernard, 55, 68, 71, 87, 98–101, 110, 119, 126–27, 141, 229
Moran, Lord, 46–47, 102
Morison, Samuel Eliot, 58
Moscow, 67
Mountbatten, Lord Louis, 49, 173
Munich, 192
Murillo, Bartolomé Esteban, 33, 115
Murphy, Ambassador Robert, 7, 31, 48–49, 51–52, 58, 78, 100, 126, 227–29, 261, 269, 274, 281
Mussolini, Benito, 74, 76–79, 82–83, 126, 183, 185, 246, 260, 263, 264, 268
Mydans, Carl, 24

Naples, 15, 30, 75, 109, 142, 157, 186, 205, 206
Napoleon, 102, 123, 260

Napoleon III, 260
Navy, Allied, 216
Navy, U.S., 91, 96, 146, 174
Nazis. *See* Germany; Germans
Nepalese troops, 203
Nero, 260
Netherlands, 80
Nettuno, 142, 161, 199
New York *Times*, 86, 101, 243
New Zealand troops, 33, 177, 180–81, 202, 205, 216
Newsweek, 82, 210
Normandy, 76, 109
North Africa, 60, 91, 111, 141, 145, 150, 157; *see also* North African campaign (TORCH)
North African campaign (TORCH), 31, 34–37, 44–45, 47–55, 66, 77, 89

Oklahoma, 172
Oran, 45, 51, 67
Osborne, Sir D'Arcy, 257
OSS (Office of Strategic Service), 37, 119, 163, 182, 219, 234, 240, 258
Ovenden, A. W., 266
OVERLORD. *See* Channel invasion

Pacific war, 33, 95, 143
Paris, 67, 209
Partisans, Italian, 182–83, 186–91, 234, 244, 258
Patton, Gen. George S., Jr., 36, 47, 55, 60–61, 71–72, 101, 111–12, 114, 149, 166–67, 172, 271
Pavolini, 102
Pearl Harbor, 34
Pearson, Drew, 72
Petrograd, 67
Philadelphia *Bulletin*, 42
Pius XII, Pope, (Vatican): criticism of official conduct, 4–5; relationship with Kesselring, 80–81; urges neutrality status of Rome, 82, 188, 242–44; authority over Roman Church Property, .82; receives diplomats of both sides, 82–83; preferred treatment by Germans, 83–84; appeasement policies denounced and defended, 84–87; provides sanctuary, 86–87; during German occupation of Rome, 105; meeting with Gen. Keyes, 112, 276–77; orders investigation of Monte Cassino abbey bombing, 181–82; distrusts Partisans, 192; considers Communism worse menace than Nazism, 192–95; character, 192–93; position of weakness, 194–95; aids Jews and escapees from Nazis, 195–97; gives thanks for salvation of Rome, 270; audiences with and evaluations by Americans, 274–77
Pius XII and the Third Reich, by Saul Friedländer, 4, 84
Pogue, Forrest C., 39
Poland, 80, 100
Polish troops, 33, 202, 206, 212–14, 216, 248, 275
Pond, Hugh, 92
Porter, Gen. Robert W., Jr., 19, 29, 61–68, 81, 112, 116–18, 121, 132, 178, 185, 211, 235–37, 249, 272, 282–83
Presidential Greatness, by Thomas A. Bailey, 57
Princeton University, 21
Pronestina, Via, 253
Pyle, Ernie, 128–30
Pyrenees, 150

Quebec Conference, 33, 74

Radcliffe, Capt. Taylor, 250–52
Rapido River, 3, 17, 79, 112, 145, 151–56, 160, 166, 175, 206, 209, 215, 216, 280
Rasella, Via, 190–91
Ravello, 269
Reese, Col. Al, 15
Ribbentrop, Joachim von, 83
Rider, Gen., 156
Rodriguez Islander troops, 202
Rome, 3–4, 51, 78, 115, 122, 147, 158–59, 209, 213, 274, 280, 283–84; U.S. breakthrough, 11–29; race for and fall of, 30, 33, 233–38, 244–49; "open city" conflict, 81–83, 188, 242–44; Vatican property, 82–83, 85; German treatment, 83; Churchill optimistic about capture of, 102; conditions after Allied landings, 102–5; Churchill urges capture, 122, 124; capture agreed upon at Teheran, 124; slow progress toward capture, 127–30, 141; nearby landings proposed, 141–47; roads, 142–43; delay in capture costly, 157; Allies miss chance to capture, 160–63; anti-Allied feeling, 182; Allied bombardment, 182, 188; skepticism of citizens, 182–83; resist-

ance against Nazis, 185, 187–90, 196; Germans use city militarily, 188; German reprisals against citizens, 190–91; Vatican weakness, 194–95; Jews and escapees from Nazis aided by Pope, 195–97; Escape Line, 196–97, 267; desired as prize by all nationalities, 202, 204; Hannibal's attempts to capture, 209; reaction to Allied offensive, 219–20; Anglo-American conflict over right to capture, 223–33; race for, 233–38, 244–49; German evacuation of, 234, 238–42, 256–59; controversy over neutrality status, 242–44; liberation, 244–60, 277; inhabitants' reaction, 253, 255–60; post-liberation difficulties, 263, 266–68; U.S. reaction to capture, 263–67; celebrations, 264–67; reprisals against collaborators, 267; political situation, 268–69, 273–74; world leaders' reaction to liberation, 270

Rome Escape Line, The, by Maj. Sam Derry, 196

Rommel, Gen. Erwin, 71

Roosevelt, President Franklin D., 31, 44, 45, 48, 61; "Big Three" alliance, 33–34; concessions to Stalin, 34; agrees to North African campaign, 34–35; postpones cross-Channel invasion, 35; appoints Murphy representative to Eisenhower, 51–52, 126; upset over "Darlan deal," 53–54; approves code name for French invasion, 54–55; at Casablanca, 56–57; and British flattery, 56; at Washington Conference, 73–74; at Quebec, sets date for Channel invasion, 74; insists on "unconditional surrender," 74–75; foe of Nazis, 74–75; desires abdication of Victor Emmanuel, 78; at Teheran, 109, 121, 125; Cairo meeting with Churchill, 121–22; leans on military leaders, 122; mediator between Churchill and Stalin, 124; agrees to Anzio landings, 145; meets Clark in Sicily, 147; and bombing of Monte Cassino abbey, 181; Pope disapproves of, 193; reproves Russians, 198; discusses spring offensive with Clark, 203–4; regards Rome as prize, 228; broadcasts Rome capture, 270

Rotterdam, 82

Russia; Russians (Soviet), 33–34, 56, 58, 75, 77, 103, 109, 120, 124, 125, 133, 176, 198, 212–13, 270, 283

St. Peter's, 82, 105, 252, 270, 272

Salerno, 4, 15, 20, 21, 80, 87, 91–99, 101, 102, 103, 147, 152, 157, 159, 206, 219, 260, 278

San Francisco *Chronicle,* 264

San Pietro, 152

Santa Croce, 187

Sardinia, 136

Scotland, 45

Scott, Capt. Jack L., 28

Scrivener, Jane, 103–5, 187, 220, 239, 255–56

Senger und Etterlin, Gen. Frido von, 80, 111, 176, 229–30

Sevareid, Eric, 7, 9, 24–25, 130, 150–51, 247, 266, 273. 277

Shaffer, Max E., 11–14, 22, 26, 29

Sheehan, Fred, 154

Sherwood, Robert, 122

SHINGLE, 145

Sicily (HUSKY), 36, 60–61, 67–68, 71–72, 74, 80, 89, 95, 101, 111, 113, 126, 147, 149, 157, 278

Simonds, Sgt. Hubert A., 25

Singhalese troops, 202

Sions, Harry, 7, 133, 135–36, 184, 196, 274–76

Sloan, Gen. John E., 7, 253

Smith, Gen. Bedell, 36, 43, 47

Smuts, Field Marshal J. C., 46

Somme, the, 57

Sora, 239

South African troops, 202, 275

Souza, Capt. Ben, 218–19

Soviet Cultural Bureau, 272–73

Spain, 15, 85–86, 123

Stalin, Josef, 31, 33–35, 44, 57, 58, 84, 109, 119, 121–25, 193, 228, 270

Stalin, Svetlana, 125

Stars and Stripes, 132–34, 136, 185, 265

Stilwell, Gen. Joseph, 56

Stimson, Sec. Henry L., 31

Stovall, Col. Oran C., 16, 29

Strategy, Allied: in Italian campaign, 14; 36th Division breakthrough at Velletri, 11–18, 22–29; drive for and fall of Rome, 30; planning for and political intricacies of North African campaign, 31, 34–37, 44–45, 47, 48–55; landings in North Africa, 51; halts German counteroffensive in

Tunisia, 55; victory and benefits in North Africa, 55; in Sicily, 71–72; American, at Salerno, 91–94; British landings, cautious advance, 97–98; Fifth and Eighth Armies link up, 98; strategy destroyed by politics, 102; Allied attack maintained, 109; stalemate, 109–10; shift to OVERLORD, 110; Mediterranean theater versus OVERLORD and ANVIL controversy at Teheran, 121–25; capture of Rome and OVERLORD date agreed upon, 124; Italian campaign secondary, 125; Anzio landings proposed, 141–47; armies coordinated to take advantage of landing, 145; hoped-for achievements at Anzio, 145; doubts about Anzio, 148–49; offensive to divert enemy from Anzio, 150, 160; at Rapido River, 151–56; landings and seige at Anzio, 156–71, 173–74; offensive at Cassino, 158–59, 174–79; misses chance to take Rome, 161–63; bombing of Monte Cassino abbey, 179–82; German misapprehension about, 199; spring offensive, 201–7; endorsed by U.S. government, 204; successful execution of offensive, 208; French breakthrough, 208–11; II Corps thrust, 210–13; Poles capture Monte Cassino, 212–14; slow British drive in Liri Valley, 214; breakout from Anzio, 216–19, 230, 250; II and VI Corps link up, 219; Alexander and Clark disagree on, 225–33; drive to capture Rome, 233–38, 244–49; American task forces enter Rome, 250–52; northward move, 270–71; withdrawal of troops to southern France, 271; debate over, merits of, 278–80

Strategy, German: defense of Rome, 11, 15–16, 18–19; in Italian campaign, 14; in Tunisia, 54–55; in Sicily, 71; plans to defend Italy, 79; Allied speculation about, 89, 97, 109, 144, 158; improvisation and resistance in North Africa and Italy, 89–90, 102; at Salerno, 91–93; opposition to British, 98; determination in southern Italy, 102; superiority in numbers, Kesselring holds "Winter Line," 110, 128–29, 142; resistance, 122; Gustave Line defense, 145, 154, 174–76, 205–6, 211, 215, 221; against amphibious landings, 149; at Rapido River, 152–56; countermeasures at Anzio, 157–67, 173–74; attack Allied offensive at Cassino, 159; defensive measures at Cassino, 174–77, 180–81, 205; failing manpower makes Anzio position hopeless, 197–98; weakened by Allied deception and attack, 201–2; flexibility and terrain advantage, 203; misapprehension about Allied spring offensive, 205–7; Hitler and Caesar lines defense, 206, 211, 221; inability to contain French, release reserves, 210–11; blow up roads, 211–12; loss of Monte Cassino, withdrawal to Hitler Line, 213; unable to hold Hitler and Gustav lines, 214–15; attempts to hold against Allied victories, 215–16; offensive power cracked, 216–18, 221; criticized by German generals, 221; still effective, 222; defense against Clark's plan, 234; defense against Allied encirclement of Rome, 238; withdrawal from Rome to north, 238–44, 256–59; delaying actions and defensive maneuvers, 244–46, 253; fighting continues in north, 277; blunders and successes, 278–80

Swazi troops, 202
Sweden, 218
Switzerland, 197, 198
Syro-Lebanese troops, 203

Taranto, 98
Tasso, Via, 187, 190, 265
Tedder, Marshal Lord, 71
Teheran Conference, 3, 57, 109, 121–25
Terracina, 211–12, 218, 229, 235
Texas National Guard (Texans), 15, 20, 29, 95, 97, 151–56, 218
"They'll Never Forget Mark Clark," by Sid Feder, 153
Thompson, Frances, 265
Tiber River, 83, 242–43, 245, 248–49
Time, 93, 154, 242
Tittman, the Hon. Harold, 86, 182
Tokyo, 281
Tompkins, Peter, 7, 78, 163, 182, 219, 234, 257–58, 267–68
TORCH. *See* North African campaign
Truscott, Gen. Lucian K., Jr., 11–13, 15, 17–18, 22, 95, 127–28, 146, 153, 165–66, 171–73, 202, 205, 211, 216, 221,